How Does a Policy Mean?

How Does a Policy Mean?

Interpreting Policy and Organizational Actions

Dvora Yanow

GEORGETOWN UNIVERSITY PRESS / WASHINGTON, D.C.

Georgetown University Press, Washington, D.C.
© 1996 by Georgetown University Press. All rights reserved.
Printed in the United States of America

10 9 8 7 6 5 4 3 2 1   1996

Library of Congress Cataloging-in-Publication Data

Yanow, Dvora.
  How does a policy mean? : interpreting policy and organizational
  actions / Dvora Yanow.
        p.   cm.
  Includes bibliographical references.
  1. Policy sciences.   2. Corporate culture.   3. Social values.
  I. Title.
  H97.Y37   1996
  320'.6—dc20
ISBN 0-87840-611-5 (cloth: alk. paper).
                                                    95-42087

We shall not cease from exploration
And the end of all our exploring
Will be to arrive where we started
And know the place for the first time.

T.S. Eliot, Little Gidding

Contents

Preface

How does a policy mean? The reader may be startled by this locution. Isn't it ungrammatical? Shouldn't the title read *"What* does a policy mean?"

In 1959 John Ciardi, English professor, poet, critic, essayist, translator, and poetry editor for the *Saturday Review*, published his book *How Does a Poem Mean?* In it, he sought to explain how it is that poems convey their many and varied meanings to us, their readers. He looked at word choice, sounds, symbols, metaphors, rhythms, with multiple examples of each. The book was one of the required texts in my high school English class over twenty-five years ago. But it was not until recently, while working on the analysis that comprises this book, that I began to make sense of the title.

First, to the grammatical structure: it is correct usage, though odd, the adverb "how" modifying the verb "mean."

Like Ciardi, I am asking: What are the various ways in which we make sense of public policies? How do policies convey their meanings? Who are the "readers" of policy meanings? To what audiences do policies "speak"? I am intentionally using the oddity of the locution in the hope of provoking thought on these questions. More recently developed theories of textual interpretation locate meaning not in the text alone, nor exclusively in the author's intentions, but also in the experiences that readers bring with them to their readings. These theories encourage us to look at the interactions among author, reader, and text for ways in which meanings are created. So it is, also, in

policy and organizational contexts—in particular during policy implementation which is the interface of these two arenas.

The analysis presented in this book grows out of my experiences
in an Israeli agency charged with implementing national social policy.
The book explores the agency's language and acts and the settings in
which these were enacted. It should be of interest to political scientists
studying questions of public administration and policy, and to students of organizations, especially those interested in cultural approaches that focus on meaning-making and interpretation.

But unlike most studies of organizational culture, which have
rarely looked beyond the boundaries of the organization being studied, this one looks at the societal context of the values, beliefs, and
feelings engendered by and embodied in organizational artifacts. This
is, or should be, the hallmark of public sector organizational culture
studies, if not of all such studies: that we examine the relationship
between meanings made within the organization and those made
within the polity of which the organization is a part. For the two are
not separable: workers, managers, and executives do not leave their
societally bound values and beliefs at the office door at 9 a.m., only
to reclaim them at 5 p.m. as they leave. The embeddedness of organizations in societal contexts is clearly evident for public sector agencies
implementing public policies, as it is for departments in private compa-
nies charged with implementing federal policy (such as human resource management departments charged with affirmative action/EEO
or Americans with Disabilities Act policies). Certainly, general societal
values concerning work, sexuality, emotionality, and individual and
social responsibility influence how these are enacted in *all* workplaces.
But most studies of organizational culture treat it as if each company
or agency created its culture de novo, out of the null and void, without
examining the extent to which organizations reproduce or react against
the societal or national culture in which they reside.[1] In taking a
cultural approach to the analysis of how an organization communicated policy meanings, this book examines the extent to which an
implementing agency enacted national values.

I did not set out to conduct this research from a particular ideological or philosophical position. What initially drove the research was,
first, a desire to understand what it meant to be a Jewish Israeli living
in Israel, and later, a desire to make sense of what I had learned. One
of the things that I learned fairly early is that Israeli life is experienced

in forms far more varied than what is typically known of them in the United States. It is not just that there are agricultural *kibbutzim* and urban cities and towns. Within each of these categories are multiple other ways in which Israelis further differentiate among themselves. One of these other forms—development towns—figures centrally in this narrative.

What started me on the analytic tack I ended up taking was an acquaintance's passing comment about communities as "symbol-sharing groups." And so my initial investigations were into the literature on symbols, metaphors, myths, rituals, ceremonies, and so forth. These readings were undertaken in the context of Martin Rein's work on the fact-value dichotomy in policy analysis and Donald Schon's insight that metaphors are present not only in poems but also in policy and professional language, where they are linked to ways of seeing and understanding. Bringing language analysis, particularly of metaphors, into policy and organizational studies was my homecoming to John Ciardi and other literary approaches that I had left behind in turning to study the social sciences.

In the early 1980s the field known as corporate or organizational culture exploded, and I found others moving along the same path as I, although with a difference: I continued to think of my work as crafting an "interpretive" approach to policy and organizational studies. Reading in the meaning-focused literatures of symbolic anthropology and literary criticism brought me to the philosophy of science and social science and to the history of thought among German philosophers and related American and French theorists underlying interpretive and critical approaches. Feminist theories developed at this time gave me a way of talking about silences in public discourse, which typically exist around those areas that are most vital to us as a society and with which we are most uncomfortable. Feminist theories teach us to look for the assumed, but hidden norm against which all are measured. But this form of analysis need not be limited to studies of gender: the same principle of the silent norm exists in other matters and has often led to the silencing of those who do not fit the norm. Some of those tacitly known, yet nonetheless communicated meanings may concern the status of particular groups of "Others" in the population. In the United States we have recently come to see this played out around issues of race and ethnicity, class, and gender. In Israel, the case setting of this book, a central silence, and one which figures in my analysis here, concerns the existence of "ethnicity" among Jews.

But that our public discourse is silent on some issues does not mean that we are ignorant of them. This attention to public silences complements Polanyi's (1966) notion of "tacit knowledge." Much organizational and policy analysis has focused on that which is or can be made explicit; and yet, as Polanyi suggests, there is much in human life, in organizational, policy, and other spheres, that we know and that can be understood which is not explicit, and perhaps cannot be made explicit.

This book focuses on some of those areas of organizational and policy practice that are known tacitly and understood through communication by symbolic means. Tacit knowledge in part enables silences in public discourse. I make some of those silences speak here, partly in theoretical terms, partly in terms of a specific case. Public policies do communicate meanings, and they do not always do so through the explicit use of language with a singular, clear meaning. We can no longer afford an understanding of the policy process that ignores these points.

Anthropologist Paul Stoller (1986, p. 71) has remarked, concerning beginnings of tellings: "Lyrical, revelatory beginnings reflect, generally, a humanistic or critical interpretation to follow. Beginnings with theoretical contentions or general assumptions, by contrast, signal a more positivistic approach." Coming on this passage after having completed all but the last chapter of this book, I laughed. Chapter 1 starts: Let us begin with a story. And what follows is an interweaving of humanistic and critical interpretations. I have two hopes for the writing of this book. One is that I have given due weight and clarity to the theoretical contentions that underpin interpretive policy analyses. The other is that both case analysis and theoretical discussion are revelatory, and that both are done in an appropriately lyrical fashion.

NOTE

1. One exception, both in theoretical treatment and in case analysis, is Ingersoll and Adams (1992), who explore the ramifications within the Wash-

ington State Ferry System of a societal preference for a rational-technical mode of administrative practice. A partial exception is those studies that examine industry cultures—e.g., Phillips (1994) on museums in Los Angeles County and on the California wine industry and Weiss and Delbecq (1987) on the high-tech industry of Silicon Valley in California and Route 128 outside Boston. But even such studies have not yet explored how these industry-wide cultures reproduce or vary regional or national cultures.

Acknowledgments

Acknowledging debts incurred in pursuing research takes many forms, from sparse listings of names to more detailed accounts of relationships and happenstances. Narratives of either form often hint at the shapings and histories of ideas that undergird the evolution of a research project. "Here lie the roots of this research story," they seem to say. And so I will tell here a story different from the one that begins Chapter 1, though closely related to it.

This book owes serious intellectual debts to two anthropologists with whom I have had little contact other than through their published work. One is Clifford Geertz, whose story about Cohen, the Berbers, and the French, drawn from his field work in Morocco, spoke to me on so many levels when I encountered it in the midst of trying to decipher my own stories from Israel. On the one hand, it conveys so much of the texture of interchanges among Spanish and French Moroccan, Iraqi, Romanian, German, American, and other urban and rural residents and bureaucrats among whom I had lived and worked, and whose lives and works I was trying to explicate. At the same time, the essay on thick description that it glosses (or does the essay gloss the story?) provided me with much theoretical and philosophical material to go on. I felt catapulted out of the rut of instrumental-rational methodological reasoning with which I had been struggling. It nigh saved me from abandoning graduate study in frustration. What's more, it is writing that is at times elegant, at times entertaining—remarkably readable for social science (surely a backhanded compliment, though not intended as such, for Professor Geertz). As I reread the essay today, nearly twenty years after I first encountered it, its simultaneous simplicity and complexity again make me breathless.

The other is Mary Douglas, whose work deciphering symbols was among the first I happily encountered. What drew me into her early collections of essays were those on biblical texts: the practices of ritual sacrifice, and "Deciphering a meal" and its implications (as I saw them) for the continuing practice of *kashrut* (Jewish ritual food practices). It was from her work that I first learned procedurally how to ask about meaning: how to "estrange" an object or a practice, how to ask what else might be going on. Her later work on institutions and thinking was also important for me as I struggled to find an appropriate language to talk about collectives knowing and taking action in ways that are different from what individuals do. Her analysis of the wine industries of France and California helped me understand why I had such difficulties navigating the local wine shop shelves in San Jose, coming with an Easterner's familiarity with French wines.

To Murray Edelman I owe both intellectual and personal debts. The intellectual ones are perhaps the easier to speak of. When I first read his work in symbolic politics and symbolic language, I was encouraged to continue along the path that I had begun. But he was also honest about the difficulties he had encountered in his pursuit of that path: in a letter in 1981 he suggested an avenue of thought that I might explore and then warned me not to do so, as I would likely encounter great opposition. Our more recent correspondence has been less pessimistic about such academic matters, and he has often encouraged me to stick with it.

The first draft of this manuscript was completed while I was a visiting professor in the Department of Public Administration at Leiden University in the Netherlands and presented there to a faculty and doctoral student seminar. My deepest gratitude to Henk Wagenaar for making my stay there happen; and to him, Paul 't Hart, and Mark Bovens for bringing the seminar to fruition. I could not have hoped for a more challenging and encouraging ambience. To the seminar members, my thanks, especially to Aletta Winsemias, Arjen Boin, and Paul 't Hart for detailed responses and marginal comments that forced me to disentangle what had by then become to me self-evident arguments. My thanks also to Anne van 'der Zwalmen and Annette Reugers for producing that manuscript.

Steven Maynard-Moody surpassed the obligations of collegial reciprocity and returned a set of questions and observations that, although I have not followed all of them, have helped make this book a better one. His clear positions enabled me to clarify my own.

Several people were instrumental in breaking intellectual or procedural logjams in the development of this work. I thank Doug Torgerson for first pointing out to me that I was talking about implementation not only as interpretation, but also as text; and Earl Jones for noting that communities are symbol-sharing groups. The significance of his comment for my thinking went unnoticed by me, but Scott Cook picked up on it, and his attention to this detail was what allowed me to define the research question that led to my understanding of the cultural dimension of public policies and their organizational enactment. Bill Trueheart also made what for him was surely an incidental observation in a chance meeting and conversation about our respective research, suggesting that David K. Cohen would be interested in what I was doing. "Trueheart was right," Cohen wrote in a subsequent note and directed me to Geertz on the Balinese cockfight and to Terry Deal, who was at that time developing his thoughts on corporate culture. Sitting in on Terry's seminar while working on an initial analysis of this material gave me a forum for thinking through some of its aspects at a time when few in the Cambridge organizational or policy worlds were thinking in cultural terms. In a similar fashion, Alan Hoffman sent me to David Harman, to whom I am most grateful for creating the institutional arrangements at JDC-Israel that made the second phase of this research possible. Dror Rotem, at the time head of manpower planning there, listened to and read parts of my analysis, corroborated my initial hunches, and kept me up-to-date on agency events for some years afterwards.

Several colleagues read parts of the manuscript, including some initially developed as conference papers, journal articles, and essays. Guy Adams championed the manuscript as a whole, as he had earlier two of the chapters in article form. Jon Jun provided an opportunity for me to put down in writing for the first time parts of Chapter 1. Chris Bellavita's comments on an early draft of that essay regarding his grasp of what I meant by an interpretive approach to policy analysis enabled me to refine what it was that I did mean. Helen Yanow, my mother, has always been an astute critic. I have benefited from her critical reading of an earlier version of the case study presented in

Chapter 3. She watched many of these events unfold from a different vantage point as program officer for children's services for Malben and JDC-Israel from 1972 to 1980, and her reading was most helpful in contextualizing the narration, smoothing its rough edges, and catching my errors of language use. Scott Cook, Steven Maynard-Moody, Henk Wagenaar, and Ed Wachtel gave insightful "readings" of what it could mean to be a metaphoric supermarket, helping me sharpen those arguments presented here in Chapter 5. Charles Goodsell provided an opportunity to polish a large part of the argument that appears in Chapter 6. Guy Adams, Scott Cook, Martha Feldman, Harvey Goldberg, Steven Maynard-Moody, and Dennis Palumbo read and critiqued drafts of the article that is the basis for Chapter 7. Suzanne R. Thomas-Buckle, Leonard G. Buckle, and Gary Marx helped shape the first version of what is now this book. Lee Bolman, Jo Hatch, Michael Lipsky, Martin Rein, Deborah Stone, and Jay White also read and commented on various parts in earlier configurations, as Hal Colebatch did on the whole manuscript.

To my students in the Department of Public Administration at California State University, Hayward, especially Dave Moffatt, Dan Morrissey, Linda Cherry, and Kevin Lynch, I am indebted for showing me that these ideas had not only intellectual and analytic merit in the Israeli world out of which they grew but practical worth elsewhere as well, in their ability to explain such varied areas of professional policy and administrative practice as philanthropic fund-raising for voluntary agencies, U.S. federal agricultural policy, drug and alcohol practices among American immigrant communities, and art museums. I owe a similar debt to Mike McCoy, who wrote to ask if I could elaborate on "how to do it" as he set off on his own international relations dissertation research in China.

The final manuscript was prepared while I was a visiting scholar at Stanford Law School. David Rosenhan made that possible, giving me a pair of giant's shoulders of *mentshlichkeit*—of humaneness—to stand on and aspire to.

These publishers have graciously permitted the reprinting of the following materials: Harcourt, Brace for permission to reprint the stanza from T. S. Eliot's poem "Little Gidding" that appeared in *T. S. Eliot, The complete poems and plays 1909–1950* (copyright 1952); Walter de Gruyter for permission to reprint parts of Chapter 1 which first appeared in "Interpretive policy analysis: Notes toward a theory,"

Chapter 23 in Jong S. Jun, ed., *Public Policy in the Pacific Rim* (copyright 1994). Three chapters are based on previously published journal articles: an earlier version of Chapter 5 appears as "Supermarkets and culture clash: The epistemological role of metaphors in administrative practice" in *American Review of Public Administration* 22:2 (June 1992); Chapter 6 is revised from "Reading public policy meanings in organization-scapes: The Israel Corporation of Community Centers" in the *Journal of Architectural and Planning Research* 10:3 (Fall 1993), special issue on "Architecture as a setting for governance," edited by Charles Goodsell; and a version of Chapter 7 appeared as "Silences in public policy discourse: Organizational and policy myths" in the *Journal of Public Administration Research and Theory* 2:4 (1992). None of these previously published essays has been reproduced here in its entirety. All have been changed to bring them into accordance with the argument presented in the book.

At times, manuscripts are held back from publication to protect the identities of agencies or actors in those agencies and community members who enabled insight and who might be harmed in some fashion by disclosure. Narrations of such analyses, with their inclination to highlight the shortcomings of agency practice relative to the lofty ideals of policy goals, often read as indictments of people who began with only good intentions. In publishing the analysis two decades after beginning the first research phase, my hope is to avoid wounding people in this fashion. I believe that the insights into the processes of interpretive policy and organizational analysis are still timely.

I regret, though, that what I have learned in this work has not led directly to material improvement in the lives of the development town residents among whom I worked and who made me a "daughter in their homes." But we have seen silences about "ethnicity" increasingly broken, and as it becomes less a verboten subject of Israeli public policy, my hope is that the attitudes that enabled discrimination against them will also dissipate. I rest, in the end, on the knowledge that in our work together, we altered one another's lives, immeasurably, and mutually. This book is dedicated to them and to four others who have shaped my life: my father, Albert Yanow, from whom I learned a love of scholarship; my mother, Helen Vogel Yanow, from whom I gained the critical and social consciousness in which to anchor such scholarship; the late Paul N. Ylvisaker, who as professor and dean, dissertation reader and boss, but mostly as friend, kept me anchored in a world of academic endeavor oriented toward social justice; and Scott Cook, my colleague, partner, and friend, who facilitated this work in myriad ways.

1

Policy Implementation and Organizational Actions: Interpretations and Texts

Let us begin with a story.

The late Zalman Aranne, Israel's Minister of Education and Culture in the 1960s, is remembered by his associates as a bright, sharp, creative, and innovative administrator. More than anything, say those who worked with him, he was noted for his curiosity and his openness to new ideas and schemes.

Aranne began to voice his curiosity about the "new society" of immigrants in Israel's planned New Towns called "development towns," in new neighborhoods of the large cities, and in other immigrant settlements. He was concerned about their social and cultural lives, aware that parents' problems influenced their children's studies and development and that there were clear social and economic differences between the residents of his country's rurally located development towns and those of the urban centers.

Research conducted by the university's communication studies department had just revealed that patterns of leisure time activity, including reading, differed along lines of income and educational achievement. Aranne wondered what the New Town residents did in the evenings and on weekends. How did they spend their nonworking hours?

One fall day in 1966,[1] according to the story related by many of their associates, Aranne called one of his special assistants, Hayim Zipori, into his office.

"I know how people in the cities spend their time," Aranne is reported to have said, "but I don't know what people in the development towns do. Hayim, I want you to find out for me how those people spend their free time. Fly over the development towns, lift up the rooftops, and find out what people do in the evenings."

During the four-month period that Zipori was on the road researching this question, Aranne was visited by Ralph Goldman, then director of the Israel Education Fund (a disbursal arm of the United Jewish Appeal), and some potential donors from the United States.[2] Goldman, a social worker trained in U.S. Jewish Community Centers, wanted to know whether Aranne didn't think that "community centers" would be an institution suitable for solving some of Israel's social problems. Goldman and his guests elaborated on the idea and left.

The next day, Aranne called Ya'el Pozner, head of the ministry's Comprehensive Schools Program, into his office, as she related in an interview.

"Do you know what a community center is?" she recalls he asked her.

"I think so," she says she replied.

"Do you know," he said, "three Americans were here, and they asked me whether it wouldn't be a good idea to set up something like this in Israel. I don't know what this thing is. Why don't you set up a committee and decide."

Both Zipori and the research team under Pozner's direction revealed that New Town residents had few avenues for social, recreational, and educational activities without traveling to the larger cities. This perhaps was also contributing to the large out-migration from these towns, and the cities were becoming crowded. Pozner and her committee recommended establishing a network of community centers where development town residents could see the latest music, dance, art, and theater performances, take classes in a wide range of subjects, and be involved in planning these activities as well. Doing this in their own towns might help them feel less like second-class citizens.

With Aranne's endorsement and active backing, in 1969, after a few years of planning, the national government passed a law creating the Israel Community Center Corporation to provide social, recreational, and educational activities for town residents. Funds were sought for new buildings and staffs, and within a year seven Community Centers were in operation. In the first year of operations the Housing Authority offered to provide funds for community development workers,[3] if the Centers would be their base of operations. The agency accepted the proposal, and within a period of months community organizers were canvassing local residents, inviting comments on Center activities, and extending the Centers' services. Ten years later there were over a hundred Centers throughout the country, administered locally with overall direction from agency headquarters in the capital.

And yet attendance at Center events, participation in programs, and membership remained low relative to the number of potential participants in each community. Moreover, although the Centers came to offer a wide variety of social, educational, and recreational activities, the problems of poverty, second-class stature, and ethnic conflict which had initially prompted Aranne's concern continued unresolved.

This "gap" between policy intentions and agency outcomes could be explained in many ways: ambiguities in policy language; the lack of appropriate incentives to induce cooperation on the part of ministerial or local agency staff; poor organizational design of the agency; blocked communication flows between national, regional, and local levels of government.[4] These approaches share the presumption that the nature of the problem is objectively real and concrete: that problems exist in the world as unambiguous facts, and that the purpose of policy and implementation analysis is to mirror that reality as closely as possible. In this view, we can take action to correct the problem when we are able to capture its definition appropriately and correctly. Both problem and solution are seen as real elements in the world, much in the same way that trees and cats are real. The existence of none of these depends on human perception or understanding: trees and cats exist whether or not humans see or understand them. If we cannot narrow the "gap" between policy intentions and outcomes, we simply have not grasped "the nature" of the problem, seen it in the right light, or hit on the correct solution to it. These are the assumptions of a positivist approach to the social or human world in general, and to the policy world more specifically.

But this leaves aside the human quality of policies, including analysis: that policies and their analysis are a human activity, and that human perception is not a "mirror of nature" (Rorty 1979) but an interpretation of it. That is, the human sciences, including policy analysis, yield an interpretation of their subject matter rather than an exact replica of it. From this point of view there is no single, correct solution to a policy problem any more than there is a single correct perception of what that problem is. For this contrasting set of assumptions, we need an interpretive approach to policy analysis.

WHAT IS INTERPRETIVE ANALYSIS?

The intellectual roots of an interpretive approach to policy analysis lie in the work of European social philosophers of the late nineteenth and early twentieth century (including Wilhelm Dilthey, Edmund Husserl, Max Weber, Alfred Schutz). These interpretive thinkers developed the German idealist thought of Immanuel Kant and others of the mid- and late 1800s, in opposition to the positivist thought of those times. I use the term "interpretive" here as an inclusive label, to refer to the hermeneutic and phenomenological philosophies developed in Germany and elsewhere in Europe, as well as to the schools of symbolic interactionism and ethnomethodology developed in the United States in later decades of the twentieth century. Many of the ideas that mark these philosophies are also shared by critical theorists (the so-called Frankfurt School of Theodor Adorno and Jürgen Habermas) and by French philosophers (e.g., Jacques Derrida, Michel Foucault, Paul Ricoeur) whose writing is often subsumed under the heading of postmodernism. Many of these ideas also have themes in common with various feminist theories, of both U.S. and continental origin.[5]

What these schools of thought share is an attention to the differences between humans and social institutions as subjects of knowledge, on the one hand, and the physical and natural world on the other. They have challenged the supposition of the nineteenth-century positivists (Henri de Saint-Simon, Auguste Comte, John Stewart Mill, and others) and their twentieth-century intellectual heirs that the methods appropriate to the study of the physical and natural sciences were equally appropriate to the study of the human sciences.[6]

This supposition marked the positivists' contribution to the advancement of scientific thinking beyond metaphysical explanations. The revolutionary aspect of their work lay in the argument that universal laws or generalizable principles deduced through use of the scientific method could be developed to explain human behavior much as such laws were being developed to explain the natural and physical world, rather than appealing to lucky stars or fate(s) or theological explanations. So, if an apple fell on one's head, it was not because Zeus was throwing thunderbolts and one hit the tree, but because of something called "gravity" that worked in Egypt and Canada just as it worked in Rome. Similarly, a king's kindness or a worker's vengefulness could be explained by principles of behavior that were universal. These universal principles or laws would allow us to know, predict, and thereby control the human world, much as they allowed us to act similarly with respect to falling objects and other elements of the natural or physical world. Positivist science made an argument for a world that could be known through rigorous, repeatable steps of discovery by a neutral observer making neutral, impartial observations following the rules of the scientific method—rules which themselves would afford a set of neutral observations. In this manner, this knower would discover facts about the subject of study, facts that could be generalized to other similar subjects and that could be distinguished from values. This would move the explanation of human behavior beyond the metaphysical realm into the arena of scientific progress.[7]

Interpretive theories have challenged the notion that vengeance and apples could be known in the same way. An interpretive approach to the human, or social, world shifts the focus from discovering a set of universal laws about objective, sense-based facts to the human capacity for making and communicating meaning. Unlike apples and other elements of the physical and natural world, humans make meanings; interpret the meanings created by others; communicate their meanings to, and share them with, others. We act; we have intentions about our actions; we interpret others' actions. We make sense of the world: we are meaning-making creatures. Our social institutions, our policies, our agencies are human creations, not objects independent of us. In restricting their explorations to knowledge based on the experience of the senses, positivist philosophies of human endeavor neglect some of what we take as essential elements of human life: meaningful experiences, such as the appreciation of a sunset; novel and creative acts; emotions and motivations; social institutions; cultural belief systems; conceptual communication, including both written and spoken words and nonverbal acts. These are not captured in sets of laws that look at physical and mental regularities. Since the world of public policy entails these things, we need a human science that can help us understand them, understand the actions and interactions and intentions of others, understand ourselves in organizations and societies, question the production of knowledge and the nature of that knowledge. These are all matters that constitute the interpretive paradigm.[8]

Interestingly, this same development of ideas was played out in the policy sciences in the 1960s and 1970s. The extension of Program, Planning, and Budgetary Systems (PPBS) from the Department of Defense to various social policy arenas recapitulated the argument of positivist science that the methodological rigor of the scientific method could and should be extended from the physical world to the social world. PPBS brought the language of target groups, delivery systems, and policy impacts to the realm of housing, health, education, and welfare. But social policies are not projectiles aimed at "target" populations.[9] Criticisms of PPBS recapitulate the interpretivists' argument that the social world needs a science based on attributes of humans, rather than one based on trees and falling objects (whether apples or missiles). The social world needs an understanding of the policy process as not only an instrumental process. It is also about the inculcation of values and the validation of status,[10] things that cannot be measured according to rational techniques, especially since the latter require that everything be made explicit and unambiguous—whereas legislative and organizational processes require ambiguity at times, and tacit knowledge, which cannot be made explicit, is an important and very real part of human life.[11]

Positivist knowledge does not give us information about meanings made by actors in a situation. When we read a policy, we see more than just marks on a page; we hear more than just sound waves. As Richard J. Bernstein (1976) wrote, describing Schutz's views on this subject:

> A human actor is constantly interpreting his [or her] own acts and those of others. To understand human action we must not take the position of an outside observer who "sees" only the physical manifestations of these acts; rather we must develop categories for understanding what the actor—from his [or her] own point of view—"means" in his [or her] actions. . . . [I]n focusing on action, we can and must speak of its subjective meaning.

That is, interpretive approaches contest the possibility of neutral, unbiased observation. Prior experience, education, training, and so forth constitute the "frame" or "lens" through which one sees the world and makes sense of what is seen. All knowledge is social knowledge, as Karl Mannheim noted (quoted in Burrell and Morgan 1979); observation and "facts" are theory-laden; and what we take to be objective "facts" may well be affected by the observer (as Werner Karl Heisenberg noted with respect to physical bodies in motion). This means that knowledge is not produced through disembodied reason: knowledge is context-specific, as is the "knower" producing that knowledge.

How we make sense of human acts was the subject of extended attention among nineteenth-century and later antipositivists. The distinction drawn between the physical world and the human world extended beyond subject matter to method. Explanation (*erklären*, in German) was understood to be the method of the physical sciences, leading to the discovery of universal, predictive laws; whereas understanding (*verstehen*) was seen as the method of the human sciences that would lead to the discovery of context-specific meaning. First developed as a distinction in the mid-1800s by Johan Gustav Droysen, the concepts were elaborated by Dilthey, Weber, and Schutz, among others, writing in the late nineteenth and early twentieth centuries. It is worth emphasizing the link between subject matter—what the researcher wants to know—and method. Both are intertwined, also, with the researcher's assumptions about the "reality status" (Berger and Luckmann 1966, p. 106) of the subject matter and the likelihood of its "knowability."[12]

Given human variety, creations of human activity may be interpreted differently by others. That means there is the possibility of multiple meanings, of varieties of interpretation. There are the possibilities of miscommunication and of noncommunication, of meanings that are shared or not shared, of meanings once shared that are later dismantled.[13] This is a striking contrast with a positivist view that there is one set of discoverable, universal, objective laws governing human behavior.

It is the case, however, that we often succeed in communicating. If we, indeed, live in a world of multiple meanings, how is this possible? Phenomenological reasoning offers an explanation that has come to be widely known as the social construction of reality, after Berger and Luckmann's (1966) title. The argument parallels Kuhn's (1970) about how scientists working together come to see their subject matter in the same way. Through a process of interaction, members of a community—whether it is a community of scientists or some other group—come to use the same or similar cognitive mechanisms, engage in the same or similar acts, and use the same or similar language to talk about thought and action. Group processes reinforce these, often promoting internal cohesion as an identity marker with respect to other communities: the familiar "us-them" phenomenon. Cognitive, linguistic, and sociological practices reinforce each other, to the point where shared sense is more common than not.[14]

Interpretive philosophies contend that human meanings, values, beliefs, and feelings are embodied in and transmitted through artifacts of human creation, such as language, dress, patterns of action and interaction, written texts, sculpture. They differ, among other ways, along the lines of what artifacts they attend to as their subject of study. Hermeneuticists, for example, building on established techniques for analyzing biblical texts, apply these to works of literature and art as human artifacts, and extend them to a treatment of action as text. Symbolic interactionists and ethnomethodologists look at patterns of interaction, including language use, in an effort to discover the commonsense, taken-for-granted assumptions which guide human action in everyday situations. Phenomenologists see not only social institutions as human constructions, but also the individual "Self" as an artifact of human creation embodying meaning.[15]

Too much of policy analysis, implementation studies, and descriptions of the policy process is shaped by the assumption that all human action is literal and instrumentally rational. It is as though Merriam's (1934) credenda of power—the cognitively known, rational elements of politics—were the only part of politics worth studying, to the neglect of the miranda of power—the symbolic elements that also carry values and feelings. In the world of administrative and organizational studies, the case is much the same. Even in the subfield of organizational culture, which one might expect to be different, studies have largely focused on values and beliefs, the more cognitive aspects of human action, to the exclusion of feelings, the more emotional and less instrumentally rational aspect.[16] Yet Merriam's formulation itself is misleading, if taken as a reflection of practice rather than as an analytic distinction. Credenda and miranda interact. They work together to shape human action in political, policy, and administrative arenas.

An interpretive approach to policy analysis, then, is one that focuses on the meanings of policies, on the values, feelings, and/or beliefs which they express, and on the processes by which those meanings are communicated to and "read" by various audiences. It gives miranda equal weight with credenda, treating both as human artifacts communicating meanings. In analyzing public policies or the actions of organizational implementors, such an approach focuses on policy and/or organizational artifacts as the concrete symbols representing policy and organizational values, beliefs, and feelings.

SYMBOLIC RELATIONSHIPS: LANGUAGE, OBJECTS, AND ACTS AS ARTIFACTS

A symbol is something—usually concrete—that represents something else—usually an abstraction; as in, a dove is a symbol of peace. A symbol is a social convention: people have agreed on it as a stand-in for the meaning it conveys. As Warner (1959, p. 455) put it, "Each culture has its own sounds, noises, and silences which arouse the attention of its members and have agreed upon significance." Symbolic meanings, in other words, are public, not private or personal meanings, and they are historically and culturally specific: at another time, in another place, for another group of people, a dove may be dinner or simply a greyish white bird. A symbol may accommodate several meanings, depending on context and meaning-maker. The home provided by housing policy may represent security and status, shelter and wealth. The power of symbols lies in their potential to accommodate multiple meanings. Different individuals, different groups may interpret the same symbol differently.[17]

Symbols serve to set those who share their meanings apart from other people or groups who do not share them, at the same time that they unite those who do. "An exalted name, a flag, and shared heroic memories are the kind of images that bind a nation" (Gottschalk 1975, p. 14). Knowing these names, traditions, and other symbols is important itself as a symbol of membership in the nation, community, organization, or group. "Not to know them is not to belong" (Hunter 1974, p. 67). Symbols come to be evidence of the meanings that a group holds, believes in, and practices.

Human artifacts stand in a symbolic relationship with the values, beliefs, feelings, or meanings which they embody and/or engender. Artifactual symbols include symbolic language, symbolic objects, and

ARTIFACTS

Language, Objects, Acts

MEANINGS

Values, Beliefs, Feelings

Figure 1-1.   Artifactual expressions and their related meanings exist in a symbolic relationship: Artifacts are the more visible embodiments and expressions of tacitly known meanings. Their use recreates or changes the underlying meanings.

symbolic acts. These embody three dimensions of human meaning-making: emotive, cognitive, and moral, corresponding to feelings, values, and beliefs (Gagliardi 1990). As shown in Figure 1-1, the artifact is the concrete manifestation or expression of the more abstract value, belief, feeling, or meaning.

All language, objects, and acts are potential carriers of meaning, open to interpretation by legislators, implementors, clients or policy "targets," concerned publics, and other stakeholders. At the same time, they are tools for the recreation of those meanings and for the creation of new meanings. Through "artifactual interaction," our often daily engagement with symbolic language, objects, and acts, we reembody them with meaning at the same time that we use them to communicate those meanings and to create extensions of those meanings.

Values and so forth, since they are abstract, are difficult to know about or discover directly. They are hard to "pin down," to make concrete and imageable. In part, this is because values and meanings are often known tacitly, rather than explicitly. We typically do not speak to one another about our values and beliefs in everyday encounters in the post office or on the street (e.g., "Hello, I'm Michael and I value freedom and individuality"); or if we do, we often present what we think we believe or value, or think we ought to value, or what we would like the other person to perceive as our value, yet these may not be the values we act out. For example, Mary, observing Michael, may ask him to corroborate or correct her interpretation. But asking Michael to state his values absent an action context may elicit a story about the values he preaches rather than those he practices, and the two are often different. The proverb "Do what I say, not what I do" captures this distinction.[18]

Nevertheless, we do know a great deal about what others value and believe, because we communicate these values and meanings through such artifacts as dress, action, language, and so forth that have acquired meaning in certain contexts, where members of those contexts commonly share those meanings. We know—because we have learned through socialization and other forms of teaching—how to interpret the meanings of artifactual symbols in their contexts. We communicate, in other words, through artifactual interaction, inter-preting the more concrete symbolic representations (e.g., Michael's clothes, posture, gestures, reported observations, and the like) that embody our and others' values, beliefs, feelings, and meanings. We are able to understand one another without always making our mean-ings explicit, by drawing on tacit knowledge of the symbols' meanings. This is especially true of nonverbal language and built space. As Polanyi (1966, p. 4) noted with regard to tacit knowledge, we "know much more than we can tell." The consequence of Mary's holding a certain value or belief or feeling in a particular way may be understood by observing her actions and interpreting them, inferring from action to meaning(s). Although not spoken of directly, these values, beliefs, and feelings are known, tacitly, and communicated through the cul-tural artifacts that express them—the objects, language, and acts of everyday life. By interpreting such symbols, we strive to understand the meanings they are vested with and their moral (belief), cognitive (value), and affective (feeling) bases. Our knowledge may be wrong—we have made an interpretation that is not in keeping with the actor's intent; but in acting on that knowledge, we may discover our errors of interpretation.

It is important to emphasize the contextual nature of such knowl-edge. It is also important to note that it is only provisional knowledge, subject to change as circumstances and individuals change or as our (mis)interpretations are corrected. This lack of universality and eternity stands in marked contrast to positivist notions of the certainty of knowledge. It is also essential to understand that symbolic purposes are not the same as functions in a structural-functionalist sense. Such purposes are not essential to the organization, and the symbolic means of communication that are identified are not the only way of accomplishing these purposes.[19]

This focus on interpretation of meanings made by actors in policy and agency contexts lies at the heart of an interpretive ontological and epistemological stance. Interpretation of artifactual meanings is the methodology of an interpretive approach. In this sense, the methods of interpretive analysis that focus on the ways in which meanings are made and conveyed are, at the same time, the subjects of study. The medium of communication is intimately connected with the message it communicates.[20]

There has been a tendency in some discussions of symbolic politics to treat that concept as distinct from "real" politics, as if symbols and their meanings were not "real" or as if material redistributions and instrumental actions were the only "real" elements of political and policy acts. The distinction is, however, erroneous and misleading. Policies and political actions are not either symbolic or substantive. They can be both at once. Conceptually speaking, even purely instrumental intentions are communicated and apperceived through symbolic means. In practice, policies are intended to achieve something material or expressive, or both. To do so, they have recourse only to symbolic representations to accomplish their purposes, and these purposes can be understood only by interpretations of those representations. There are no unmediated, directly apperceived policy or agency actions.

Dunn (1981, p. 2) brings a marvelous example of the blurred boundary between "symbolic" and "real" politics. The commandant of the castle of Hochosterwitz, in the province of Carinthia, was under siege in 1334 by the forces of the Duchess of Tyrol. The castle, perched on a high promontory, was invulnerable to direct attack, but its defenders were down to their last ox and two bags of barley corn. The duchess's troops, on the other hand, were increasingly restless, no end to the siege was in sight, and there were urgent political affairs to attend to at home. At this point the commandant had the last ox slaughtered, its abdominal cavity filled with the remaining grain, and the carcass thrown down the cliff in front of the attackers. The duchess and her troops abandoned the siege.[21]

INTERPRETING POLICIES: ARTIFACTS AND POLICY MEANINGS

Symbolic elements that represent and convey policy meanings include the language, objects, and acts associated with a policy and its implementing agency. As the organization charged with implementing a policy goes about taking the various actions that constitute implementation, it creates these symbols anew or uses existing ones, at times invested with new meanings. These symbols include such things as buildings, programs, program names, organizational metaphors, rituals, ceremonies—indeed, potentially all those organizational artifacts that, together with the values, beliefs, and feelings they embody, constitute the culture of the organization.

It is not only legislative language that may be symbolic, but also language used by the implementing agency in brochures, speeches, and so forth. Symbolic objects may include the substantive remedies or actions proposed by a policy. For example, U.S. housing allowance programs that enable families to acquire housing provide access not only to physical shelter, but also to the other values in contemporary American culture conveyed by homeownership or the head-of-household's ability to provide shelter. The fact of being in a physical structure possessing a roof and four walls means more than a statement of relative status and financial position. Homeownership has come to represent a congeries of attitudes and behaviors associated with such varied values as deferred gratification ("saving for a rainy day," for example) and conspicuous consumption (cf. Sopher 1979). Warner's (1959, pp. 44–50 passim) comments on the contents of homes are illustrative of values that a housing policy may entail:

> The decor, furnishings, paintings and their arrangements . . . are all symbolic objects . . . which refer to the manners and morals . . . and express the significance of the people and their way of life . . . [; they] also evoke and maintain in people sentiments about who they are and what they must do to retain their

. . . images of themselves and keep before them an interesting and justifying vision of the [meaning] of their world.

A housing allowance program, in other words, which offers one the means to acquire housing through purchase or rental brings with it the cultural values symbolized by its substantive elements.

A policy may also work symbolically through its enactment. The very process by which a policy is moved onto the legislative agenda is a symbol that represents the ideals of democratic government: equality, freedom, popular representation, among others. We see in the "dance of legislation" (Redman 1973) concrete examples that "democracy" exists: the *forms* of legislature reassure us (Edelman 1964). The message sent is that "government" is indeed responsive to the needs and demands of its citizens, and that citizens' claims on government for action are legitimate. Government responses speak not only to those directly involved in pressing for response, but to broader publics as well (Lipsky 1970, p. 176). Gusfield's (1963) discussion of Temperance, Prohibition, and Repeal provides an extended example. Prohibitionists, finding their values under attack from the immigrant, urban, Catholic lower classes, used legislative politics to attempt to quiet "the fear that the abstainer's culture was not really the criterion by which respectability was judged in the dominant areas of the total society" (p. 110). Ratification of the Prohibition amendment was understood as public affirmation of Dry norms, a symbol of the power, prestige, and hence dominance of those norms, despite the difficulties of its enforcement. Prohibitionists used legislation to make a public identity statement—to themselves as well as to their opposition—that validated one status, one set of values, beliefs, and feelings, over another.

Symbolic language, objects, and acts are often separable only analytically. Typically, they are intertwined. In the 1992 Republican National Convention in Texas, for example, the massive columns that soared from the stage toward the roof reminded many of the architectural designs of the Third Reich, serving thereby as symbolic objects to convey feelings about fascist belief systems (which not a few people saw further reflected in Pat Buchanan's address eliminating "feminists" and homosexuals from the Republican Party's "big tent"). The act of giving such a conservative as Buchanan air time at the convention symbolized for many the values of the Republican Party, and his words, as well as Vice President Dan Quayle and others' invocation of "family values," are examples of language that symbolically conveyed value, belief, and feeling abstractions that were nevertheless known, albeit tacitly. In the community center example with which this chapter begins, an interpretive approach might analyze policy wording, names, and titles used by implementing agencies— the community center name, for example—and organizational metaphors as forms of symbolic language. The design, landscaping, and decor of agency buildings and substantive agency programs are symbolic objects which an interpretive analysis might examine. Symbolic acts could include such categories as agency ceremonies and rituals— annual meetings, in-service training sessions which repeatedly ask "What are our goals?" and so forth. Such an analysis would focus on the meanings of artifacts such as these to various actors in the situation.[22]

Unlike approaches to policy analysis grounded in positivist philosophy, interpretive approaches consider a hard and fast distinction between facts and values to be ontologically untenable. If the world as we know it is perceived and understood through theoretical constructs, there is nothing "factual" in an objective sense about human acts and events. Yesterday's certain fact is today's illusory belief—as in the known fact in 1491 that the world is flat. Even numbers, those elements that we take to be the most "objective" and "factual," may "lie," as Gusfield (1981, pp. 55–60) and Stone (1988, ch. 7) show so well.

We need, then, to see policy analysis as a process of inquiry that seeks to ask questions, rather than as a collection of tools and techniques designed to provide the right answers (Dunn 1981, p. 3). The "right answers" approach begins from the assumption that the perception of the problem is accurate, whereas the "inquiry" approach problematizes the very definition of the problem. When we problematize the "framing" (Rein 1983, Rein and Schon 1977) or the "design" (Dryzek 1990, Schneider and Ingram 1993) of the policy problem and the assumption of legislative "intent," we invoke a communications theory of policymaking that emphasizes the creation, transmittal, and interpretation of policy meanings. The channel metaphor underlying traditional communications theory begins with the dyad of transmitter and receiver, linked by a channel through which communication flows—or does not—as in the diagram. Later systems theories added a feedback loop.

Channel

Transmitter(s) $>$ $>$ $>$ $>$ $>$ $>$ $>$ Receiver(s)
flowing information

This model encourages us to ask such questions as who are the transmitter(s) and receiver(s); what is (are) the transmitter's (s') intention(s); what is received, and how does it compare with the intention (is there distortion, for example)? It expands the traditional view of the policy process as legislators communicating to implementors who communicate to clients. It can include communications by both legislators and implementors to other policy-relevant publics: a broad group of stakeholders, including citizens groups, unions, political parties, public agencies, even policy analysts, any or all of whom may have an interest in policy outcomes. The range of receivers is broadened.

But the model is not without problems. For one, the channel regularizes communication, rather than seeing multiple, possibly non-congruent messages being sent by multiple transmitters to multiple receivers all at the same time. Second, by freezing action at one point in time, the model imputes intentionality and suggests that this intention is discoverable. Third, the language of "receivers" and "audiences" implies a passive listener, even if the listener becomes a sender in turn. This omits the active construction of meaning that a listener must engage in to make sense of what has been heard.[23] Moreover, the language of this model focuses on cognitive processes and oral transmission and reception of meanings. It leaves out visual and emotive processes and content, the sorts of things that are communicated by built space and other objects and by nonverbal acts (gestures and the like), as well as textual processes of communication and interpretation. It also assumes explicit and intended communication, omitting the communication of knowledge that is tacit, as well as the possible making of meanings that were not intended by the sender. None of these constraints, however, necessarily obtains in policy and adminis-

Agenda-setting ------ > Legislation ------ > Implementation

Figure 1-2.   Traditional model (simplified) of policy process as a series of stages. (Feedback loops are not shown.)

trative processes. The channel itself is an unnecessarily constraining and regularizing image. Not all communication is so controlled.

Implementation has typically been presented as a stage in the policy process, following agenda-setting (including problem definition) and legislation (policy formulation and adoption), and itself followed by evaluation (and at least one textbook includes termination), as illustrated in Figure 1-2.[24] Influenced by systems theories, these models often include one overall and one or more internal feedback loops.

The stage model suggests a linear, unidirectional, instrumental policy process that is also future- and progress-oriented, and hence incremental as well, although it also implies a finite end point. Seeing implementation actions as organizational actions invokes the traditional model of a hierarchical organization or bureaucracy, illustrated in Figure 1-3. This model, too, suggests a linear, unidirectional (top-down), goal-oriented, finite set of behaviors.

In an implementation context, as suggested by the addition of a systems perspective (see, e.g., Edwards 1980, Mazmanian and Sabatier 1983, Nakamura and Smallwood 1980), the traditional hierarchy becomes more complex with added intergovernmental dimensions, as in Figure 1-4.

Here, the various problems identified in the second-generation implementation literature (Goggin et al. 1990) can be seen: structural problems of authority, responsibility, control; individual and interpersonal issues of motivation and incentives; systems problems of coordination and communication across governmental levels; and power issues such as domain, leadership, negotiation/bargaining (Yanow 1987a, 1990).

Studies of street-level bureaucrats by Lipsky (1978, 1979) and others (Prottas 1979, Weatherley 1979) begin to modify the top-down linearity of the organizational model, as shown in Figure 1-5.

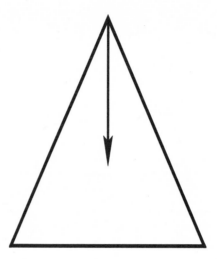

Figure 1-3. Traditional model of organizational process: Bureaucratic hierarchy marked by lines of authority and responsibility.

Street-level bureaucrats are seen as actively interpreting agency rules and regulations, and these enacted interpretations are interpreted in turn by clients as constituting policy. The theory brings clients into the picture, moving in the direction of more active "targets" and bidirectional, rather than linear, action.[25]

Approaching implementation interpretively, with an emphasis on context-specific meanings, brings organizational analysis of implementing agencies within the context of a particular society's values. These organizations are not treated as divorced from a value context, as they appear to be through other "lenses" of implementation analysis. This suggests a model of an intergovernmental and intra-agency policy process in two dimensions, time and geographic space, where policy meanings may change over both dimensions. The model is sketched in Figure 1-6.

Assuming a single meaning when a policy is initially legislated, that policy may come to convey additional meanings as it is implemented over time and at successive organizational or governmental levels (either within an agency or across a federated agency). But that assumption of an initial single meaning may be faulty. Prior debates and policy meanings may, and often do, influence current understanding.

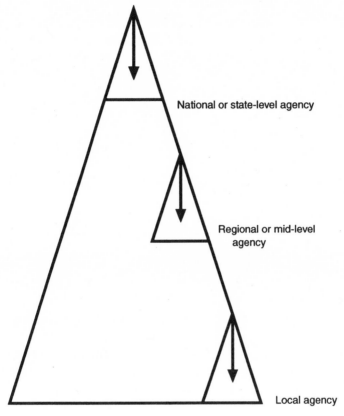

National or state-level agency

Regional or mid-level
agency

Local agency

Figure 1-4. Intergovernmental implementing agency: Traditional hierarchy as elaborated by implementation theory.

In this way, we may see how "policy" as a concept has itself been variously understood, referring at times to a piece of legislation and at other times to a set of practices. The model suggests that the meanings of the concept themselves evolve over the life of a policy issue.

In this view, interpretations, as Stone (1988, p. 21) has noted, are more powerful than "facts." That makes the policy process, in all its phases, a struggle for the determination of meanings. It becomes very important for an implementing agency to establish its identity, internally, and its image, externally, early on as it communicates policy meanings to its various "audiences" or "readers." The case study

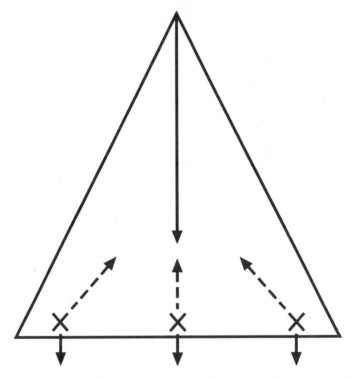

Figure 1-5.   Traditional hierarchy as modified by street-level bureaucracy theory: Agency staff as active interpreters; clients as less passive "targets."

that illustrates these arguments in this book focuses on the agency's founding years and initial decade of operations, to show how policy meanings—some explicit, some tacitly known—were established, conveyed, and read, misread, and not read. As presented here, the case involves more actors and details and covers a longer period of time than most implementation cases. But such is the nature of a thick, rather than a thin, description of the convoluted, intertwined, overlapping webs of meaning that are significant to the actors in the situation described, which they themselves learn to "read" and which anyone else entering that situation and attempting to comprehend it must also navigate.

This approach entails the following assumptions: (1) implementation may cover a wide range of symbol-sharing communities, some

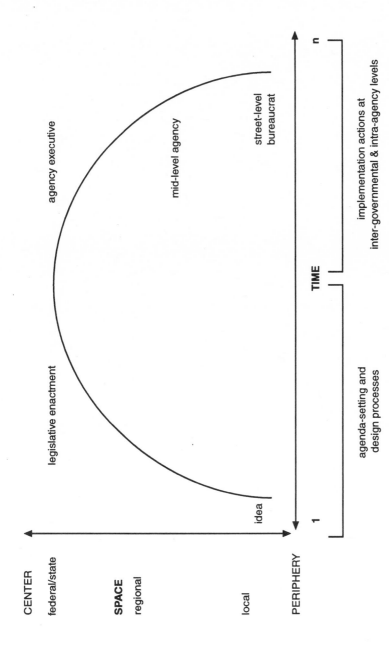

CENTER
federal/state

SPACE
regional

local

PERIPHERY

legislative enactment

agency executive

mid-level agency

street-level
bureaucrat

idea

TIME

1

n

agenda-setting and
design processes

implementation actions at
inter-governmental & intra-agency levels

Figure 1-6. A time and space model of the policy process.

21

but not all of which overlap; (2) interpretations of symbols and the making of meaning(s) change over time; (3) actors who share symbolic meanings at one time may not share them at another time in the course of implementing a policy; (4) relationships among actors, policy goals, and implementation may change over time. These are the meaning-centered assumptions that underlie the relationships drawn in Figure 1-6.

IDENTITY STORIES: PUBLIC POLICIES AS TEXTS, CLIENTS AND OTHERS AS READERS

Moreover, from an interpretive point of view, policies are seen not only as instrumentally rational, goal-oriented statements, but also as expressive statements. Taylor (1988) defines expressive acts as those which have meaning for individuals; they are not only the instrumental communication of information. Expressive behaviors, he said, give voice to something within a repertoire of shared experience. At the group level, then, public policies may be seen as expressive statements or expressive acts when, through them, a polity expresses its identity. We tell ourselves who we are, in terms of what we value; we may communicate that identity to others as well. The local governments of such U.S. cities as Hayward, Berkeley, Oakland, and Santa Cruz in California, for example, as well as Cambridge, Massachusetts and others have declared themselves Nuclear-Free Zones, posting signs to that effect on the streets. Yet, these cities' governments are unable to stop the transshipment of nuclear materials across their borders, since such shipment moves over federally funded highways and federal law supersedes local law. The policy is expressive: it is a statement city residents make to themselves and to one another, as well as to more distant publics, about their values and identity.[26]

Seeing policies as expressive of meaning, and not just as instrumentally rational, emphasizes different aspects of the communication of policy meaning. It emphasizes policies' role in the public expression, inculcation, and validation of values, beliefs, and feelings, as well as in the distribution of material goods, thereby validating self-esteem, respectability, and other "status goods." A policy may be seen as a claim on government—a claim for attention, at least, and possibly for material response. When government responds to a claim for attention with returned attention, even when not backed by material response, the validity of that claim is legitimated, and the claimant's status as reasonable claimant is validated. This is accomplished through various policy issues (e.g., housing, family and work, immigration—the specifics change over time) that are or become symbolic stand-ins for the value debates of the period, which values are communicated tacitly. In the language of U.S. democracy, the response acknowledges and reinforces the idea of government "of, by, and for" the people: the people claim, and the people respond. From an interpretive point of view, these expressive aspects of the policy process are anticipated, not seen as aberrant. Since implementing agencies enact governmental responses, they are part of this cycle of value inculcation and status validation.

Traditional policy and organizational analyses impute instrumental rationality where it may not have existed. We see cause-and-effect relations after the fact, but in attributing intention to the causality, traditional analysis ascribes both instrumentality and intentionality before-the-fact to policy actors and events. We cannot know for certain, however, that the patterns we are seeing retrospectively in policy actions "actually" resided in them. Our ex post facto reasoning is the reflexive process that phenomenologists, after Husserl and Gadamer, assert is basic to human knowing. It is like the apocryphal story of the baseball umpire who, when asked whether it's a ball or a strike, proclaims, "They ain't nothin' till I call 'em." The pattern is in our perception of the events, not in the events themselves. We "see" governmental actions as government responding to problems; yet these very actions may have been expressive acts rather than instrumentally rational ones intended to cause particular effects or achieve certain explicitly stated goals. Given the value contemporary Western society places on instrumental administrative (and other) rationality, acts that appear to be goal-oriented may themselves be expressive of this value.

We complicate the picture further if we consider not only public policies as "texts" that are interpreted as they are enacted by implementors, but also consider those enactments as "texts" that are "read" by various stakeholder groups: clients, potential clients, legislators, other agency personnel, other citizens, and at times foreigners as well. Reader-response theory—a literary theory of textual meaning developed since the 1970s—refutes an earlier argument that the meaning of a text lies in the text alone. Nor does the meaning of the text reside in its author's intentions. Rather, a text's meaning lies also in the eyes or mind of the reader (see, e.g., Iser 1989). In one view, meaning resides not in an object—not exclusively in the author's intent, in the text itself, nor in the reader alone—but, rather, is created actively in interactions among these three, in the writing and in the reading.

The argument holds for policy practices as much as it does for academic or literary ones. In policy, law, and government, it is expressed when action is measured against legislators' intent, the court's intent, or the Constitution's or Founding Fathers' intent (e.g., in Judge Bork's arguments in the late 1980s about establishing "original intent"; see Teuber 1987). Applied to the policy context that is our concern, we may see that meaning is actively created by implementors as well as by legislators, but also by clients and potential clients, by other agencies and ministries or departments, and by policy-relevant publics, in interactions among themselves and with various policy-related artifacts, including, but not limited to, the literal text of the enabling legislation or the agency's mission statement.

The meanings created in these other readings may, at times, be crucial to implementation success or failure. The ability of the Polaris missile developers to convince Congress that they were successfully implementing their charge before they had a missile to show for their work was key to further funding essential for implementation. They did so not by showing a finished product, but through the symbolic act of spending the whole of their allocated budget (Sapolsky 1972)— an act that was "read" by Congress and that brought additional appropriations.

In this sense, not only is legislative and other language a "text" that is interpreted by implementors and others; those interpretations—in the form of agency language, objects, and acts—themselves become "texts" that are "read"—by those actors and others. A text or "text-analogue" (Taylor 1971)—that is, action, object, or spoken language treated as text—is interpreted by its "readers"—agency staff, clients, and so forth.[27] But these interpretations prompt or come in the form of responses—acts, language, or objects—which themselves are then treated as texts and interpreted. This circular process of action-text-interpretation is diagrammed in Figure 1-7.

What these various stakeholder- and critic-readers interpret are

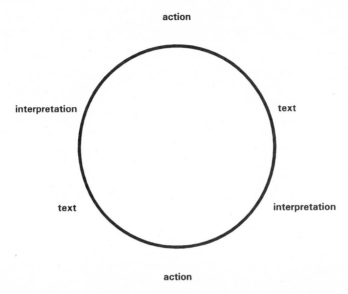

Figure 1-7. Action is treated as a text and interpreted; interpretations come in the form of actions.

the organization's image and identity: an image that is projected to external stakeholders (potential clients and personnel, funders, policymakers, other interested publics); an identity that is conveyed to internal agency personnel, to guide them in their tasks. In order to implement a policy mandate, an organization must be able to communicate to policy stakeholders what that mandate is, as well as its intentions for action, not to mention its ability to carry out that action. Such communication must be internal, so that organizational members know what the organization is about, and it must be external, to any publics whose potential actions are germane to the operations of the organization. Such readers may include legislators and legislative appropriations committees; potential personnel and clients; agency headquarters, regional, and field staff; administrators, professionals, and executives of cognate agencies with related areas of activity; fundraisers and philanthropists; and supporters and detractors in the general voting public. A new agency especially needs to establish its distinctness, if not its uniqueness, with respect to other agencies that might serve similar or related purposes, constituting potential threats to its continued existence in times of scarce resources.[28] But such communication need not be—and typically is not—made through explicit language alone.

In the context of policy analysis and implementation, this means that we may no longer see clients (for example) as passive recipients of a policy's meaning, but as active readers themselves of legislative language and agency objects and acts. Implementation difficulties, in this view, may no longer be fixed by repairing ambiguous policy language, because in this view not only is language inherently multi-vocal—capable of carrying multiple meanings—but clients' and others' interpretations cannot be predetermined or controlled. Such a view moves us decidedly away from the military metaphor of policy analysis that sees clients as passive targets to be hit by policy missiles.

Interpretive analysis as discussed above has been criticized by critical theorists for undervaluing the seemingly objective reality of social institutions and for ignoring the matter of change (e.g., Fay 1975). Critical theorists argue that interpretation's emphasis on understanding meanings is not enough, that understanding needs to be anchored to action (Beam and Simpson 1984). While these criticisms may be appropriate to the social philosophies that underlie interpretive policy analysis, the limitations they identify need not be characteristic of interpretive policy analysis itself. There is nothing about such an analysis that is antithetical to problems of change. In fact, the origins of much of the work to date that could be called interpretive policy analysis (e.g., Colebatch and Degeling 1986, Feldman 1989, Fox 1990, Hofmann 1995, Jennings 1983, 1987, Maynard-Moody and Stull 1987, Palumbo 1991) appear to be a desire not only to explain agency performance, but to make it more just, more equitable, more effective. The same drive that has marked implementation studies—to improve the match between implementation and intention in order to achieve more equitable policy outcomes—may in fact mark interpretive analyses. The difference is that the latter accept the multivocality of political life as human reality. In this sense, recommendations to eliminate ambiguities of policy language are seen as deriving from a mechanical metaphor of social reality that is an inappropriate understanding of human reality.[29] Several theorists (e.g., Hawkesworth 1988, Jennings 1983, Schneider and Ingram 1993), in fact, argue that interpretive analysis presupposes or requires an ethical commitment to a more democratic policy process and analysis.

LINKS WITH POSTMODERN AND OTHER
THEORIES OF MULTIVOCALITY

The interpretive philosophies of the 1920s and 1930s are at last making inroads into thinking about public policies. Modernism asked questions about the physical and social worlds. Its answers—in the form of generalizable, universal principles independent of a specific context—were to be achieved through disembodied reason. Postmodernism, like interpretive theories, calls for an end to the search for universal principles abstracted from the specifics of a particular time, place, context. It argues that disembodied reason is not possible: policy analysts are situated knowers thinking and writing from particular points of view. All subjects of policy analysis are situated "knowns," and we cannot understand them and should not take action with respect to them without understanding the contexts in which they are situated. Feminist theories, in particular, underscore the notion of a situated knower: that knowledge is privileged by a point of view, and each researcher, each policy analyst, each individual perceives, understands, and acts out of a particular context—family and community background, education and training, experience. The knowledge we produce as situated knowers is colored by that context, by our cognitive structures, our circumstances, traditions, history, social environment. There is no external, objective point from which to observe and analyze. Recent narrative theories present active "readers"—meaning-makers—of policy action-as-text rather than more passive receivers or audiences or targets. All actors in a policy situation—from legislators to implementors to clients to voters—are, in this view, active constructors of policy and agency meanings.

These observations should, in fact, extend to what I have written here. I have, up to this point, largely adopted the conventions of modernist modes of impersonal, seemingly objective narrative common to policy analysis. This chapter, for example, presents itself as timeless, universal truth spoken from a detached, objective point of view. Because of the way the research was originally framed, the book is presented largely in a modernist voice. But, in fact, it is nothing more (nor less) than one voice, presenting one interpretation, one way of understanding the matters discussed herein. This one voice speaks from her experience and education, her contextualized situation; other voices may interpret these same matters differently, and still others might continue to opt for a positivist approach to the subject matter. From an interpretive point of view, positivism is just one more way of seeing, one more form of human endeavor. It is not a privileged position, a metadiscourse providing final answers to all questions.

HOW DID ONE POLICY MEAN?

This book presents the case of the Israel Corporation of Community Centers (ICCC) as a series of stories, explanations, or tales about ways in which policy meanings were communicated to various audiences. Following a methodological discussion in Chapter 2, the case is presented in Chapter 3 as a "realist" tale[30]—a seemingly objective, historical account of the development of the legislation that led to the creation of the ICCC and of its early years. This first account includes an explanation of the social and political environment out of and in which the ICCC grew, defining and narrating such key elements as immigration to Israel, the development towns and population dispersal, immigrant absorption, ethnic and class distinctions and their geographic manifestations, and so forth. This historical narration is presented as if all the events were objectively factual, although in choosing which events to highlight and in composing the narration, I have obviously made choices that reflect my particular view. In this sense, it is an authored tale. But the author is not visible in the telling, and the problem of meaning is not faced here directly. That is, I present the story as if there were only one story, only one way to tell the events, only one meaning for all participants and audiences.

After an interlude in Chapter 4 that invites reflection on the realist tale, I turn to the problem of meaning head on. The next three chapters proceed from examples of language use which had as their primary audience members within the organization; to examples of objects that communicated meaning to external audiences near and far; to examples of acts that, while engaging organizational members primarily, situated the problem of agency meaning and policy implementation in the context of general sociopolitical concerns. Chapter 5 focuses on an organizational metaphor that shaped agency actions as an example of the role of language in communicating policy and agency meanings. Chapter 6 looks at built space as an example of agency objects that communicated meanings symbolically. Chapter 7 examines agency acts in the form of rituals that enacted policy and organizational myths.

In each of these three retellings of the story, the communication of meanings and their multiple possible interpretations by various audiences is at the center of the tale. Each retells the same story from a slightly different angle, so that after the fourth telling, we have a Picasso-like word portrait of a public policy and its implementing agency. This ordering of perceptions, proceeding from language to objects to acts, seems to follow the order in which new members make sense of an organization: first, seeing it whole, largely in terms of its language, as it presents itself; gradually moving toward a more complex view, nuanced in terms of spatial and power relations and the contradictions between stated intent and action.[31]

In light of the various facets of this portrait, we can no longer suggest with compelling logic that the agency would have achieved its policy goals and narrowed the gap between intentions and outcomes if only the language of the enabling legislation had been more exact. Rather, when seen as expressive acts and not solely as instrumental ones, public policies and their enactments may be "read" as telling national identity stories. Chapter 8 makes this case for the ICCC. At this point, we see that legislation is the interpretation and enactment of prior debate and idea history; that implementation is at once the interpretation of policy "texts" and the creation of a "text" (in the form of agency actors' enacted interpretations of policy texts) which itself will be interpreted, together with legislative texts, by clients, community members, policy-relevant publics near and far, evaluators, legislators, policy analysts, and potentially many others. Observations about the communication of policy meanings as one form of interpretive analysis are extended in Chapter 9. It is a view of the policy process that brings communications (oral, visual, and textual) and dramatism together: we are all in a very large setting, actively watching and acting in and enacting the play of societal meanings, communicating them to ourselves and to others through our own actions and through others' actions that validate or undercut our own values, beliefs, and feelings.

𝕿𝖍𝖊 𝖂𝖔𝖗𝖑𝖉 𝖎𝖘 𝕱𝖑𝖆𝖙

∽ Class of 1491 ∽

This framed sign hangs in David Rosenhan's office at Stanford Law School.

NOTES

1. Zipori's first report to Aranne carries a March 1966 publication date. However, the report refers to an "earlier study" dated June 1966. Since all other informants corroborate a later publication date, I have concluded that the March 1966 date is a typographical error which should read 1967. Otherwise, these events would have to have taken place in the fall of 1965, a timing not supported by other evidence.

2. The stories about Aranne, Zipori, Goldman, and Pozner are based on my interview with Pozner and on Lavi's published interview with her (Lavi 1979). Others, including David Harman and Dan Ronnen, also reported Aranne's instruction to Zipori to "fly over the rooftops," which by 1980 had entered agency lore.

3. "Community development" is known in French as "l'animation" and in American English as "community organization." It is a professional subfield of social work in the United States, and an outgrowth of British and French colonial practices, with affiliated university-level degree programs. The practice in Israel has been informed primarily by its British roots, although leaning more and more toward American models since the late 1960s.

4. Indeed, in analyzing the implementation studies literature, one can find a correspondence between the level of the implementing agency being

analyzed and the perceived nature of the implementation problem (Yanow 1987a).

5. In the following paragraphs I will give a very brief overview of these ideas. The history is told in greater detail in many other sources, including Abbagnano (1967), Burrell and Morgan (1979, ch. 6), Dallmayr and McCarthy (1977), Passmore (1967), Polkinghorne (1983), and others cited in the next several notes. Also, several excellent discussions of the limits of positivist approaches to policy analysis have been published. See, e.g., Beam and Simpson (1984), Fay (1975), Fischer (1980), Hawkesworth (1988), Kelly and Maynard-Moody (1993), and Martin Landau's foreword to, as well as the essays in, Portis and Levy (1988). For an overview of feminist and postmodern theories, see Nicholson (1990).

6. The logical positivism of the Vienna School philosophers (e.g., Moritz Schlick, Otto Neurath, Kurt Gödel, Rudolf Carnap) is considered the intellectual descendant of nineteenth-century positivism (see Abbagnano 1967), although others contest this linkage of the two sets of ideas.

7. The distinction between facts and values lies at the core of policy analysis as it has traditionally been presented. Hawkesworth (1988, especially ch. 4) presents a detailed and very clear summary of the insupportability of this distinction.

8. I use the word paradigm in a Kuhnian sense, to mean something akin to a religious conviction that organizes one's perception of the world. Paradigms are no more interchangeable or ephemeral than convictions of other sorts. They are "ways of seeing" or *weltanschaaungen* (worldviews), conditioned by family and community backgrounds, education, training, experience, and so forth—but that cannot be removed or replaced like a pair of eyeglasses. Moving from one paradigm to another requires an experience often likened to a religious conversion or a gestalt shift (as Kuhn [1970, pp. 62–65 and 114–15] illustrates and discusses so clearly). From a positivist paradigm, an interpretivist argument makes no sense; and while many interpretivists, having been "converted" from a positivist view, can still make some sense of a positivist argument, most cannot comprehend how someone could still believe a positivist argument. See Kuhn (1970, 1977).

9. Much of the language of policy analysis is marked by a military metaphor—seeing clients as "targets," for instance—brought and introduced, perhaps, by Robert McNamara when he moved from the (U.S.) Department of Defense to the Ford Foundation, along with the PPBS that he brought with him from there. DeHaven-Smith (1988) has also noted the imagery of social policies as missiles.

10. Maynard-Moody and Stull (1987) also make this point.

11. Edelman (1980), among others, has noted the relationship between the degree of ambiguity of policy goals and their potency. See also Cohen and March (1986) and March and Olsen (1976) on ambiguity and organizations.

12. See Polkinghorne (1983, ch. 1) for an eminently readable history of these ideas.

13. Gray, Bougon, and Donnellon (1985) present an interesting discussion of the construction and de-struction of shared meaning.

14. See Part II of Berger and Luckmann (1966) for an elaboration of this process, beginning with a prototypical first and second persons and proceeding with the addition of another generation in time. See also Geertz (1983b) on what is "common" about common sense.

15. This discussion is obviously highly condensed. For more extensive presentations of these various approaches, see, e.g., Ricoeur (1971) and Taylor (1971) on hermeneutical approaches, Berger and Luckmann (1966) and Schutz (1967) on phenomenology, Mead (1934) or Charon (1985) on symbolic interaction, Garfinkel (1977) on ethnomethodology. See also Rabinow and Sullivan's (1979) introduction and collected essays for an overview of "the interpretive turn" in the context of the social sciences.

16. Gagliardi (1990) notes that most studies of organizational culture have neglected built space and the feeling component (which he calls pathos) that is so strongly present there, attending instead to values and beliefs, what he calls the moral (ethos) and cognitive (logos) components. Witkin (1990) attributes this neglect of the aesthetic dimension of organizational life to the conception of organizations as "rational-technical machinery" (p. 326) that emphasizes cognitive processes at the expense of the nonrational. This would explain why built spaces and their affective responses become more visible elements of analysis once one takes an interpretive approach to organizations.

17. It may be useful here to distinguish between "signal" and "symbol." Unlike a symbol, a signal—e.g., a traffic light, a stop sign—is task- or action-oriented. Both are representative, but a signal is more immediately purposive.

18. Vickers (1973) and others have noted this sort of discrepancy. Argyris and Schon (1974) refer to it as the difference between one's "espoused" theory (what I say) and one's "theory in use" (what I do).

19. Feldman (1994) also makes this distinction.

20. This, of course, was Marshall McLuhan's notion (1964). Edelman (1995) explores such interconnections in the realm of art and politics.

The stance outlined here is represented in some of the work in organizational culture (e.g., Gagliardi 1990, B. A. Turner 1990). Schein (1985) presents organizational culture as a layering of artifacts, values, and assumptions (p. 14), without noting their representational relationship and the necessity of artifacts for the communication of culture. Deal and Kennedy (1982), by contrast, appear to emphasize only the artifactual component of organizational culture. My argument here is that artifacts are a necessary but not sufficient component of culture. They are linked as embodiments or symbolic representations to their meanings (values, beliefs, feelings). This is a mutually reinforcing and recreating relationship, carried out through our daily interaction with the artifacts of our creation. But see Hatch (1993a) for a different interpretive approach.

21. Dunn cites as the source of this story Paul Watzlawick, John Weakland, and Richard Fisch, *Change: Principles of Problem Formation and Problem Resolution* (New York: Norton, 1974), p. xi.

22. Organizational culture studies provide many examples of these various kinds of symbols. See, e.g., the essays collected in Frost et al. (1985,

1991), Gagliardi (1990), and Pondy et al. (1983), or the Fall 1983 issue of *Administrative Science Quarterly*.

23. In their analysis of how people "receive" their views of the world from television news broadcasts, Neuman, Just, and Crigler (1992) found that, unlike communications theories that would lead us to expect audiences to be passive targets of a unidirectional line of meaning-making, hearers of TV news actively engage in the construction of meaning by interpreting what they hear.

24. Such models are found, e.g., in Anderson (1990, p. 36), Palumbo (1988, p. 19), Theodoulou (1995, p. 86), and many other public policy textbooks.

25. This is one of the implications of Lipsky's (1978) title, "Standing the study of public policy implementation on its head."

26. The awareness of more distant publics typically depends on the news media, and the media were happy to comply when the local legislations were initially passed, given the dramatic nature of the antinuclear statement. Since then, however, national awareness has largely fallen off, although on visiting these cities one sees the signs proclaiming their status posted on the streets.

27. See Ricoeur (1971) and Taylor (1971) on treating acts as texts. I have developed this argument in respect to built spaces in Yanow (1995a). The reference to Iser is unintentionally ironic, because he argues there, in response to Stanley Fish, that it is inappropriate to extend the metaphor of text analysis to acts—a view not shared by Ricoeur, Taylor, or apparently, Fish.

28. In these circumstances, an established agency might pose a threat by arguing that the new one duplicates its services, thereby seeking to absorb the new agency or its funds. Indeed, spending allocated budgets becomes, at times, an act symbolizing that the agency is successfully implementing its mandate, as Pressman and Wildavsky (1979, p. 137) and Sapolsky (1972, ch. 8) discovered.

29. Stone (1988) makes a parallel argument when she contrasts the market model of policy analysis with the model of the polis.

30. Van Maanen (1988) discusses "realist" and other forms of presenting ethnographic research. The construction of ethnographic texts has been given much attention of late (see Clifford 1988, Geertz 1988, Marcus and Fischer 1986). Many of their points also hold for written presentations of other types of research. See, e.g., McCloskey (1985) on economics and Fischer and Forester (1993) on policy analysis. On organizational theory, see Golden-Biddle and Locke (1994), Hatch (1993b), Kunda (1992, appendix), O'Connor (1995), Smircich (1995), Van Maanen (1995), Yanow (1995b). I return to this in Chapter 2.

31. Martin (1992) follows a similar path in progressing from unitary views of organizational culture to views of subcultures to a more fragmented, multivocal view of contradictions.

2

How Do You Know When You've Found an Organizational Metaphor? Reflecting on Methods

> Believing, with Max Weber, that man is an animal suspended in webs of significance he himself has spun, I take culture to be those webs, and the analysis of it to be therefore not an experimental science in search of law but an interpretive one in search of meaning. It is explication I am after. . . .
> —Clifford Geertz (1973, p. 5)

"How do you know when you have found . . . ?" is a question commonly asked by those first coming to interpretive methods, whether in application to language, acts, or objects. While symbolic anthropologists typically engage procedures for identifying conceptual categories and their labels (whether of kinship structures or tools or origin myths), these questions and techniques have rarely been included in political science curricula, and not much more often than that in organizational studies or administration coursework.[1] Moreover, issues pertaining to the writing of research have remained largely unexamined until very recently, even in anthropology.[2] Much has been written on ethnographic, participant-observation, and other such methods, and I will not reproduce that material here.[3] But other areas do warrant attention. One is a more general set of issues that arises around the intersection of these methods and questions of meaning: e.g., how does the researcher discover and know when an object, act, or language element has symbolic meaning for policy and/or agency actors? What weight should be given to researchers' meanings when these are not explicitly expressed by situational actors? A second set of issues concerns the constructions of meaning in the presentation of research findings in articles, books, and other academic narratives.

A formal account of the methods used in the research presented here might begin as follows: The case study of the Israel Corporation of Community Centers (ICCC) in the chapters that follow is based on participant-observation and nonparticipant-observation, interviews, agency records and files, and newspaper accounts, gathered in two separate undertakings. But while this is an accurate encapsulation of what I did and the kinds of sources I drew on, it does not address a concern that is central to many who contemplate undertaking this kind of work: How do you recognize an organizational metaphor as such when it comes up in an interview or in an agency document? And even if you perceive its metaphoric nature, how do you know that it is significant or meaning-ful for the organization? The same questions can be, and are, asked about symbolic objects and symbolic acts.

There are many texts on sources of data and how to "collect" them: how to conduct open-ended interviews, what participant-observation means, and so forth. What sorts of data I gathered, from what sources, and under what conditions is related in the next section. But that sort of account does not really convey how meanings are made of those data. Researchers' sensemaking transpires both during field research—during conversations and observations—and later on, often away from the research site, while writing research reports and analyses.

The distinction between data "collection" activities—observation, interviews, participation—and data "analysis"—making sense of what has been "collected"—may have some temporal reality (I am "in the field" before I am at my desk) but is conceptually artificial. Much sensemaking goes on, of necessity, while observing, interviewing, participating, as well as prior to "entering" the field. Nevertheless, there are techniques of analysis that may be brought into play later on, as one begins to write a formal presentation of what one has seen, that are typically not invoked while one is immersed in the daily life of the research setting. I will follow here the convention of treating the collection and analysis of data as analytically separable acts, although they are, in practice, interwoven.

In the following, capital letters for Center or Community Center refer to the ICCC Centers; lowercase letters refer to the generic idea of community center or to non-ICCC centers.

COLLECTING DATA

I was both a participant and an observer, under circumstances I shall shortly describe, in one ICCC Community Center from November 1, 1972 through February 1973, and in a second from mid-March 1973 until the end of August 1975. Five years later, in September 1980, I undertook follow-up interviews, document analysis, and further observation for nearly five months under different auspices, also described below. While the fieldwork recounted here is based primarily on my experiences in the second Center from 1973 to 1975, it is leavened and balanced by experience in the first Center, visits to and observation of other Centers, extensive conversations with staff from other Centers, and work on a national in-service training committee based in ICCC headquarters that began in the spring of 1974, as well as by the subsequent interviews, observation, and archival research done in 1980–81. Since then, I have followed the agency through newspaper and colleagues' accounts, supplemented by occasional interviews with Joint Distribution Committee-Israel or ICCC staff and consultants. The case, then, focuses on the founding of the ICCC and its first several years of development.

I went to Israel a second time in late August 1972, having spent the 1969–70 academic year as a university student in Jerusalem. Jerusalem served then, as now, as a magnet for Jewish Americans committed to the idea of a Jewish state. Wanting to get a sense of what the "real" Israel was like, I intentionally chose to live and work elsewhere than in Jerusalem with its extensive American expatriate population (although in many ways I would have preferred a more urban location to the rural areas where I ended up). I began working as a community organizer for the ICCC in a development town in the middle of the country nearly a three-hour bus ride, making connections, from any of the three major cities (Haifa, Tel Aviv, Jerusalem). One of the first Community Centers to open, it operated an extension in a distant neighborhood populated by recent arrivals from Soviet Georgia. Although I spoke Hebrew, they did not. It was difficult to outline a workable program. The winter was wet, and cold. The ICCC made housing arrangements for Center directors and some community workers so they could live in the remote development towns where they worked. My apartment had no heat, no heater, broken windows, and country-sized rats. I was not greatly saddened to leave when the Center declared bankruptcy.

During this time, the ICCC had been conducting in-service training sessions in two-day sessions once a month for its community organizers throughout the country. Aside from the academic and social aspects, these gatherings were wonderful opportunities to hear case studies of the particular circumstances of residents and Centers in development towns and urban neighborhoods in all their variety. At the session following my departure from the first Center, one of my colleagues introduced me to a Center director from a town on the coast who had been looking for an organizer for some time. I proceeded to spend the next two and a half years there, initially as a community organizer, later supervising a staff of three full-time organizers, a street-gang worker, and a unit of over fifty volunteers, and later still also as director of adult education programs. I left to continue full-time graduate study and pursue the analysis and ideas that are presented here.

My participant-observation was not initially undertaken, then, for purposes of degree-related research. Rather, I undertook research according to the norms of professional community organization practice, including the requisite field notes.[4] I entered the field with the explicit intention of learning about the lived experience of Israel as a society and polity. It soon became clear to me that development towns constituted a settlement category other than any with which I was already familiar: the city with its neighborhoods, the kibbutz, the moshav (another form of agricultural collective). Their mix of people—Soviet Georgians with Moroccans, Indians with Poles, Tunisians, Algerians, Libyans, Persians, and so on—made the development towns unlike other more ethnically homogeneous settlements. I enrolled in graduate programs, first in urban studies and then in city and regional planning, to understand the development towns in their social and physical planning contexts. Course research for these programs also guided some of my observations of agency and community activities.

My field notes recorded the plan of the town, mapping income, country of origin, family size, and other demographics onto physical layout; a "map" of existing social service agencies and voluntary associations with their areas of service provision and political party affiliation; a sociometry of leadership—who speaks to whom, on what occasions, and, as important, which members of the community were not on speaking terms. Data were gathered from extensive interviews and conversations with town and agency leaders (including the mayor, vice mayor, local government department heads, agency directors, community organizers in other agencies, school principals and teachers, heads of political parties and their affiliated health, labor, women's, and youth organizations, and prominent troublemakers and juvenile delinquents—the equivalent of today's gang leaders), as well as with residents I called on in their homes or encountered while walking around the neighborhoods or in shops. I was present in the Community Center or elsewhere in the town in the morning, during the midday hours (when offices traditionally closed and people ate their large meal and rested), afternoon, and evening (the Center stayed open until 10 or 11 p.m., depending on the day). Since the Center organized holiday activities, I was there for those celebrations as well: Chanuka, Purim, Independence Day. As Center hours were extended, I started staying or returning on weekends (Friday and Saturday afternoons and evenings). After some time, as I began to know people more informally, I was invited to weddings, births, and other family gatherings and attended funerals.

My field notes also contained reflections on what I observed, transcriptions or summaries of conversations, notes on meetings. I attempted to understand how organizational and community members (including local agency and government staffs) made sense of their daily lives and surroundings, as well as of the Community Center. Interviews and conversations were oriented around the town's Community Center as a specific place and as a concept: was the person with whom I was talking familiar with the Center and, if so, what was his or her relationship to it? In taking the Community Center as the specific focus of the conversation, I was able to learn much about the person's family and immigration story, town history, voting patterns, and political intrigues—who came from where and who was related to whom, which usually overlapped with party lines.

When I returned to the United States in 1975, I took a number of questions with me to full-time graduate work: What is the meaning of "community"? What is the history and philosophy of community organization and development? What is the history and purpose of community centers? How do these efforts in nonformal education at the micro-level relate to national social policies? (I also took what I was told was a Moroccan Hebrew accent and an understanding that what it meant to be an "Israeli" was highly context-specific.) The question that continued to dog me was, given that community organizers and Center directors in the field were working in an agency that had been created by the national government to accomplish certain social policies, why was it so difficult to get things done in the field? This question led me to the burgeoning literatures in policy and implementation analysis and in organizational theory and behavior. But I also came to find these fields' insistence on exclusively literal meanings, goal-oriented action, and the politics-administration dichotomy limiting in their ability to help me understand what had happened in "my" development town with its Community Center. In assuming the existence of a single, accurate way of expressing and understanding policy and agency purpose, these theories did not—and could not—explain the existence of multiple and often conflicting understandings that I had found in the field.

The exploration of an alternative approach that took as its starting point the "reality" of multiple interpretations sent me back to Israel for a second round of research, entailing both written and oral sources as well as observation. This was undertaken between mid-September 1980 and February 1, 1981 under the auspices and hospitality of the Research and Planning Unit of the Joint Distribution Committee (JDC)-Israel in Jerusalem. (As will be seen in the next chapter, JDC-Israel assumed a large role in supporting the ICCC's development.) I had access to JDC-Israel's current files on their work with the ICCC, as well as their and the ICCC's archival files (and those of Malben, as JDC-Israel was known until 1975). These files contained correspondence, protocols of meetings, budgets, proposals, internal memos, and notes to the files. Other written sources included ICCC annual reports (1973–80); the agency's annual survey, conducted by Uri Yanai from 1976 on; and ICCC Executive Director Hayim Zipori's two surveys and his other reports and lectures.

Contemporaneous newspaper accounts provided useful background for contextualizing agency files as well as the recollections of people I interviewed. I relied extensively on the archives at the *Jerusalem Post*, the English-language daily, and to a lesser extent on the Tel

Aviv-based Hebrew dailies *Ha'aretz* and *Ma'ariv*. Agency files were especially helpful in recreating a sense of the development of the ICCC, while the newspaper columns and articles presented pictures of the mood of the times, social and economic problems, riots and demonstrations by various groups, and so forth.

Formally, I interviewed thirty-seven people in this second research phase, several of them more than once, some of whom concurrently or sequentially played different roles within the ICCC. In choosing whom to interview, I selected respondents who could tell me about different aspects of the ICCC and its Centers. I interviewed staff from agency headquarters and the field; Center directors and community organizers, the two most clearly articulated groups of Center staff workers; veterans and newcomers to the agency; staff from large Centers and small ones, from development towns and city slums, from the four general regions of the country (North, Central, South, Jerusalem); and the founders and early policymakers who were still alive, as well as former staff from the Centers' first years and two of Minister Aranne's associates. This represents a categorization of positions within the agency structure; professional groups; tenure with the agency; Center size (loosely correlated with service population size and reflected in budget, staff, and physical plant); settlement type and geographic location. Counting roles rather than individuals, I formally interviewed twelve community organizers, nine directors, six community organization supervisors, five JDC staff, five faculty from the Schwartz Program to Train Community Center Directors and Senior Staff, four members of local or national boards of directors, five ICCC headquarters staff, the *Jerusalem Post* social affairs reporter, Prime Minister Golda Meir's assistant for welfare matters, and two local residents. (There are more roles than individuals because some people filled more than one role in the agency.) I also observed Centers of different sizes and "in-house" reputations throughout the country at different hours of the day, and one of the ICCC's training sessions for new directors.

I was simultaneously carrying out a small research effort for a department in JDC-Israel exploring the nature of community organization practice in the ICCC, and introduced myself in that capacity. Interviews generally lasted sixty to ninety minutes and were open-ended. I asked directors and community organizers how their work, Center, and neighborhood compared with others they knew; about their professional background; how they saw their roles and how these related to the ICCC's goals; about relations with supervisors, colleagues, coworkers, and headquarters concerning work issues; how they communicated their goals to local residents, other agencies, and their boards. Other interviews focused on policy and agency history and development or on current agency programs and future plans, depending on the individual's role in the agency.

People were generally receptive to my requests for interviews. Community organizers in the field seemed intrigued that a former organizer would return to interview them. As a group, they were particularly encouraging of my research. For Center directors, however, the fact that I was "coming from Jerusalem" at times lent an aura to my visit that I found not beneficial for my purposes. Although I welcomed the entree that "researcher from JDC" provided, I did not want to cast myself in the role of inspector-from-headquarters. If directors perceived me in such a role, I sensed they would be more likely to slant our conversation, perceiving (incorrectly) an opportunity through me to convey desirable images back to HQ. I hoped that by reflecting on my former role as a community organizer in two ICCC Centers, I might encourage directors to share their own reflections. I was successful in this in most cases. When I was able to approach directors through mutual friends among agency staff or extra-agency contacts, such reflection was more likely. On other occasions, however, more interview time was spent in normative discussions of ideal Center practices, rather than in conversation on actual ones.

Two categories of respondents are not included among the people formally interviewed in this second research phase. Interviewing former-colleagues-turned-friends about professional matters proved a quirky art. We were unable to sustain a new role for myself as interviewer and a new definition, however temporary, of our relationship. I found myself unable to direct the conversation to agency-related matters. For that same reason, I refrained after a few attempts from further revisiting in a research capacity the two towns where I had worked. I found I could not maintain an investigative posture in the face of former "clients" and coworkers who had become friends.

Second, I was unable to interview local residents successfully about their interpretations of Center symbols. On the one hand, local patterns of hospitality preserve a certain distance between strangers which I could not bridge to discuss the questions I had. Answering questions of meaning and interpretation would have meant, for them, revealing to a stranger more than one ordinarily would. At the same time, people in development towns were by then accustomed to survey research, since they had been subjected to endless ministry questionnaires. Asking my questions drew people into a survey question response pattern, part of which was—again, because of hospitality concepts—providing an answer designed to please the researcher. The two residents I did interview formally I met for the first time and in social or work situations removed from the context of the Centers, and I was able to extend these casual conversations into more focused interviews.

Most of what I write, then, about residents' interpretations of agency symbols is drawn from the first research phase of observing and interacting with the citizens of two developments towns over nearly three years or based on interviews with others who have worked and/or lived as intimately with development town or neighborhood residents. For it is only such intimacy that allows one to begin to understand, from within, the meanings people make and the images and impressions they create and form in interpreting symbolic artifacts. No amount of survey research could accomplish this.

For this reason—difficulties of language and access that did not permit me to learn the community and its values "from within"—as well, the initial and follow-up studies excluded the few ICCC Centers built in Arab villages and neighborhoods. The analysis presented here also does not pertain to them.

MAKING SENSE

These kinds of data and methods of data collection are characteristic of the policy and implementation narratives—presented as case studies that recount events enacted by many people in the intergovernmental, interdepartmental environment of a policy sector—common in academic writing (e.g., Allison 1971, Bardach 1977, Nakamura 1990, Pressman and Wildavsky 1973, Sapolsky 1972) and in case development programs in public policy curricula.[5] These use multiple methods that invoke general modes of sensemaking to attend to various facets of human life. Navigating the bureaucracies, participating in work and taking lunch breaks, shopping in markets and traveling city streets, reading newspapers and agency documents, conversing, interviewing, listening—researchers using these modes gather information in the form of language, acts, and objects (or impressions of them), both of their own sensemaking and of actors' situational interpretations. Based on such interpretive modes of research, they present the context of meaning in which policy events, through their language, objects, and/or acts, are interpreted by relevant publics. In discussing the same events with different people, researchers begin to construct a "thick description" (Geertz 1973) of what transpired, (re)presenting an event from different angles.

More specific methods for analyzing these various forms of data have also been developed. These include, among others, semiotics and deconstruction, from linguistics and literary theory, for the analysis of oral and written language; ethnomethodology and symbolic interaction, from social psychology, for the analysis of conversations, interviews, and interpersonal or group-based roles; dramaturgy, from both literary theory and social psychology, for the analysis of acts, settings, and roles; human or social geography, from geography, urban planning, and architecture, for the analysis of physical objects, such as built spaces.[6] Each of the analytic chapters (5–7) further discusses the kinds of data and the modes of analysis used for specific elements.

But in a more general sense, how does a researcher discern that a word is being used metaphorically, and that the metaphor has implications throughout the organization, beyond a single speaker—in short, that any of these more specific analytic methods needs to be invoked?

In making meaning out of events observed and recorded, we bring into consideration whatever elements are at hand. For us to observe them, they must have what Vickers (1968) called "a foothold in the mind." I had been trying to explain the conflict between community organizers and Center directors as a conflict between two different communities. This led to a relative dead end of sociological and political definitions of "community." But this was the niche that the notion of "communities as symbol-sharing groups" took hold of. The idea of symbols opened that line of inquiry to a new realm, as the literature on symbols led to the analytic language of myths, metaphors, and so forth, from a variety of meaning-focused disciplines.

This is what I brought back to the field in the second research phase, to interviews, written texts, and observations of daily work.

Starting, as I did, with an orientation toward making sense of, and sensemaking in, an agency with respect to its implementation of a specific policy mandate, I was oriented less toward a single classification of data and more toward an intergovernmental, interdepartmental situation with its variety of data as they came to hand. The three-part categorization of human action presented in this study emerged out of the types of data that were observed rather than from a predetermined set of analytic methods. Out of these data, as I sat in my study afterwards struggling to construct a written description of the intricacies of policy implementation as it looked in the field, emerged the understanding of language, acts, and objects as artifacts expressing values, beliefs, and feelings, through whose use those values, beliefs, and feelings are communicated.

Interpretive policy analysis presupposes a commitment on the researcher's part to work with the understandings of situational actors—policymakers, agency staff, residents—and to allow the relevant categories of analysis to emerge out of those interpretations, themselves the data for analysis. At the same time, however, these data are not "collected" or "gathered" as if they were so many butterflies or seashells strewn about an organizational beach just waiting to be found. Although I did not initially have a set of conceptual boxes labeled "language," "objects," and "acts" into which to force different species of data, I did have a great big, undifferentiated box labeled "meaning"—and this box directed and filtered my attention while I was in the midst of observing, participating, and conversing.[7] After the first research phase, as I reflected on the contents of this box and read academic discussions about symbolic representations, differentiations began to crystallize. The early forms of the three-part categorization I use here emerged during reflection on the second research phase, and they have developed further since then.

The categories, then, did not develop entirely from the data, although neither did they emerge as a piece from the various literatures—symbolic anthropology, human geography, cognitive linguistics—I was reading. (I would now call these literatures "applied" phenomenology and the like: they were oriented toward analytic and methodological practices; through them I came to the philosophical literature that supports them.) In working back and forth between these literatures and field notes, transcripts of interviews, and various printed data (agency files and documents, newspaper reports, etc.), patterns and themes emerged.

Meaning-focused research requires self-reflexivity: the researcher is constantly "living" in two worlds, making sense of self ("my" world) and making sense of the community, organization, or other type of group which is being studied (the "other" world). In putting oneself in that other world, one becomes "the stranger"—the one for whom the social rules and norms are not necessarily known or transparent and immediately discoverable. In this process of intentional and reflective "self-estrangement," one creates the possibility for "puzzles" or "tensions" to emerge between what one expects to find, hear, see, feel and what one does find, hear, see, feel. It is out of reflection on these puzzles or tensions that the researcher begins to perceive that members of the group being studied have invested something with meaning that is different from hers, or that different subgroups disagree about what that meaning is. Such perception can be corroborated, refuted, or modified by further conversation and/ or observation directed to this end. Identifying that something is meaningful for a group of policy or agency actors, and identifying what that meaning is (or, in the second instance, what the conflicting meanings are) begins to establish the symbolic relationships active in the specific situation. Out of this identification emerges a sense of language that is organizationally metaphoric, acts that are organizationally mythic, objects that are organizationally symbolic, and so on.

For example, several people repeated phrases about supermarkets. Once I could estrange myself enough from the field context in which it seemed a "normal" thing to say, I began to see that it was peculiar. In what ways was the Community Center a supermarket? In the context of the interviews, it had made sense—had seemed unremarkable—because people then went on to talk about Community Centers as if they *were* supermarkets. But with distance (geographic, time, analytic) from the interviews, its strangeness emerged. I could then begin to see it as a metaphor whose meaning was significant for the group and work at it as a puzzle, drawing on what I knew about metaphors and symbolic representations of meaning.

Similarly, with respect to myths. I did not start with the idea of myth and look to "collect" some. I started with puzzles from the field. For example, why repeat the question "What are our goals?" every year? Surely, after ten years of operations, goal definitions would be clear. The question was not, "How have our goals changed since last year, or since five years ago?" I assumed that the question had some meaning, at least to the Executive Director who continually asked it, and—I hoped for his sake—for others in the agency who heard and answered it. Could I learn what sense he or they made of it? Could I make it make sense in the context of what I knew of other agency practices? That the question was repeated annually raised the possibility of it having the character of ritual; and various approaches to the study of myths drew a link to ritual as enacted myth (one of the things that has led me to identify myths as a form of act rather than language).

The puzzle of the buildings emerged also from contrasting and comparing, from estrangement and the expectations it fosters. I noticed that I could drive into development towns or urban neighborhoods where I had never been before and within five minutes usually find the Community Center. It became a test of my powers of observation and reasoning. That meant, to me, a design distinctiveness from surrounding buildings, both public and residential. It also suggested a certain uniformity of design over ten years, different architects, and different locales—as contrasted with the agency's Operating Principles that focused on local needs and characteristics. I also made a practice, in both research phases, of asking residents in various sectors of the places I visited if they knew the Community Center. When they did, they usually identified it by a particular phrase (not by its donor's name, as Centers were often called, or even as "Community Center") and described it in physical design terms ("You mean that big glass building . . . ?"). These and other experiences and observations led me to consider that the buildings themselves communicated meaning—as the literature in human geography suggests would be the case.

The idea that programs also embodied and communicated meanings in ways that were significant to and different for agency members and residents became clear from printed agency materials and correspondence (letters, memos) and conversations with residents. Once I had identified specific programs and other artifacts that seemed significant expressions of meaning to policy- and agency-relevant publics, similarities and differences between them suggested the categorical groupings of language, objects, and acts. The analyses of specific elements of all three of these categories proceeds by identifying contrasts made apparent through self-estrangement: at times, similarities and differences; at other times, presences (what attention is directed toward) and absences or silences (what attention is diverted from).

A useful starting point for analysis, then, whether in agencies, in the legislative arena, or in community settings, is the identification of "communities of interpretation"—those for whom policy and agency artifacts have (or are likely to have) common meanings. In doing so, individuals and groups for whom that is not the case may also be identified. Such identification works back and forth between symbol-sharing "communities"—professionals, class and race/ethnic groups, organizational groups—and specific artifacts whose significance to the group emerges from observations of and conversations about the ways they talk about or otherwise engage them. This is a methodological view of the relationship between artifacts and their meanings diagrammed in Figure 1-1.

Meaning-centered methods such as semiotics are intended to help make more explicit the artifactual meanings that are tacitly known and common to these groups. Part of the problem of moving between methodological generalism—participant-observation or ethnography or cultural analysis—and specific analytic techniques—semiotics or ethnomethodology (which have very specific rules of analysis)—is that meaning is far more involved than any single tool or artifact can convey. If the research objective is to develop an understanding of what and how a specific policy means, we cannot, under typical circumstances, limit ourselves to one artifact and one analytic technique.

Ironically, it is "easier" in terms of the potential for understanding to go farther away from the context of one's "native" understanding, precisely because outside of explicitly instructional contexts, meanings—taken-for-granted, common sense—are usually not made and conveyed explicitly. Aside from the classroom and job training, acculturation is one of the central instructional contexts, and while this takes place "naturally" and tacitly for a child being socialized into a family and society, it is less so for the adult stranger—whether immigrant or ethnographer. They have other contexts of sensemaking in which strange language, acts, and objects and their meanings do not make sense, happily for the ethnographer, less so (typically) for the immigrant—although both may suffer similar discomfitures of estrangement from familiar settings and practices. Such intentional estrangement is less easily obtained in an organization within one's own native culture, but it is not impossible. To the extent that language and conceptual categories are being increasingly problematized, rather than treated as "natural," conceptual self-estrangement in one's own land may become less difficult and less infrequent.[8]

WHOSE MEANINGS?

The language of metaphors, myths, and symbols is analytic language. Agency or community members typically do not speak of their own actions in these terms. The language, to pursue one example at length, used in Chapter 5 in spelling out what I have identified as an organizational metaphor—the vocabulary of shopkeepers, peddlers, clerks, goods, merchandise, turnover, and other terms that are implicated by talking and thinking about a Community Center as if it were a supermarket—is largely my language. It comes from reflecting, first, on what it meant to say, as organizational members often did, "the Community Center will be a functional supermarket." That meant identifying the phrase as an organizational metaphor—the notion of a supermarket—and asking three questions: What were the characteristics of a supermarket in Israel in the late 1960s (at the time that the metaphor came into use in the ICCC)? (That is, what did it mean in that context, at that time?) In what ways was an ICCC Community Center like those features of a supermarket? In what ways was an ICCC Community Center *not* like those features of a supermarket? It is, in short, an analysis based on context-specific similarities and contrasts or oppositions.[9] Most of the analytic ideas came from juxtaposing the meanings of "supermarket" and "Community Center" as someone living with them would have understood them. The attributes of each clarified my understanding of the other. Unpacking the metaphor in this way made some ICCC choices and practices make sense—the clashes between community organizers and Center directors, for example—in ways they had not before. Occasionally, members of the organization themselves used supermarket language in expressing their understanding of agency actions (the female director quoted in Chapter 5, for example). Some of the ideas have come from others who read the chapter in one version or another. Although unfamiliar with the historical context, they understood something about American supermarkets that had escaped my attention, but that fit with my understanding of the context.

As Feldman (1994) notes, such an analysis "relies on the researcher's intrinsic understanding of the culture" in which the metaphor or other artifact is used. The analytic technique itself does not supply the insight. The insight comes from the researcher, although the technique may help make analysis more explicit and more systematic.

What makes an interpretation of the metaphor "good" is not only its logical consistency with the idea of supermarket, but its fit in the agency's historical context. One reader of my analysis, for example, observed that supermarkets and their clerks and owners are purveyors of food, and food is a primary human need, according to Abraham Maslow's hierarchy.[10] This line of thinking suggests a way of making sense of a social service agency that offers ballet and sports classes, items higher up on Maslow's scale, while it purports to meet communities' "felt needs" of a more basic sort. A provocative idea, it exists outside of the context of the Community Center: none of the ICCC documents that I came across, notwithstanding its heavily social science and needs orientation, mention Maslow, nor did any agency founders or staff I interviewed. Unlike other interpretations of the metaphor that are grounded in views expressed in interviews or agency documents or observed practices, this one is not.

Another reader noted that supermarkets are "such bland, soul-less places where we get standardized, often low quality food." He then asked, "Was this also part of the [Centers' intended] meaning?"— drawing an analogy to housing developments as contrasted with the idealized concept of "home."[11] This is also a provocative insight into possible meanings of metaphoric supermarkets, but it is one that reads supermarkets of a particular sort in an American context of the 1990s, rather than in the Israeli context of the 1970s. There, then, they were exciting, modern innovations (over small shops and outdoor markets) that represented the heights of American achievement. There was every intention on the part of the ICCC to offer high-quality programs, and they were perceived locally as doing so.

Again, a "good" interpretation makes sense in a societal and organizational context, and dovetails with other symbolic elements. The process of sensemaking reflected in this book's case example encompasses agency members' intentions and policy-relevant publics' responses, where each of these two broad groups of "readers" themselves include numerous sensemakers, not all of them making the same sense of the same policy and agency artifacts. At the same time, the researcher brings her or his own experiences and training— "footholds"—to the situation being studied, whatever philosophical, theoretical, or methodological approach is being used. The interpretive analytic process is a constant struggle to make sense that is tied as closely as is humanly possible to the lived experiences of residents, agency members, and other policy-relevant publics.

This raises many complex issues of first- and second-level interpretations (Schutz 1973), what Geertz (1983a), citing the psychoanalyst Heinz Kohut, called "experience-near" and "experience-distant" understandings. That is, those closest to the experience—residents and Center directors, for example—may report those experiences and their understandings of them. The researcher to whom they report their sensemakings in turn makes sense of and reports these, bringing all manner of other experiences to bear. In a policy and organizational context, these experiences include not only theoretical conceptualizations of policy and organizational processes, but also the senses made and reported by actors elsewhere in the context. The participant-observer ethnographer, while experiencing firsthand the same event experienced by a Center director, for example, is also making sense (or not) of that event in light of her own more familiar cultural practices that estrange her from that event. While the experience is immediate, and "near" in that sense, it is "distant" in the sense that its understanding is mediated by other webs of understanding.

The researcher is not a tabula rasa, then. Because he also brings his own sensemaking context, a situation may arise in which he makes sense of an event which its participants regard as an erroneous interpretation. Or the researcher may find the participants' interpretations limited. Developers of participatory action research (Whyte, Greenwood, and Lazes 1989, Greenwood, Gonzalez et al. 1991) and others (e.g., Behar 1994, Kelly and Maynard-Moody 1993) have sought to address such potential for conflict in the context of the connections between knowledge and power, by involving participants in research design and its narration. The Greenwood and Gonzalez analysis of the Mondragón work cooperative was researched and written together with members of the organization. Behar allows her "informant" to speak also, moving the analytic task from a single voice of the academically trained researcher to the dual voices of researcher and "subject." Others suggest that researchers' interpretations should be corroborated with participants. Whyte discussed his *Street Corner Society* manuscript with Doc, his main "informant," who read every page, and he sent the book to several of the "boys" on the corner after it was published, as he notes in the methodological appendix published in the second edition (1955). These are, however, still far removed from the kind of work that characterizes implementation and policy analyses, where ethnographic writing is still an anomaly. But it is in keeping with an interpretive philosophical position: casting academic researchers as interpreters of meanings and creators of texts implicates us in the world of rhetorical practices designed to persuade, rather than as producers of some metapractical work of positivist science.

Although this book has not been read as a whole by people I interviewed, worked with, or observed, I did discuss various aspects of my analysis with many of them at several points during the research. During the first research phase, my sensemaking of work and daily life entailed, perforce, a corroboration of my understandings with agency and community members. The uncertainty of moment-by-moment understanding, and the initially constant need for corroboration and correction, are both the cost and the benefit of such self-estrangement. In the second phase of the project, I was constantly checking my interpretations of agency events in interviews with agency members. In addition, those parts of the analysis that pertain to community organizers were presented to a staff meeting at the JDC.

At times, and especially in the latter instance, there have been strong disagreements with my analysis. In other instances, there have been equally strong agreements with it. This itself is part of the interpretive process: that is, one would expect multiple and varying interpretations of a research report. Most of the disagreement concerned the meanings that agency actions had for residents, important because of the implications for their participation in Center programs and, hence, the ICCC's ability to implement its policy mandate. This left the question of whether to discount my own interpretations, based as they were on firsthand experience. Reader-response theory provides one answer to the problem of participant-observers' and local actors' conflicting interpretations. Both, in this view, may be valid interpretations of actions- and other artifacts-as-texts, to the extent that both are context-specific. That is, neither is necessarily privileged as the "more accurate" truth, as both reflect lived experiences that are brought to the situation. What makes one more compelling is its explanatory power—its ability to explain more elements in more detail, more coherently and cohesively. When agency members' interpretations of residents' understandings conflicted with mine, I have tended to rely on local residents' interpretations. In this situation, they are the ones providing experience-near interpretations; the dissenters were farther from that, making their own interpretations of residents' meanings from agency offices removed from the local situation.

WRITING UP

The third aspect of the engagement with data, following on their collection and analysis, is the process of "writing them up." Again, this distinction as a separate phase is analytic alone: the practice of writing entails analyzing. As Mark Twain is reported to have said, How do I know what I think until I hear what I have to say? Writing is yet another way of thinking through data. Language constructs a reality, and while the textual map may not be the territory, it constructs one and guides us in it.

Writing has rarely been considered a methodological issue.[12] Once we move, however, to a world in which multiple, even incommensurable meanings are the rule and social science is not seen as mirroring reality, "writing up" itself becomes, if not a form of research as data collection, a form of research in its presentation or representation of data. Writing practices themselves are, in this view, "ways of worldmaking" (Goodman 1978). In presenting the researcher's view of policy and agency actors' views of their world, research narratives construct that world. Researcher-writers' rhetorical skills play a role in conveying veracity and validity—the researcher really was at the research site, as any reader can tell from all the detailed descriptions and quotations—creating "good" interpretations.

And yet, authors are not alone in worldmaking. Readers share this responsibility. Reader-response theory helps us understand this formulation, maintaining not only that meaning is indeterminate, but also that readers are not simply passive recipients of authors' intended meanings but also active constructors of meaning, bringing to their readings their own contexts, their own backgrounds and experiences. Meanings entail "authors" (in the language of texts), "texts" (literal ones or "text analogues"), and "readers," themselves the constructors of meaning. Text-based metaphors capture this sense better than the dramaturgical language of actors, settings, and audiences: in policy and agency situations, "readers" are also "actors," actively creating meanings as "authors" in their own right (although they may be less powerful in other ways). "Audience" is too passive. An interpretive analysis—one that is focused on meaning—needs to explore all three.

Since interpretive science does not claim to mirror the world, one may ask what other criteria for a good interpretation are. As noted above, a good second-level interpretation (that made by the researcher or policy analyst, for example) is one that most persuasively accounts for meaning to the actor in the event—persuasive, that is, both to the actor and to other readers. Good interpretations are those that rest on and provide "thick descriptions" (Geertz 1973) of their subject matter: that find symbolic expressions of the values, beliefs, and/or feelings in several modes of language, objects, and acts. Language, metaphoric or otherwise, fits together with objects and acts. The three categories are separable only analytically. In practice, they are interrelated. The "thicker" the description—the more details of lived experience, the more modes of symbolic expression that are discovered and described, the more nuanced and layered the text—the more one is ascertained of the validity of one's interpretation.[13] And so it is with the requirements of such thickly detailed description in mind that I present, in Chapter 3, an extensive history of the background and founding period of the ICCC.

Another researcher might equally well have written a story different from mine after experiencing the same interviews and events, and each story could be a "good" one. The nature of its "goodness" would be judged in part by its ability to "resonate" with other readers and researchers because they share sufficient consensus regarding meanings and interpretations. Individual experience and interpretation take place in the context of societal norms (Taylor 1971). These provide a measure of common understanding that makes interactions possible. Some of us may want to call this consensus "truth" or "objective reality," as we agree to the conventions of an "inch" or a "mile." This measure will be "tighter" or "closer," the stronger the cultural ties that bind us. From this point of view, policy analysis must be, to borrow Geertz's phrase (1973, p. 5), an interpretive science in search of meaning. Interpretive analysis of policy events is a thick description of meanings conveyed and made and their interpretations.[14]

This is not an argument against or denial of human inconsistency. Ethnographic and other types of interpretive research discover a world in which humans give expression to their values, beliefs, and feelings in multiple overlapping ways, through multiple and overlapping artifacts. In finding these, the meaning-focused re-searcher creates a picture of organizational or communal or other public, shared life that is, in some respects, like a Cubist portrait: one attempts (but never wholey succeeds) to portray the subject in all its details from various angles, as the portrait assembles elements to-gether from multiple angles, exposing the contrasting planes and the logically incompatible perceptions. This is the closest we can approxi-mate its "reality"—a reality constructed of actors' readings of it.

SUMMING UP

Interpretive analysis is not "impressionistic" analysis. The processes entailed in producing thick descriptions and in understanding how meanings are being conveyed and what those meanings are invoke their own methodological rigor. As with reports of experimentation, survey research, and other deductive forms, the (re)presentation of research results—the rhetorics of research narratives—plays a strong role in convincing readers of the "goodness" of the interpretation. A choice of method entails how "reality" (at times in the form of data) will be treated, but it also rests on presuppositions about reality at the same time that it creates those data. Assumptions about the know-ability of those data are similarly implicated. And the received view of science "supplies the methodological underpinnings" for its social science applications (Polkinghorne 1983, p. 59). That is, ontological and methodological assumptions about what policy analysis can dis-cover create the way we see policy processes as unfolding and create the data that we identify as those processes. In this sense, philosophi-cal presuppositions may be said to underlie different modes of policy analysis.

But in a policy and organizational context, it is not only "explica-tion" that we are after, to demur for a moment from Clifford Geertz. The normative embeddedness of policy analysis marks it as different from the practice of anthropological ethnographies. We explicate for a purpose: to clarify for other parties so that they may have a better understanding of how their "authored" meanings are being (mis)un-derstood. Stone (1988, p. viii) noted that although her approach might be seen as having some affinities with critical, postmodernist, and feminist theories, she "did not start out to be . . . self-consciously a practitioner of any of these schools." Like her, I came to this research without a base explicitly rooted in a particular philosophy of social science. Indeed, this seems to characterize the recent work of several "applied" interpretive scholars (e.g., Colebatch 1995, Hofmann 1995): trained in positivist orientations toward decisionmaking, policy implementation, and so forth, we discover, often while we are in the field in the midst of a research project, the limitations of such theories for usefully explaining the subject of our explorations. In casting about for more useful directions, we focus on the problem of meaning, and out of that—as a very practical, research-oriented, rather than philosophical, set of concerns—we come to interpretive philosophies and their related methodological concerns. The next generation to undertake interpretive approaches to policy and organizational analysis, one hopes, will be trained and proceed differently.

NOTES

1. For example, the organizers of the second annual interdisciplinary organizational studies doctoral student conference found it necessary, after their first year's experience, to develop a new evaluation form for reviewing papers based on other than statistical methods. At least one of the organizers spent considerable time and effort learning how ethnographic work is typically evaluated, filling in, apparently, a gap in his doctoral program curriculum.
2. See Van Maanen (1988); see also Clifford (1988), Geertz (1988), and Marcus and Fischer (1986) on the rhetorical aspects of ethnographic writing, and McCloskey (1985) on writing in economics.
3. See, e.g., Spradley (1972) and Whyte (1955, appendix; 1984); and Geertz (1973, ch. 1) for a more philosophical discussion. The *Handbook of Qualitative Research* (Denzin and Lincoln 1994) covers a variety of methods and issues in meaning-focused research.
4. This was done to meet the requirements of my supervisors in the community organization divisions of Amidar and the ICCC, and at the urging of my mother, who sensed that I was undertaking an unusual fieldwork project. Family members, I think, often play an unsung role in field research.
5. I am thinking of Harvard's Kennedy School of Government, Graduate School of Education, and Institute for Educational Management (in which I took part between 1976 and 1982 as casewriter) which established case writing, publishing, and teaching programs in the mid-1970s that came to be used in other policy programs elsewhere as well. Of course, the use of case studies in the policy and administration curriculum (such as the Inter-university Case Program) dates to the late 1940s and early 1950s (see Stein 1952).

6. See Feldman (1994) and Denzin and Lincoln (1994) for an overview and illustration of many of these. References to other works are cited in Chapters 5 to 7.

7. I am drawing here on Kuhn's (1970, p. 5) language: "research as a strenuous and devoted attempt to force nature into the conceptual boxes supplied by professional education."

8. Estrangement, as I have been using it here, is comparable to Garfinkel's "breaching experiments" to violate common understandings (Feldman 1994). Estrangement situates the breach in the researcher's commonsense understanding of the world. Garfinkel's method shifts the locus of sense-breaching to the community resident, agency member, or other situational actor. This reflects the different interests of the two approaches: the ethnographer's focus on understanding specific situational meaning, the ethnomethodologist's on exploring processes of meaning-making.

Community studies such as Whyte's (1955) are an example of highly successful estrangement within the researcher's native culture. See also Agar (1980). This difficulty of "local estrangement," however, may explain in part why interpretive approaches have not been widely found in a public policy analysis that largely studies elements of its own culture. Myths, metaphors, and other things symbolic and known tacitly are much harder to see without estrangement.

9. This approach to the analysis of organizational metaphors has much in common with a semiotic analysis that focuses on similarities and oppositions of meaning. See Feldman (1994, ch. 3) for a summary and further references.

10. K. C. Bjornsen, Department of Public Administration course paper, California State University, Hayward, 1993.

11. The observation is Steven Maynard-Moody's.

12. But see Richardson (1994) for an exploration of writing as a method of inquiry.

13. Though some suggest that validity is a holdover from positivist concerns. See, e.g., Kvale (1995).

14. I am following a Geertzian cultural theory rather than the one developed by Douglas (1982, e.g.) and her followers as "grid-group" analysis, which has begun to enter the world of policy analysis (see, e.g., Ellis and Coyle 1994 or Thompson, Ellis, and Wildavksy 1990). Although she may not have intended it to be used so, it has come—at least in the policy world—to predetermine the elements of culture that are deemed significant. Thick description, as I understand it, leaves the determination of significant categories to each study. Indeed, they emerge out of the study itself, rather than arriving with the method. From the intellectual antecedents discussed in Thompson, Ellis, and Wildavsky, in fact, one sees the structural-functionalism and ontological realism that characterize that sort of cultural analysis; whereas followers of Geertzian interpretive cultural analysis are guided by different assumptions.

3

The Israel Corporation of Community Centers, Ltd.

The story of the founding of the Israel Corporation of Community Centers (ICCC), its growth and struggle to establish itself through the creation of an internal identity and an external image, is also the story of an agency created to aid in the "absorption" of new immigrants into Israeli society. What the nature of "Israeli society" is and would or should be has been the subject of debate since before the founding of the state in 1948. Even the question of who is a "new" immigrant has not always been clear. And what "absorption" (*klitah*, in Hebrew) means has also largely not been discussed in policy circles or in public forums, unlike in the United States or Canada where reflecting on the meaning of "the melting pot" and "the mosaic" have long been part of national public discourse. The following account describes the central social issues surrounding the founding and first period of the ICCC and how the Corporation staff presented its goals to themselves and to others. It is a thickly detailed narrative of events and issues intended to provide a background for understanding the various policy and agency meanings, authored and constructed, and the various readers authoring and constructing those meanings.

Understanding the intended purposes of the ICCC requires knowledge of the history of Jewish immigration to Israel, of immigrant policy, and of the notion of ethnicity among Jewish Israelis. Israel's population more than doubled through immigration within the first two years of statehood (1948–50). Most of the immigrants from Europe, Jewish refugees from Hitler's extermination efforts, moved into cities, suburbs, and communal settlements (*kibbutzim* and *moshavim*) to be near surviving relatives and countrymen. Those immigrating from Islamic North African, Middle Eastern, and Asian countries, however, had few cousins or countrymen among prior settlers to join.

Coming from non-Western societies with limited monetary, linguistic, and other resources for survival in a nation that looked to western European nation-states as its model, they were dependent on the state for shelter, food, clothing, jobs, schooling, and so forth. The state accommodated them first in temporary quarters and then settled them in the newly created "development towns." These—Israel's "new towns"—were established between 1950 and 1963 for the purposes of dispersing the country's population beyond the sprawling metropolitan areas into the hinterlands, for various social, economic, natural resource, and military policy reasons.

Because of ethnic differences resulting from centuries of living in different societies and consequent acculturation to different customs and traditions, "Western" Jews—those coming from eastern and western Europe and the Americas—and "Eastern" Jews—from Asia, the Middle East, northern Africa, and parts of southern Europe—were largely alien to one another. Even among the religiously observant, ritual practices differed from "West" to "East." Immigrants to Israel from western Europe and the Americas were often university-educated cosmopolitans. Those from Asia and Africa were more often unlettered town and rural folk; by and large, the urban elites of these communities had immigrated to the West (largely to France and Canada) rather than to Israel. Their different settlement patterns in Israel institutionalized the separation. The development towns and some urban neighborhoods remained lower-class enclaves with high rates of unemployment and welfare, unfamiliar and even somewhat mysterious to "Westerners"; the cities, largely populated by "Westerners," became a magnet drawing upwardly mobile "Easterners" out of the development towns. Since immigrants from Europe, both Eastern and Western, and their descendants held most of the leadership positions in the army and other key political, economic, and social institutions, their cultural attributes and lifestyle became established as the norm to be desired and imitated by any who would call themselves "Israeli."

Part of the story's richness (or confusion) lies in the label applied to the Eastern category, usually called *S'faradim*. Properly speaking, *S'faradi* (the adjective or singular noun, also spelled *Sephardi*) refers to those who trace their ancestry to the Jewish communities expelled from Spain (*S'farad*) and Portugal (in 1492 and 1497, respectively). Today, this typically includes people from the modern states of Bulgaria, Greece, Spanish Morocco, among others, and S'faradi communities in the Netherlands, the United States, Latin America, and elsewhere. Jews from northern African states are properly called Maghrebi Jews, while those from Italy, Iraq, Iran, India, the Yemen, and so forth fit neither category and constitute their own separate categories. But they have collectively been referred to by Europeans as "the Tribes of the East" in Hebrew (*edot hamizrach*), or—inaccurately—as *S'faradim* (noun, plural). Historically, they have been called "Oriental Jews" in English, although the name *S'faradi* has become more widely used. Both category names—"*S'faradi*" and "Oriental/ Eastern"—create an opposition with Western Jews (*Ashkenazim*) whose ancestors arrived in Germany (*Ashkenaz*) beginning in the 800s and spread from there into Russia, Poland, and the Austro-Hungarian Empire. *Edah*—the singular for "tribe"—may be loosely translated as "ethnicity," but it is used only in application to groups of Eastern-origin Jews—those of European origin are not called "Tribes of the West."

The distinction between the two population groupings identified most broadly, *Ashkenazim* and *S'faradim*, has aspects of what would be analogous in the United States to distinctions between "White" and "Black." One finds such a distinction in some language usage: the expression "*schwarzfis*"—literally, "black face"—for example, can be found in reference to S'faradim (Bahloul 1993) in some usages of Yiddish (until recently, the German-based lingua franca of Ashkenazi Jews). Marriages between Ashkenazim and S'faradim have been considered intermarriages. But since the cities included middle-class residents of S'faradic heritage and the development towns included lower-class immigrants of Ashkenazic heritage, the fear of the development towns was not exclusively a "race"-based phenomenon. "Race-ethnicity," class, and settlement interact in a complicated pattern; they do not map exactly onto each other.

To see community centers as vehicles for acculturating immigrants may seem obvious to those familiar with London's Toynbee Hall or with the U.S. tradition of settlement houses in Chicago (Jane Adams's Hull House), New York (Lillian Wald's Henry Street Settlement), Boston (West End Settlement), and elsewhere.[1] To Israelis, it was not obvious. Moreover, the questions "who is an Israeli?" and "who is a Jew?" and "what is Israeli culture?" have been actively and explicitly debated since before the establishment of the state.[2] In 1968 it was still being debated into what, precisely, immigrants were to be integrated. The answer had been assumed in 1948: Israel was to be a Jewish state, as that was understood by primarily secular Jews from Poland, Russia, Germany, and neighboring countries. The arrival of North African, Indian, Yemenite, and other Jews who looked different, spoke Hebrew differently, and practiced different forms of the religion than the European state founders transformed the legal question of a "Jewish" state into a sociological question. Even so, the founders assumed that all (Jewish) Israelis were a single people. It is in this sense that the awakening to "two Israels," noted by one of the ICCC's founders as a central marker of the agency's creation, was such a surprise. The ideology underpinning the founding of the state, based on the utopian ideology of Zionism, anticipated a classless reunification and mixing together of (Jewish) exiles.[3] It had no room for a physically separated second class of citizens. The sudden perception of this reality, social and ethnic, came as a shock.

This "ethnic blindness" (Peled 1982, p. 105; see note 10) could also be described as a class blindness, supported by the socialist Zionist ideology that guided the creation of the state and the Labor Party. It led to a paternalism that can be seen in the ICCC case: agency founders assumed they knew what should be done on behalf of development town residents. This paternalism is also suggested by the Ashkenazic construction of S'faradic identity (see Bahloul 1994). Furthermore, seeing the S'faradi as sentimental or emotional, as Bahloul notes, implies a gendered construction: the paternalistic (male) Ashkenazi agency founder protecting the emotional (female) S'faradi client. This implied passivity is recapitulated in the military metaphor of policy analysis theory that portrays the client as a target waiting to receive a program.

If the policy process evolves over time and space and is continuous, as suggested at the end of Chapter 1, then any implementation analysis looks at an arbitrary slice of this process. To illustrate the sorts of issues an interpretive analysis might engage, I will focus on that slice of the implementation history of the ICCC that looks at the events leading up to the agency's creation and its founding years. Part of what this presentation illustrates is that it is difficult, if not impossible, to find a single point of origin for the idea of the ICCC Community Center. Even the creators of the ICCC discovered that the idea already existed, not only overseas, but also within Israel. How they presented and engaged these idea-traces is part of the policy story. Since these traces affect how the policy meaning was made and communicated, they are a potential subject for interpretive analysis. Part One of the history of the founding and first decade of operations of the ICCC focuses on the social concerns that constituted the context into and out of which the ICCC was born. Part Two focuses on organizational issues, including those that addressed these social concerns. The story begins as it did in Chapter 1, but with additional details. It is presented here as a "realist" tale (Van Maanen 1988, Kunda 1992): as if the author could be absent, but omniscient, lending the story a veracity and authenticity by the detail of the telling and the seeming objectivity of the narration.

PART ONE. SOCIAL CONCERNS

THE FOUNDING YEARS

The late Zalman Aranne, Minister of Education and Culture in the 1960s, is remembered by his associates as a bright, sharp, creative, and innovative administrator. More than anything, say those who worked with him, he was noted for his curiosity and his openness to new ideas and schemes.

Aranne had three special assistants: Dan Ronnen, David Harman, and Hayim Zipori.[4] Zipori was brought in to the ministry in late 1963 as assistant director of the new Adult Literacy Program, one of Aranne's brain children. As Zipori tells it, at the beginning of 1964 he and Program Director Yitzhak Navon[5] brought some five hundred soldier-teachers (women who fulfill their military service by teaching) to development towns and other immigrant settlements:

For me, this was my first introduction to, my most basic encounter with what was then called "the second Israel." Directly, through the soldiers, by way of home visits and home-based classes, we came to know the nature of things in the development towns, as insiders. (Zipori 1972, pp. 1–2)[6]

Zipori left Adult Literacy at the end of 1965 to begin developing a new program called "Art for the People" (*Omanut La'am*). "This operation was also directed toward development towns and poverty areas," he wrote. "Its objective was to bring theater, concerts and other passive [i. e., nonparticipatory] art activities to new audiences" (Zipori 1972). One of his undertakings was a study entitled "Organizational Aspects Connected with Bringing Artistic Productions to Development Areas," presented to the minister in June 1966.

According to Harman, however, Zipori and Aranne had a falling-out at this time over political loyalties. Zipori chose to follow a faction that was splitting from the mainstream Labor Party to which Aranne adhered.[7] Harman maintained that Aranne removed Zipori from the literacy campaign, one of the minister's pet projects, and transferred him to the more field-oriented "Art for the People" Program in order to distance him from the center of ministry activities.

However that may be, Zipori recalled that it was at this time, in the fall of 1966, that Aranne began to voice his curiosity about the lives of immigrants in the development towns and other settlements. He was concerned about their social and cultural lives, according to Zipori, in terms of art and education. He was aware that children's studies as well as their development were influenced by their parents' problems.

> Although each of us was caught up in his own bailiwick, Aranne began to weave the pieces—adult literacy, popular arts, supplementary education [i.e., elementary and high school equivalency], youth houses, sports centers—into a comprehensive whole. (Zipori 1972)

Aranne charged Zipori with finding out more about the activities of development town residents in their free time. "Fly over the development towns, lift up the rooftops, and find out what people do in the evenings" (Zipori 1967a), he is often reported to have said.

So Zipori, drawing on his development town connections from his "Art for the People" work, began a four-month journey around the state.[8] From October 1966 to January 1967, he covered some forty settlements, meeting the local residents on their street corners and in their cafes, chatting about their preferred activities, their available facilities, their desires and dreams.

It was during this period that Ralph Goldman, then director of the Israel Education Fund (a disbursal arm of the United Jewish Appeal) and some potential donors from the United States, visited

Aranne.[9] Goldman reportedly asked Aranne whether "community centers" could solve some of Israel's social problems. The next day, Aranne charged Ya'el Pozner, head of the ministry's Comprehensive Schools Program, with the mission of finding out about community centers.

> So I asked him, "What exactly do you want to know?" And then it became clear to me that for a long time he had been preoccupied by the question of what really went on in the development towns, especially during the evenings and on the Sabbath. And he thought that putting up such "community centers" in these towns might possibly be the answer for residents who might be bored.
>
> So I set up the committee. We had a sociologist, a town planner, an educator, a representative of the Housing Ministry, and a director of a community center in Haifa [among others]. We collected information on what they were doing in America in this field. But primarily we began traveling around the country in the evenings. We sat in the cafes and on the street corners. We asked people what was on their minds.

Dr. Pozner, a German-trained physicist who entered the arena of Youth Aliya (immigration) and nonformal education during World War II, remembers the social issues that were on the minds of Israeli educators at the time.

> It was as if we awoke suddenly to find that two Israels had developed between 1950 and 1960. We didn't expect it; we didn't anticipate it. In the "first" Israel, the children were well-integrated, but in the development towns, in the "second" Israel—a tremendous gap was revealed between the two populations. We had an enormously troubling problem: how to deal with this gap. There were two routes: the Reform[10] and informal education. The Community Center program fell into the latter category.

Harman remembers that Aranne "dreamed of a national network of 'something'—he didn't know what to call them, 'Aranne Houses,' perhaps." Harman also says that Pozner was brought in on the project because Aranne no longer trusted Zipori's politics since the latter had joined the splinter Labor group.

Pozner's committee began meeting late in 1966. One day, she said, a young man approached her in the hallway of the ministry building and introduced himself.

> "My name is Hayim Zipori. I've been going around to the different development towns doing a study of leisure time activities, and I hear you have a committee investigating a related idea. Could I join your committee?"

Pozner welcomed him, and he and her committee continued their work, separately and together.

In the meantime, Harman had inherited Zipori's former job in the Adult Literacy Program. He recalls that in early 1967 he engineered the establishment of the first multifunctional recreational center in a development town.

> I had an army unit from *Nahal* [a branch of the military] teaching adult literacy in Bet Shemesh, and they needed a place to meet. There were no youth movement clubhouses, no place to hold adult education classes. Mayor Look wanted to build a basketball court. I suggested putting it near the old town hall, which the Habimah Theater [troupe] used for its productions when it traveled locally. Through Zipori's connections with Habimah, we were able to get the building for our use—it became a community center!

There were also other places, Harman noted, which served as community centers. These included Tcherner House in Yaffo, set up by the Tel Aviv municipality in late 1967, and the Jerusalem YM-YWHA which had been going since the early 1950s.

Harman recalls originating the idea of a multipurpose program as well, following the 1967 war.

> I had another army unit in Netivot [a development town in the southern desert], and we conceived of the idea of laundry centers

or clubs where mothers could use washing machines in a central location and study Hebrew at the same time. And we also developed the idea of using bomb shelters [as meeting places] after that, in Dimona [another southern desert development town], to teach literacy classes.

"Community centers," said Ronnen, Aranne's third special assistant, "was an idea that Aranne learned from other people," such as himself and Harman, both of whom had been in the United States and brought Aranne ideas from there and from the professional journals they read. The American idea was a multiservice community center providing a variety of activities "all under one roof."

The notion of a community center had been around for a while, said Ronnen:

There were many youth clubs sponsored by the various political movements. There were cultural centers: there was Rothschild House in Haifa and four others following [Director Yaakov] Malchin's ideas of community centers. And there was the influence of the kibbutzim's "people's houses."

But Aranne and especially [then Finance Minister Pinhas] Sapir were sensitive to the readiness of Americans to give money to a familiar concept. Whereas they might not jump to support a "youth club" or a "pensionnaires' club," they would contribute to a Jewish Community Center sort of thing.

Zipori presented his "Survey of Culture, Youth and Sports Centers in the Development Towns and in Immigrant Cities" to Aranne in March 1967.[11] His "Survey of Culture, Art, Recreation, and Sports Activities on Sabbath Eves," delayed by the war in June 1967, was submitted in September. He reported that there were not enough public, nonpartisan facilities to support recreational activities for the nonurban people he had studied, and that much of what was available was inadequate and run-down.

Pozner submitted her committee's report to Aranne in early 1967 also. Based on their research and on Zipori's findings, the committee recommended that two or three Community Centers be set up on an experimental basis. "It was in [the southern desert development town of] Yeruham that the committee derived its motto," said Pozner. "One young fellow with whom we spoke told us, 'There's no place pleasant to hang around and kill time. Our apartments are small; our families are large. There's nowhere to go.' And we conceived of the mandate of the Community Center as providing someplace to go.

"On the other hand," she continued,

> Hayim's report proved that we weren't coming to a *tabula rasa*. Most places had programs for youth or for adults, but without coordination, and without any comprehensive view. Sometimes there was competition [between the providers of different activities]. We felt that the Community Center could introduce some order and a directed approach, if only partially.

Aranne accepted the committee's recommendations, with the single reservation that two to three Centers would be too small an experiment. Thirty was a more likely sample, he thought. He appointed a second committee, again under Pozner's leadership, charged with developing plans for building and programming the thirty experiments. The new Committee for Cultural, Youth, and Sports Centers included the Education Ministry's director of sports, its youth department director, and its budget officer; the Histadrut's (National Federation of Labor) culture and education director; Ralph Goldman of the Israel Education Fund; a representative of the United Jewish Appeal (one of the central coordinating bodies of American Jewish fund-raising); a university researcher; Hayim Zipori; and others. The committee met for a year and a half, gathering information on Jewish and non-Jewish centers in Europe, especially in the Scandinavian countries, and traveling around Israel, trying to involve local townspeople in the design of the Centers.

Zipori wrote:

> We convened those who held their fingers on the social pulse of the town and we told them we wanted to know their needs so the building design would reflect them. We divided them into subcommittees—for youth activities, sports, culture, arts . . . and collected all these ideas . . . and had them set priorities. . . . I think we were the first and only ones in Israel to go this most difficult route. . . . (Zipori 1972)

"We wanted the entire population using the Community Center to take an active part in directing it and setting its programs," said Goldman.

This means that local residents must be on the Board, feel that the Center is theirs and direct it. Although most of the funds come from the government Ministries and other public institutions who also have ideas, the main responsibility rests with the local volunteers.

. . . The innovation of [drawing on] volunteer work, of [creating] a Board of Directors which is not nominated by government or public bodies, was alien to the people. [They] . . . were accustomed . . . to get help from government. We had, therefore, to teach the community members to start thinking in different terms, to learn to help themselves, to decide what is good for them and to attempt to achieve it on their own, rather than to wait for some government clerk to decide something should be done for them. There are many things which the government must do for its citizens. However, there is no lack of things which each citizen must do himself for himself—not just to receive but also to give. (Lavi 1979)

"They didn't understand us," said Pozner:

"What are you asking us for?" they said. "Let the Housing Ministry build it, and we'll use it."

We discovered how difficult it really is to bring them to [the point where they could] identify their needs and to express what they really needed.

In Dimona we had a surprise. We were exerting ourselves in an effort to explain what a Community Center is, what they should think about and how to express their wishes. They stopped us in the middle: they were astonished that we were bringing them models from the U.S. Why were we telling them "stories"? Why, in Casablanca they had a similar institution!

We were very embarrassed that we hadn't known. They told us more about their center, where the Jewish community had organized the same sorts of social and cultural activities as we had just been describing. We asked why they hadn't recreated such a center in Dimona, and they said they had no idea that it could be done in Israel too. (Lavi 1979, p. 10)

The committee submitted a report calling for the establishment of a network of Community Centers under a single coordinating body, with a five-year building plan to be funded through the Israel Education Fund and foreign donors, and an educational-social-cultural program to be funded by the Ministry of Education and Culture through its standard regional and local allocations procedures.

According to Pozner, committee members wanted the programs of the proposed Community Centers, no less than their building design, to grow out of the field through resident involvement. They wanted an independent, public organization, not a government body. Therefore, government lawyers recommended they adopt the legal status of a "Government Corporation," established by authority of the Knesset [Parliament] under the aegis of the Minister of Education and Culture. Its shares would be owned by the government, and it would be directed by a voluntary board appointed by the minister, who would serve as its chairman or designate a substitute. The board of directors would have twenty-one members, ten of whom would be government officials and eleven members of the public. Each individual Center would also incorporate as a nonprofit entity, under the directorship of a board of local government officials and citizens.

On May 4, 1969 the Prime Minister's Cabinet Committee for Economic Affairs voted to establish the "Corporation for Culture and Sports Centers (for Youth and Adults), Limited." The government ratified the recommendation. On June 4 it was registered legally as a government corporation, and on August 11 Minister Aranne signed the papers establishing it (ICCC Annual Report 1975).

Aranne resigned his position shortly thereafter and died six months later. Elad Peled, then director-general of the Ministry of Education and Culture, became chairman of the board of the new corporation. Pozner continued to work in the ministry, becoming assistant director-general in 1976 until she retired in 1979. She also was appointed vice chairman of the ICCC and chairman of its executive board, succeeding Peled as chairman of the board as a whole in 1976. Zipori was appointed the corporation's first executive director, a position he held until his untimely death in 1983.

Zipori operated the corporation under the aegis of the Ministry of Education and Culture out of its offices and drawing on its support staff until the spring of 1971, when he moved it into separate office space in Jerusalem.

PUBLIC SOCIAL CONCERNS

Conceptions of the Centers' purpose were influenced by contemporary public perceptions of societal problems at the time of the agency's creation. A more widespread awareness of the existence of social problems grew in the late 1960s, perhaps due to the increase in physical and economic security resulting from the June 1967 war.[12] Also, Russian immigration increased dramatically in the early 1970s, from 9 in 1969 to 33,500 in 1973. Not only did this immigration highlight differences in the historical treatment of different groups of immigrants and current differences of status among them, it also focused national attention on problems of subgroups of the Israeli population, an attention that extended to veteran immigrant groups from northern Africa and Asia.[13] Israeli social policy ideas were also influenced by developments throughout the world in the recognition of social problems and in government policies to address them. Concerns about Israeli national identity and immigrant "absorption" intertwined with concerns about the fate of the development towns.

Development towns: Israel's New Towns

Israel's "development towns" were built between 1950 and 1963, for several reasons:

(1) To disperse the state's population throughout its territory, away from the growing metropolitan center of Tel Aviv in particular, to remedy regional population imbalances.
(2) To increase the extent and amount of livable space.
(3) To implement a planned regional hierarchy of town size, spatial organization, and service infrastructure.
(4) To bolster security in outlying districts by spreading a defense network and filling in frontier lands and empty spaces.
(5) To rationalize limited water resources.
(6) To create new economic and employment opportunities.
(7) To house the large influx of immigrants arriving in unplanned waves and absorb them socially and economically.

The towns were initially created as service centers for surrounding agricultural settlements and as intermediaries between the settlements and regional cities. Only later were government resources devoted to installing an industrial base, as it became clear that agriculture would not provide a sufficient economic base for town residents. This switch in their functional conception led to changes in town plans, including higher residential densities and a linear rather than radial physical layout. These changes reflected a change in planning philosophy between 1948 and 1968, from an emphasis on "back to the land" principles toward the optimization of "human and capital resources for the creation of viable urban-industrial centers" (Lichfield 1970, p. 10).[14]

The people who were settled in the development towns were, by and large, unskilled workers or those whose skills were not in demand in a growing state (cobblers, for instance). They had little formal education; many were illiterate; they came from a housing culture unlike that of Europe, the source of the state's political and social elites. They tended to have larger families than Western immigrants, and most of the development towns provided little in the way of employment opportunities. The towns on the geographic periphery of the state and in the rural hinterlands were largely removed from sources of employment, and there was little transportation joining them to factories where they might have found work. As a result of these various factors, a high percentage of development town residents were on welfare.

The towns brought together people who happened to arrive in the country at the same time, or who were sent there as housing became available. There was little other reason for people to be neighbors. The persistent rumor recited in the town of Dimona characterizes the way residents of many development towns felt. It was said that on a certain day, all immigrants who had arrived in the port of Haifa (in the north) were loaded onto a transport bus and sent into the Negev (the southern region, a desert at the other end of the country). Dimona was built where the bus ran out of gas. Relations among different ethnic groups varied. Romanians and Moroccans got along well, but Moroccans and Tunisians were typically at odds. Stereotypes developed: Kurds are stupid; Moroccans carry knives and are quick to use them. Development towns collectively acquired an unsavory reputation among the public at large.

Toward the end of the 1960s, the fact that the development towns on the whole were losing residents while the cities (Tel Aviv in particular, where over one-third of the state's population was concentrated) were gaining became a public issue.[15] The main reason given for this "reverse" migration was the lack of appropriate employment prospects, or their absence entirely, for youth returning from their army service or subsequent university studies.[16] The 1967 war highlighted the problem; it became the focus of the annual National Conference of Mayors of Development Towns in January 1969. According to the reporter who covered that conference, the continued existence of each development town would depend on its success in providing work for its youth and in "enabling them to establish families there after their army service." The problem was seen as a lack of variety of employment opportunities and vocational training. The reporter continued:

An important development is that from year to year the number of youth who study at the universities and other institutions of higher learning is increasing. These youngsters who take up advanced studies are a source of encouragement to the new towns, but there is always the anxiety among the inhabitants as to whether their children will return to the town or will seek work outside the place where they were raised. Naturally, during their studies the big city will tend to attract youth away from the small town.

The proposed solution? "In order to keep these youth attached to their home town after completion of their studies, it is necessary to improve housing facilities, amenities, taxes and credit facilities to help those starting out in life" (Dar 1969).

But facilities and amenities were allocated in proportion to town size. Where government planners once deemed it necessary to have a local population of 10,000 in order to provide adequate services, by 1969 the number had risen to 20,000, according to the same reporter. That is, to stem the tide of out-migration, one needed to provide better services; but to justify the state's expense to provide "adequate" services, one needed a 20,000 minimum resident population—at a time when development town populations varied from 6,000 average for a small town to 15,000 for a large one. Another reporter wrote at that time:

> too many development towns have remained too small to solve the problems of services, education, health, etc. . . . The lack of entertainment possibilities is one of the factors causing dissatisfaction among population of these towns, though obviously it is not worthwhile to open such establishments in some of the smaller towns.
>
> . . . It is clear today that a town needs a population of at least 50,000 in order to be able to develop independently and economically in the matters of education, cultural services, etc. The few who are successful leave them. . . .

New immigrants are not going to live in the towns, he continued. Thus, no local intelligentsia will develop in them. The small towns are condemned to a "long life of poverty," and he recommended closing some down (Tevet 1970).

Stemming this out-migration became one of the goals of the ICCC. It would do this through the provision of social, cultural, and recreational programs and facilities on site, so that development town residents would not feel that such things were available only in the big cities. It was hoped also that this would change the poor image of the towns held by their residents. Pozner recalled in an interview that at the time, when she was vice chairman of the ICCC's board of directors and chair of its executive committee, agency planners intended the Centers to be a meeting place to fill free time. In drawing people together to "hang out," they intended the Centers to provide day-care, self-help, and other services, giving neighbors with no shared history the opportunity to integrate and create a community.

The "social gap" and immigrant policies

To the national public concern for the fate of the development towns and their residents was added a general concern for immigrant integration into the national society. By 1970, as Pozner noted, people seemed to have awakened suddenly to the "social gap," as it was called, dividing—economically, socially, educationally, culturally—Israeli

Jews of European and American origin—"Israel 1"—from those who came from the Islamic states of northern Africa and the Middle East— the "second Israel." For twenty years, Israel had avoided or denied charges of discrimination. Suddenly, stories of Westerners' discrimination against Easterners were rampant.

This classification of the Jewish population into two groups reflects disparities of income, education, and social status that entail ethnic dimensions mapped onto a geographic demarcation between metropolitan areas and the development towns. Residence intertwines with ethnicity, although public discourse at the time did not reflect this.[17] Israel's elite and middle classes include Eastern Jews, and there are Jews of Polish and Romanian origin among the development town poor. Place of residence of "new" immigrants—those arriving after 1948, the year in which Israel was founded—reflects national immigrant policies.[18]

Immigrant policies changed over time, as did the ethnicity (or country of origin) of the immigrant pool.[19] In the 1950s and early 1960s, the government had neither the time nor the resources to develop an immigrant "absorption" program. In all, 1,209,000 people immigrated to Israel between 1948 and 1964, adding to a pre-statehood population of 452,000.[20] The housing shortage was severe; resources were rationed. Those who had family already in Israel were usually helped by them to settle, often in cities and suburbs. Those who had desired skills and/or capital were able and allowed to contend on the open market and settle themselves in cities, towns, or agricultural areas as they chose. These were mostly educated refugees from the urban centers and towns of Europe.

The remainder—mostly rural North African, Polish, Romanian, and Middle Eastern immigrants—were incorporated in what became known as "direct absorption." They arrived without capital or family contacts, and they lacked—or were told they lacked—desired and useful skills. In most cases, they came without their communal leaders. The latter, the lay and religious elites of these communities, typically immigrated to France, England, Canada, the United States, and South America. The traditional religious leadership which came to Israel was dispersed and not integrated into the bureaucratized rabbinate of the state.[21] These immigrants depended on the state for housing, employment, and all other help. Since the major social policy

during those years was population dispersal (for security, water resource, and economic reasons), the state directed them to the development towns, the primary instrument of population dispersal.

Immigrant policy changed in the mid-1960s, as did the immigrant
pool. Between 1968 and 1972, the fourth wave of post-statehood immigration brought 205,000 Jews from western Europe, Latin America,
the British Commonwealth, the United States, and the USSR. With
the exception of the Soviet Georgians, these were professionals, academics, or entrepreneurs, largely financially independent. In 1965 the
Jewish Agency opened residential *ulpanim*, intensive courses in basic
Hebrew, to address the needs of academic and professional immigrants (*Facts About Israel* 1977, p. 92). Unlike the "direct absorption" in
which immigrants were sent directly to settlements, these immigrants'
"indirect absorption" took place through residential hostels that were
largely subsidized by the government and that offered job counseling,
school placement for children, and other assistance in addition to the
language classes. With this temporary residential base, these immigrants had time as well as independent capital to purchase housing
on the open market, sometimes with government loans. Alternatively,
they were eligible for government housing of a standard by now
much higher than that which had been available to earlier immigrants,
including those settled in the development towns.

Government policies toward these later immigrants sought to
encourage the apparent readiness of these so-called "Anglo-Saxons"
to immigrate in large numbers for the first time in the state's history.
In order to offer a standard of living that would compare favorably
with what the Western immigrant was leaving behind, the state extended tax rebates and customs exemptions to these new immigrants.
For example, they were excused from the 100 percent customs duty
levied on cars, ovens, refrigerators, and other "luxuries," a tax that
veteran citizens and "new immigrants" from the 1950s and 1960s had
to pay.

The result appeared as a pattern of conspicuous consumption,
making visible the "social gap." The development towns—with their
concentrations of poor, unskilled, unemployed, nonliterate adults and
their children—became noted for their lack of such "luxuries" and
other indicators of material well-being: e.g., for overcrowded housing
conditions and high percentages of welfare recipients, as well as for
disparities in educational achievement and occupational distribution.

Cities and older towns stood in marked contrast. The economic, social, and cultural differences of the so-called two Israels was played out along both geographic and ethnic lines. To the physical isolation of development town residents was added a cultural isolation.[22]

One commonly used indicator of disparities between population groups is housing density.[23] "Western" families, averaging four persons, and Asian-African families, averaging seven persons, were originally housed in apartments of identical size. In 1957, more than half of the Asian-African population lived with a density of three or more persons per room. Among Westerners, 75 percent lived at a density of 1.3 persons per room.[24]

Another indicator is educational attainment. Among the poor, secondary education was often prohibitively expensive. Until 1969, schooling was compulsory and free through eighth grade only. Then, compulsory and free schooling was extended through ninth grade, and in some development towns, through tenth grade. In the early 1970s, one year of high school cost more than one year of university, because of government subsidies to universities.

Features specific to the development towns exacerbated the problem of high schooling costs. Since most were located in remote areas of the country, it was usually difficult to attract qualified teachers (as well as other professionals). The quality of schooling and other services, therefore, was generally inferior to that in the cities.

Educational attainment among development town residents was markedly lower as compared with urban residents, due to these and other factors, including the tradition among immigrants from Asia and Africa of adolescents working to help support the family. Tables 3-1, 3-2, and 3-3 summarize some of these data. While the data show improvement over time, those of Eastern heritage lagged behind those of Western heritage. The negative image of Eastern immigrants had been established by the time of the ICCC's founding.

The percentage of development town residents needing welfare support was also very high, due to such factors as selective assignment of unskilled workers and their families to these towns and continual out-migration of upwardly mobile people. In one town, for example, 60 percent of the families in 1972 received monthly support payments, and an additional 30 percent received biannual "gifts"—food, clothing, and shoe allowances, for instance, for the New Year and Passover holidays.

TABLE 3-1.   High School Attendance: Percent of
pupils beginning first grade who continued on
through 8–12 grades

Country of origin	1965–69	1972–76
Israel/Europe/America	56.6	65.6
Africa/Asia	23.2	44.0

Source: Central Bureau of Statistics (reported in the *Jerusalem Post*, 1/26/81).
Note: Statistics present the figures as indicative of ethnic distinctions rather than geographic distinctions. The reader should bear in mind that immigrants of African and Asian origin constitute the majority of development town residents, but the problem was generally not presented as a settlement problem.

This picture of two Israels, divided geographically and ethnically, is encapsulated in the words of one woman explaining why she chose not to move to a development town despite government incentives to do so: "I wanted my children to learn good Hebrew—and to really know what Independence Day is all about," she told a reporter (*Jerusalem Post*, 5/6/77)—pointing to the widespread image of the inferiority of the towns' educational and cultural systems. The negative image

TABLE 3-2.   University Attendance: Percent of total
students registered in Israeli universities

Country of origin	1969–70	1977–78
Israel	5.8	10.4
Europe/America (includes foreign students)	79.0	69.6
Africa/Asia	13.6	17.0

Source: Central Bureau of Statistics (reported in the *Jerusalem Post*, 1/26/81).
Note: Statistics present the figures as indicative of ethnic distinctions rather than geographic distinctions. The reader should bear in mind that immigrants of African and Asian origin constitute the majority of development town residents, but the problem was generally not presented as a settlement problem.

TABLE 3-3. Higher Education Attainment, 1970: Percent completing 11 or more years of schooling

Country of origin	Immigrant generation	Second generation
Europe/America	47	80
Africa/Asia	18	40

Source: Katz and Gurevitch (1972).
Note: Statistics present the figures as indicative of ethnic distinctions rather than geographic distinctions. The reader should bear in mind that immigrants of African and Asian origin constitute the majority of development town residents, but the problem was generally not presented as a settlement problem.

had been adopted by development town residents themselves: "Anyone who is successful, leaves," one remarked, a sentiment heard repeatedly.

Some people associated the towns' success or failure, in part, with another set of issues: the newly reported increase in leisure time, and recreation as the solution to the problem of what to do with it. Their lack of cultural and recreational facilities was used to explain part of the difficulties the development towns were encountering.

Leisure time and the development towns

Toward the end of the 1960s, the Israeli public became cognizant of the concept of "leisure time," time free after work and family chores, and the notion of its "constructive use." The main tenets of this concept were conveyed by Hillel Raskin of the Hebrew University's Department of Physical Education and Recreation:

Today, we live in a leisure age, in which the character of society and the quality of life of people are determined to a great extent by leisure time activities. In this leisure age, for better or for worse, culture is fashioned by patterns of behavior of people mainly during leisure. The spontaneous and voluntary leisure activity of people may enrich or impoverish the quality of both individual and cultural life.

. . . The central problem posed by leisure is the question of how a civilization, in which leisure is the right of each and every individual, can assist each of its citizens in achieving an optimal balance in his free choice of his needs for rest, entertainment and participation in social and cultural life.

. . . The problem of the exploitation of leisure for both individual and social development in modern society is one which should occupy a special place in the society's order of preference. Appropriate leisure behavior of the individual in society will not develop on its own, but as a result of education, social conditions and the possibilities available. (Raskin 1979)

The first research on Israelis' use of leisure time was undertaken in 1966. This pilot study, sponsored by the Institute for Applied Social Research and the Hebrew University's Communications Institute, focused on two cities. After television was introduced into the country two years later, the researchers returned to update their study. A larger effort was completed in early summer 1970: following Minister Aranne's request before he left office, 4,000 interviews were conducted in 56 settlements throughout the country. Researchers reported the use of leisure time as a function of education and stage of life ("a mix of age and family statuses"). Attendance rates at theater, concerts, and museums were found to reflect the level of educational attainment. Concert audiences—the reference seems to be to symphonies—were "limited, almost absolutely, to adults, graduates of higher education institutions." Researchers' findings included the following:

- Religious observance and education are the factors that determine behavior and value differences in culture.
- In general, it seems that housing conditions have no particular effect on the individual's ability to read or on the amount of time devoted to reading.
- Residents of small or new settlements complain about the lack of appropriate possibilities for leisure entertainment and the lack of appropriate company with whom to socialize.
- Populations of the same age and schooling across different settlement types evidence no difference in their demand for cultural activities.

- The ethnic factor (i.e., differences between Westerners and Easterners) does not influence educational activity.
- Easterners attend theater and concerts less than Westerners of the same age and schooling. Among the second generation, the gap remains for those of average or low schooling, but it narrows among those who attain higher education. (Katz and Gurevitch 1972)

According to the ICCC's statistician, this research—especially the pilot study and its immediate follow-up—became part of the basis for defining a social need for cultural and recreational facilities. He also noted that it influenced Zipori's vision of the purpose of the Community Centers. Leisure concerns were soon joined by quite a different set of social issues.

The Black Panthers

Government efforts in the late 1960s to early 1970s to improve the lot of the development towns—through tax incentives, industrial development, housing schemes, educational plans—were at worst ineffectual and at best, inconsistent, because the different ministries varied in their definitions of what constituted a development town. The social agenda in Israel following the establishment of the state in 1948 had focused on "absorbing" immigrants, as more and more arrived in the aftermath of changing political circumstances abroad. Attention had been focused on state-building and on incorporating these people into a modern, Western state. Building new communities, housing, and roads, expanding manufacturing and providing jobs, teaching a new language, and expanding the network of schools—these constituted the public agenda of the 1950s and 1960s. There had been at least one expression of ethnic tension in riots in 1958 in the Wadi Salib neighborhood of Haifa. But the existence of social problems among immigrant groups—that many had *not* been "absorbed" into the population—was a new idea to many in the late 1960s and early 1970s. The impact of the social programs of the Kennedy and Johnson administrations in the United States, as well as the professionalization of social work, influenced public perceptions of what was socially "problematic" as well as perceptions of an appropriate role for government in "intervention" and "treatment."

The decade of the 1960s saw no public protest of development town conditions. When protest did begin, it started in the city slums populated almost exclusively by residents of Eastern heritage. Several reasons are offered in explanation of the seemingly sudden end to this quiescence. The "second Israel," feeling insecure about their social position before the 1967 War, had substantial numbers fighting alongside Westerners, and fighting valiantly and well. Having "proved" themselves in battle, they felt that they "belonged" and could now demand and expect the status and treatment they perceived that Westerners enjoyed. Also, the increased feeling of security from external attack after the 1967 War enabled a new focus on internal social problems. Furthermore, the postwar influx of Western immigrants was greeted by government concessions on taxes and by apartments of a new, standard, larger size. Easterners, who still had to pay 100 percent customs duty on automobiles and appliances, and who now felt cramped in their smaller apartments, saw themselves done out of conditions they claimed were also rightfully theirs.[25]

Protests started in January 1971 in Jerusalem's Musrara section. Young Israelis of Eastern background demonstrated outside the Knesset building in Jerusalem. According to *Jerusalem Post* (3/1/71) reporters, their main complaints were the lack of job opportunities and poor, crowded housing conditions. They were demanding social rehabilitation through vocational guidance and an end to "Oriental ghettoes" and slum conditions, as well as "clubs and better roads in our areas" (*Jerusalem Post*, 3/12/71). The demonstrators adopted the name "Black Panthers" from the American group. They posted signs around the city such as the following:

ENOUGH!
We are a group of exploited youth and we are appealing to all
    others who feel they are getting a raw deal.
Enough of not having work;
enough of having to sleep 10 to a room;
enough of looking at big apartments they are building for new
    immigrants;
enough of having to stomach jail and beatings. . . ;
enough of unkept promises from the Government;
enough of being underprivileged;
enough discrimination.
How long are we going to keep silent? . . .

We are protesting our right to be treated just as any other citizen in this country. (*Jerusalem Post*, 2/5/71)

A 22-year-old Black Panther told a *Post* reporter:

All this talk about Russian Jews bugs me. They never made any fuss about the Jews in Iraq. We know why they want the Russian Jews: it's because they think they're all scientists. They think Oriental Jews are stupid. (*Jerusalem Post*, 2/5/71)

In a country that had enjoyed a history of public social consensus, the public demonstration of dissent was taken as an extreme and shocking gesture. As seems to have happened with the earlier Wadi Salib riots, the demonstrators were initially dismissed. After a community organizer in the Jerusalem Municipality's Social Welfare Department leaked a story about the incipient demonstrations, his unit and department heads "decried the story as cheap, sensational and largely untrue" (*Jerusalem Post*, 2/5/71). The "Black Panther" label alienated many otherwise-potential supporters. The name itself conjured up an image "of an Israeli Huey Newton parading about Dizengoff Circle in Tel Aviv [then the fashionable center of Israel's "society"], brandishing a[n] Uzi submachine gun" (Iris and Shama 1972, p. 37). Then-Prime Minister Golda Meir said, "They are not nice boys." A Labor Ministry official claimed that "they have not looked for work seriously" (*Jerusalem Post*, 3/1/71).

Public expressions of sympathy for the Black Panthers came first from abroad. A clinical social worker from California who frequently visited Israel wrote a letter to the editor of the *Jerusalem Post* (2/15/71), saying that she was reminded of her experiences in the Los Angeles ghettoes twenty years earlier, prior to the Watts riots. "To be sure, no one seems to know exactly what a Panther is" in the Israeli context, she wrote.

But presumably, people in Israel think of the Panthers as a militant, violence oriented group which is politically aligned with Fatah [the Palestine Liberation Organization] and the Third World movement.

I suspect that "Panther" means something quite different to young gang members. While the Panthers are often considered "outsiders," the truth is that they are frustrated would-be "insiders." They want money, status, and a say in determining their own destiny. They feel they have been forced to take the revolutionary stance because there is no other way to make an impression on the "Establishment."

It is easy to see why the young gang members of Jerusalem are angry and frustrated. They see the new apartments in Ein Kerem and Ramat Eshkol [two middle-class neighborhoods] filled with newcomers. But they continue to live in their miserable hovels and dark alleys. There are plenty of jobs, but none for them of the type which will raise their self-esteem. There are schools, but none suited to their particular needs. They are forgotten.

And most tragic for them, even the army will not have them. Since in Israel the army has much status and is the badge of true "belonging," rejection from the army amounts to rejection from society.[26]

Speaking of the alleged discrimination, Deputy Prime Minister and Minister of Education Yigal Allon told a reporter "that the large majority of Oriental [i.e., Eastern] immigrants had come to Israel with no property at all, but they had been able to get homes and jobs, and they benefit from progressive social services. Pockets of poverty still existed, but these would be eradicated—he hoped, within a very few years" (*Jerusalem Post*, 5/23/71).

Police Minister Shlomo Hillel, himself of Iraqi background said:

> The economic and social gap is one of the world's most painful problems, and Israel suffers from it more seriously than most—because of the need to create a country in a generation or two. Scars had remained in Israeli society from the days of mass immigration, some of them still open and painful, but they proved that Israel's society was vigorous and alive. (*Jerusalem Post*, 5/25/71)

Israel Katz, then director of the National Insurance Institute, was among the first vocal Israeli sympathizers. He cited the following statistics:

- Easterners were 55–60 percent of the total Jewish population, but:

—10% of Members of Knesset were Easterners;
—90% of prison inmates were Easterners (*Jerusalem Post*, 8/4/71).

* 92% of all families with 5 and more children were Easterners, and:

—the average Eastern family size is 1.5 times that of the average Western family;
—per capita consumption of the average Eastern family equaled 67% of the average Israeli Jewish family's per capita consumption in 1959; it equaled 43% of the latter's in 1969 (*Jerusalem Post*, 11/10/71).

* Among Easterners, 1 student in 20 matriculates high school; among Westerners, 1 student in 3 matriculates high school (*Jerusalem Post*, 11/10/71).

Speaking in May 1971, Katz said:

[G]iving money to the poor sounded very good, but in a modern state what counted was social services for the whole population. There can be no talk of social services just for the poor. Poor neighborhoods have poor services, partly because people don't know how to secure their rights. . . . The people who can demand good services are the middle classes, and that is why services should be universal. Otherwise we are running the very serious danger of having two populations. (*Jerusalem Post*, 5/25/71)

Six months later, he said:

Israel's Black Panthers have made an important contribution to Israel by increasing the nation's sensitivity to its social problems. While every social indicator showed enormous progress in absolute terms for every sector of Israel's population, the majority of Israelis today demand progress in relative terms too. There are groups in Israel which have not been truly absorbed. (*Jerusalem Post*, 11/10/71)

Juvenile delinquency and the Katz Commission

The new awareness of and focus on social problems drew the public's attention to the existence of juvenile delinquency and its concomitant problems of drug use and prostitution. The number of juveniles referred to probation services grew from 3,650 in 1966 to 11,000 in 1968, leveling off at over 10,000 through 1970. Recidivism increased from a steady 32 percent to 38 to 40 percent.[27]

On February 21, 1971, the government decided to constitute a committee to study these problems. In May, Prime Minister Meir appointed sociologists, psychologists, educators, and other social policy experts to the Commission on the Plight of Underprivileged Youth, under the chairmanship of Katz. The Katz Commission, as it became known, was seen by many as a response to the Black Panthers' demonstrations and "the swing in public attention toward the plight of the poor" (*Jerusalem Post*, 11/15/72)—a correlation the prime minister denied, citing her early initiative in forming the commission as proof of her own personal concern for social problems (*Jerusalem Post*, 3/28/73).

The commission met for over a year, delivering its three-volume report on November 12, 1972.[28] Its recommendations included changes in existing patterns of formal and nonformal education, health care, and recreational facilities, as well as a minimum guaranteed income. The chapter on community work states:

One of the outstanding problems . . . is the absence of knowledge and clarity regarding methods and substance appropriate to the needs of youth; and especially . . . against the background of the fact that the majority of the existing methods and content are taken largely from the social and cultural world of the established middle classes.

The Katz Commission in particular created impetus, legitimacy, and budgets for the Community Center effort, the ICCC statistician stated in an interview. The new public focus on social problems led to new roles for the Centers.

PART TWO. ORGANIZATIONAL ISSUES

THE SOCIAL MANDATE OF THE ICCC

These various issues and concerns—immigrant absorption, ethnic disparities, leisure time and recreational facilities, out-migration—are reflected in the planners' and founders' views of the Community Centers' roles as they saw them then. Pozner recalled that the Center was to be a meeting place to fill free time and to integrate residents of the community. It was to turn "a commune into a community and housing into a neighborhood," she said, playing on the Hebrew forms of these words.[29] The Center would stand out as a magnet and pull people together. In their leisure time they would hang out together, meet for entertainment, and thereby acquire additional education and solve other problems: the provision of infant care, a day-care center, self-help, and social welfare services. "The great thing about it," said Pozner, "was that as the work developed, we learned about problems that existed—spontaneously. And the 'social problem' aspect joined the 'leisure time' concept—as we learned that the problems weren't characteristic of leisure time" (by which she meant, of an excess of free time with nothing to do).

According to Zipori (1972, pp. 12–13), members of the committee under Pozner's direction that recommended the initial agency plans saw one of three approaches as describing the purpose of the Community Center: individual-oriented education, community-building social change, or social services-oriented improvement. The first approach viewed their purpose as educating the population. Regardless of how that was translated into practice—whether it meant adult education or supplementary schooling for youth, whether in the arts or in academics or in physical education—the emphasis was to be pedagogic. Personnel in the field were to be well versed in psychology, teaching techniques, and educational problem-solving skills. Their aim would be to effect individual change in the person attending the Center. Of course, there was no opposition to this view, he recalled; debate concerned the relative emphasis or dominance that the educational approach would hold in Center theory and practice.

The second major view was the welfare or social approach, which placed group development at the heart of the Community Centers' work. The central problem for the Centers to undertake, as seen from this approach, was not merely effecting changes in individuals' values but rather more comprehensive social change: to cause a settlement of immigrants who had been brought together by way of refugee camps (ma'abarot) or transferred directly from their ships to weave the fabric of an active social grouping and community.

The third view became known as the services approach: services for the citizen, the family, the group. The Centers' purpose was seen as raising the level of local services, emphasizing quality of service provision (what a decade later might have been called a focus on "excellence"), in order thereby to raise the level of the population.

All three approaches were reflected in the committee's recommendations, Zipori noted, and this comprehensiveness became one of the hallmarks of the agency's program: it was an innovative outlook, as compared with other social policies and projects.

In his April 1971 "Report and Background Material" on the ICCC prepared for a conference with the director-general of the Ministry of Education and Culture, Zipori presented a "Definition of Purposes" of a Community Center. He wrote:

The Community Center was to be a vehicle for:

a. Social integration, by creating a meeting place for all sections of the population;
b. [Instilling] social and cultural values;
c. [Teaching] enlightened utilization of the individual's and family's leisure time;
d. Improving services to the citizen in the spheres of culture, recreation and entertainment.

The Center will merge and combine all existing types of activities. The Center will be a social and cultural creation of the community itself. It should provide a base for the development of initiative, and the members of the community are partners in the responsibility for its operation. Centralization of activities will bring about the large increase in the number of participants in group activities in the social, cultural, artistic and sports areas. The Center will take the place of the "street" and the various "cafes" and will fill the leisure hours with cultural content. Activities will be guided and controlled and will take place in a cultural and pleasant atmosphere. The varied choice of activities will meet the needs of all age groups and will be suited to the demands and inclinations of the individual, the family and the social group— all under one roof. (Zipori 1971)

As one observer saw it, the Centers are designed to:

a. Assist the various immigrant groups in their respective communities to more effectively integrate into Israeli society.
b. Help development towns to become more attractive places within which to live.
c. Provide supplementary education for the children in these towns.

Reporting on his October 1970 round of the existing seven Centers, the observer noted that "the actual program . . . focused primarily on school age children. . . . There is a definite plan to emphasize young adult, adult, and senior adults activities, but, to date, there has only been limited success in these areas."[30]

Goldman was asked in an interview why he thought at the time "that a replica of an institution that proved good for the American community would be good for Israeli society." He replied:

I grew up and was trained in community centers, so the subject is in my blood. I believed that despite the fact that the community center was an American institution in character, it could help in the development of the new State, mainly in absorption of new immigrants that began streaming in from all over the world. [It could be] a tool for social and cultural integration, in every sense. . . . There are some universal languages—painting, for instance, music, dance. The community center is the only place where each [immigrant] can speak his own language and still be understood by the others.

We must not forget that the community center was established in the U.S. at the end of the last century by Jews for Jews, who came from all over the world, to ease their integration in the new community. The community center achieved this goal. (Lavi 1979)

ORGANIZATIONAL LOGISTICS AND GOALS[31]

Pozner's interministerial planning committee handed over to the new ICCC an initial five-year plan to build forty-two Centers, calling for a budget of 40 million Israeli lirot, equivalent at the time to US$11,250,000. In its September 14, 1969 meeting, the ICCC's board of directors approved the appointment of the first two Center directors and mandated the establishment of local boards of directors for those two Centers in cooperation with the Local Councils (the elected local governments). The next five Centers were opened in 1970, followed by the eighth and ninth in 1971.

By then, "the social gap and the distressed conditions in . . . slum quarters in the large cities . . . gave birth to the urgent need to widen the network of Community Centers," and an additional five-year plan was submitted in June 1971 ("Community Centers in Israel" 1971). It called for construction of some thirty additional Centers in seventeen municipalities and a budget of IL50 million, more than the initial 42-Center budget had called for.[32]

By the Yom Kippur War of October 1973, nineteen Centers were built and operating, with another six using school buildings in the afternoon and evening hours. Building funds for the ICCC enterprise came from private donations, mostly foreign, channeled through the Israel Education Fund. Operating funds came from the various departments of the Ministry of Education and Culture. Local allocations followed their normal disbursal pattern: the ministry's departments budgeted funds by region, and their regional counterparts distributed the moneys to local council or municipality departments. Agreements were made locally, regionally, and/or nationally that the Centers would receive these moneys and assume local responsibility for providing recreational and nonformal educational programs.

Three of the nine members of the local Center boards of directors were to be regional ministry staff; another three were to be Local Council members. These six were usually the parties responsible for the allocation of ministry funds. Their board appointments seemingly were to ensure the smooth flow of money to the Community Centers. The other three board members were to be local lay leaders. Problems arose at the onset, however, regarding the particular personages to be chosen for these slots and the manner of their choosing. Even by 1975, few lay board members had been appointed; the matter remained problematic.

The network of interorganizational connections was wide and varied from the beginning. Some ten different departments of the Ministry of Education and Culture were involved with funding and programming, among them the Department for Youth, the Sports Authority, the Department for Bible Education, the Adult Education Division, the Department of Libraries, and the Art for the People

Program. The Ministries of Welfare (Department of Community Work), Immigrant Absorption (Department of Social Absorption), Housing (Association for House Improvement), and Defense (Youth and Nahal Division) were also involved. In addition, various voluntary associations (such as Rotary International, B'nai B'rith, the Moroccan Immigrants Society) and public sector organizations (including Amidar—the Government Immigrants Housing Corporation, Workers Councils, the Histadrut/Labor Federation's Department for Neighborhoods, and the Joint Distribution Committee-Israel) gave advice and money and were encouraged to cosponsor activities.

The ICCC made a distinction between "cooperation" and "partnership," as illustrated by their experience with the Histadrut (the National Federation of Labor) in 1972. The Histadrut proposed to Zipori that the ICCC take over several of their youth movement facilities, personnel, and budgets, according to Goldman. In return, the Histadrut wanted "formal representation for its leaders on the boards of the local Centers." They also wanted priority treatment for some of the Histadrut groups in using Center facilities.

The ICCC board, wrote Goldman, responded, almost unanimously that if

a Histadrut leader happens to be interested in Community Center work and is prepared to join a board of the Center ad personam, naturally he would be welcomed. But under no circumstances should we allow "*official*" Histadrut or Labour Council representation on the boards of the Centers. Just because a man happens to be chairman of the Local Labour Council or other Histadrut agency is no reason why he ex officio should serve on the Center Board. . . . Such representation, it was argued, would produce a board of vested interests, rather than a board which is primarily motivated by community interests and concern.[33]

Headquarters staff was small in the early years: Zipori, an accountant, a lawyer, an architect/interior designer, a director of community organization (after 1971), and one or two secretaries. (See Figure 3-1.) By late 1974, field-workers felt the need for counseling and supervision by field-based staff, rather than by the executive director based in Jerusalem. Two years later, headquarters staff had grown to include seven regional consultants to local Center directors, as well

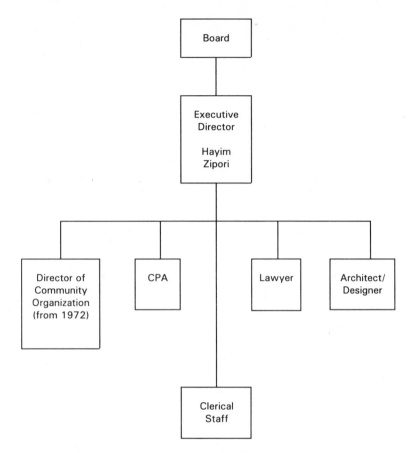

Figure 3-1.   ICCC Central Office: Early years.

as national coordinators for music, parent-child relations, toddler programs, and camping. (See Figure 3-2.)

By 1980, there were also an associate director, a director of planning and evaluation, three consultants on programs for infants, a director of development, two directors of a newly acquired camping site, a spokeswoman, a coordinator for Project Renewal (a national neighborhood rehabilitation program), a director of community schools, two consultants on art, a coordinator for Judaism and Tradition, a director of community services, a publications editor, a personnel director, a coordinator of adult education, two consultants on programs for the aged, three community work supervisors (and sev-

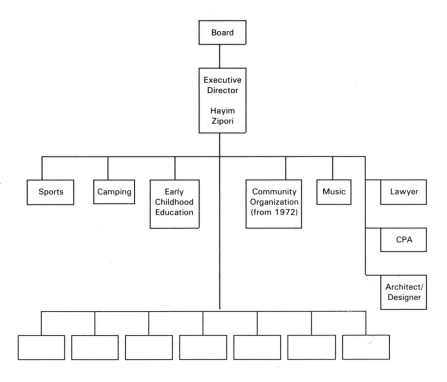

Figure 3-2. ICCC Central Office: Late 1970s.

eral others hired on a contractual basis), and nineteen clerical work-ers—a staff exceeding fifty people.

Center staffing and personnel development were critical prob-lems during the first phase of operations. Since the enterprise was new and its functions somewhat ambiguous, early applicants for Center directorships presented a wide range of qualifications and experience. Zipori recalled that the first pool of applicants numbered seventy-five; only seven or eight were suitable. Those involved in hiring felt that there was no model in Israel of the director's job which could serve applicants as an example. The scarcity of qualified applicants was exacerbated by the fact that few Centers were located near the country's population centers. Becoming a Center director in Mitzpe Ramon in the southern desert, for instance, would be the American equivalent of exile to the proverbial Oshkosh. Zipori concentrated hiring efforts on new immigrants with experience in community centers overseas and on returning Israeli emissaries with similar experience. In the fall of 1971, the one-year, post-B.A. Schwartz Program to Train Community Center Directors was inaugurated at the Hebrew University in Jerusalem in the School of Social Work with the cooperation of the School of Education and supported by JDC-Israel.[34]

Center directors were to be employed under contract with the ICCC itself, rather than by a local Center. Zipori's rationale was:

(1) To ensure uniform staff qualifications.

(2) To prevent the hiring practices that, to our sorrow, are accepted in many settlements where personal preferences, political payoffs, and nepotism form the basis for employment.

(3) To guarantee mobility from one Center to another without loss of seniority and other benefits.

"In this way," he said, "we are trying to guarantee the execution of work according to the spirit, intentions, and directions which we want for the Centers. Otherwise, we doubt that it would be possible to withstand all the pressures while carrying out the changes" (Zipori 1972, p. 23).

Directors' employment benefits were made superior to those of workers at comparable civil service levels in other agencies. In addition to a higher salary, said Zipori, the director's position "as the representative of a central body sent to work in a particular settlement or neighborhood . . . gains him a special status that's pretty strong" (Zipori 1972, p. 24).

Each director was to hire his own staff, under contract to the Community Center, not to the central agency. A typical ICCC Center had several departments under the overall supervision of the director, organized by age group and/or by function. One Center might have departments of Youth, Adult Education, Elderly, Sports, Art and Crafts, and Community Organization, as well as a library. (See Figure 3-3.) Department heads were responsible for programming activities in their units, hiring teachers to conduct the activities, purchasing equipment, recruiting students, and finding funds and donors to supplement the Center's budget to operate these programs. Department heads plus the director came to be known as the Center's senior staff.

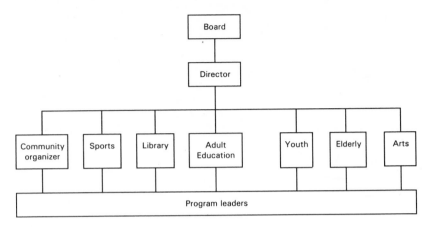

Figure 3-3. A Typical Community Center.

A typical Center might offer some or all of the activities listed in Table 3-4. New activities were added with time and changing tastes: "weight-watchers" clubs, for instance, were added in the late 1970s.

Staffing a Center was no less difficult for the directors than it was for Zipori. Department head positions were also new and unknown. Since most local residents were considered to lack the requisite training for these positions, the jobs required their incumbents to relocate to places distant from their homes. The Schwartz Program's title was changed after a few years to include "Senior Staff"; it added some department heads to the network.

In 1971 Amidar, the Government Immigrants Housing Corporation, approached the ICCC with an offer to fund community organizers who would operate out of local Centers. Amidar had a Community Organization (CO) unit. Its staff included former union and party organizers; few were university-trained, but Amidar provided in-service training. The organizers operated out of local Amidar offices, which were often small or otherwise not conducive to satisfactory work performance. The ICCC's new buildings, located in the immigrant settlements where much of Amidar's housing stock was also found, were apparently attractive as potential CO work sites. In 1972, Amidar and the ICCC signed a one-year contract to cosponsor community organizers in Centers. That fall, the ICCC hired two supervisors and eleven new organizers, ten of whom were college graduates with degrees in social work or one of the social sciences, and they joined a training program with Amidar's other new organizers.

TABLE 3-4.   Typical Areas of Community Center Programming

Sports:	karate judo wrestling weight lifting tennis field exercises	basketball soccer swimming Ping-Pong gymnastics
Dance:	folk dance ballet	jazz modern
Hobbies:	drama jewelry making batik photography metalworking film clubs	ceramics sewing knitting woodworking enamel work psychology
Music:	drums recorder violin music appreciation	guitar accordion piano
Art:	painting	sculpture
Library:	free book loan homework help	children's library authors' lectures
Education (adult and supplementary):	English Arabic mathematics literacy "parenting"	Hebrew French Bible Talmud lecture series
Activities:	immigrant absorption student council concerts, theater local arts and crafts exhibits	senior citizens street-gang work mobile art exhibits Housing Project committees Citizens Information Center

At the time, the senior staff in some of the smaller or more remote towns consisted only of a director and a community organizer. Relations between community organizers and their coworkers were characterized by all the problems of a generally more educated group with professional loyalties to CO practice encouraged by the training sessions and organizational allegiance to the agency's central office that managed their hiring. These tensions were exacerbated by the newness of the CO profession in Israel and the relative vagueness of its occupational description and by the structural arrangement that gave the organizers three supervisors: the Center director, the CO director at ICCC headquarters, and an Amidar CO supervisor. Moreover, the similarity of principles of professional CO practice to the ICCC's statement of operating principles made the community organizers, in their own eyes, the arbiters of Center practices. Their professional supervisors in headquarters and Amidar expected them to teach their directors and colleagues about community organization, which the supervisors and, hence, the organizers themselves considered to be the proper professional method of Center work. Their organizational supervisors, the Center directors, resented what they regarded as undue meddling in their affairs by employees of another organization—the CO supervisors from Amidar. Intra- and interorganizational tensions abounded.

The Amidar contract was not renewed, but the principles of CO practice had taken root. The ICCC undertook to retain and support all local CO personnel and the two supervisors. JDC-Israel probably influenced this decision. For one, JDC's senior staff were social workers, some of them from American community center backgrounds where social work was seen as an integral part of center work. Goldman, by now associate director of JDC-Israel, had retained his connection with Zipori and his influence on the ICCC's development. Second, Zipori was looking for direction, especially in a professional context. The Americans had extensive center experience, and it is likely that the lure of American ideas bolstered the attraction that professionalism itself held. Third, JDC had money. Although the ICCC absorbed the salaries of the organizers, at least initially, JDC could fund the supervisors, especially since personnel development was one of its own central concerns.

The ICCC's relationship with JDC grew because of the joint appeal of professional advice and financial support. JDC, in turn, sought someone experienced in center work and social work education to serve as liaison to the ICCC. They were able to draw a series of experienced center men from overseas, initially for one-month assignments and then for longer terms. One of them, Ernest Segal, arriving just before the 1973 war, introduced the concept of in-service training that greatly advanced the level of staff professionalism. He was succeeded by Arnulf Pins, a social work educator with center experience, who influenced professional development at both the JDC and the ICCC, the latter in the areas of CO practice and general personnel practices.

Personnel and program development in the ICCC were influenced not only by the JDC but also by the succession of social and political events that played out before and during the ICCC's founding period. These are reflected in its mission statements at the time, as it sought to establish its organizational identity and public image.

The ICCC mission: 1969–73

Before the first five-year plan matured, a second five-year plan was added, incorporating urban slum areas into the ICCC's province. Zipori presented these changes in a May 1971 letter explaining his postponement of a scheduled trip to New York. The delay

> was made necessary by our preparations for a major undertaking on the part of the Centers in connection with a new plan in the battle with poverty, in consequence of the arousal of sensitive groups to the subject of the social gap.
>
> We have just crystallized a program to build another 30 Community Centers in distressed areas of the large cities (until now we have attended to development towns only), and it was submitted two days ago to [Finance] Minister Sapir. . . .[35]

That the Community Centers were expected to help narrow the social gap is also seen in their involvement with other agencies around these aims. For example, in its September 1971 meeting, the Public Council for Community Work—which included Pozner, Zipori, and representatives of the Ministry of Welfare—discussed "Social and Economic Gaps in Israeli Society: the Contribution of Community

Work [i.e., Community Organization] to Narrowing the Gaps" (Protocol, 9/7/71).

At the time, the Centers were described as "a new experiment following a thorough investigation and study of the possibilities to advance weak communities *in need of social integration and community development*." The statement continues:

> Last spring, when the Israel public's attention was drawn to the problem of poverty by the "Black Panthers," the mayors of the development towns and large cities began to plead for more Community Centers in their poverty stricken areas. There was a general feeling that Community Centers can advance social integration and reduce ethnic tensions.[36]

The various social concerns of the time, interwoven with earlier conceptions of the purpose of the Community Center, can be seen in the following description of the ICCC's mission, quoted at length from its first promotional brochure, published in 1971.

> The amount of leisure time at the disposal of modern society is continuously growing. People who have ample means use this time in a variety of well directed ways, but in new immigrant development towns and in the city slums there simply isn't any spare money in the people's pockets. Their possibilities for entertainment or the utilization of their free time, therefore, are very limited. Youth spend their free time aimlessly hanging around the street corners, and their elders fill their days with meaningless occupations.
>
> Once in a while a cultural event comes to the small town. After the curtain goes down, the artists pack their sets and move on to the big city. The local Culture House very often does not fulfill the needs. It offers very little and its appearance is depressing. This is not the place for both teenagers and adults.
>
> Eventually the social desolation prevailing in many immigrant development towns brings about depression and spiritual degeneration and leads the youth to a street life, the outcome of which is unfortunately predictable.

The brochure continues:

In 43 development towns and immigrant centers, cultural life was sorely lacking. Cultural and social activities in those towns were run by various and strange [estranged?—ed.] bodies, when one often did not know what the other was doing. Veterans returning from the army could not stand the social desolation of the town where they had lived many years, and a number left their families and turned towards the beckoning lights of the big cities, while their brothers looked at them with envy, hoping to follow them some day.

There was a lack of capable instructors and professionals who would be able to provide fruitful cultural activities for the residents of these towns, as well as a lack of funds and appropriate facilities.

This problematic situation could only be solved by the founding of such Community Centers that would integrate most of the social and cultural activities of immigrant settlements, widen the horizons of and attract both young and old.

This picture is contrasted with the experience in the developed countries:

For example—America, where Community Centers are often found in cities quite a distance from the cultural scene. Among trees and green landscape, large facilities have been erected to serve as centers for the widening of horizons for the whole community. Those who want to stretch their limbs at sports will find football and basketball fields, special physical education equipment and a swimming pool. For those interested in cultural activities there are libraries, clubs, lectures and many other edifying activities for their leisure time.

The committee's purpose [the reference is to Pozner's committee] was to adapt all this to the realities of Israel in general and the development towns in particular. They were convinced that in Israel it was also possible through Community Centers to bring about fruitful meetings among the various social groups, whether this was in Ashkelon or Afula, Dimona or Yavneh. These and other places are known for being melting pots which absorbed communities from different countries, with differing customs and cultural backgrounds and forged them into one community.

The Centers were also meant to be a place where positive use could be made of leisure time and where entertainment of a higher quality could be offered. . . .

The text then turns to a detailed picture of the envisioned Center:

The Community Center will be located in the center of each town, within everyone's reach. It will be a large building, spacious and comfortable. In the center of the facility, a big auditorium will be built for performances which had to be staged in less suitable halls in all sorts of places. The stage at its focal point will be able to accommodate shows with many participants.

Every room and corner in this building has to be put to maximal use. Thus, for instance, the dressing rooms can be used as club rooms, the entrance hall can be used for exhibitions, and so on. . . .

The Center will also include a Friendship Club, structured on the model of the homey clubs one finds in some kibbutzim. The equipment of this club will include comfortable armchairs, a counter and self-service expresso machine, periodicals, table games like backgammon, checkers, chess and other accessories that will bring the members together and offer them a pleasant atmosphere of social and cultural well-being which is often absent from their impoverished dwellings.

They also proposed that Community Centers offer adequate activities for pre-school children and for retired senior citizens. A wide range of courses would be geared to people with different needs and tastes: they will range from dance and ceramics to drum instruction, weight lifting, sauna and judo. The athletic minded will go for the weight lifting equipment and those more intellectually inclined will opt for the chess club.

The committee also decided that a library is a must in every Center. It will be run by professional librarians and will include study rooms for adults and children, music rooms and audio-visual equipment.

Youth will be able to dance in a discotheque proposed for every Community Center. Possibly the spacious air raid shelter in every Center could be used for dancing.

A real Community Center would include a Nursery. The parents would be able to leave their children in the trustworthy professional hands of the nursery teachers, while they would profit from other useful occupations in the Center.

Community Centers must have genuine sports activities. It was decided to recommend a swimming pool, a lighted basketball field, tennis courts, a gymnasium and table tennis rooms.

And still the list of clubs and activities to be included in these Centers according to the original plan was not complete[:] Drama Clubs, a Classical Film Club, Folklore Clubs, the plastic arts such as painting and sculpture, artistic photography, music, theatrical performances and other similar entertainment.

Also to be included in the Center's activities were: Popular Education on high school and college levels, Popular Science Clubs, Natural History and Topography and others. Youth would gain from supplementary education courses as well as a variety of sports activities.

The Center would be the place where authors would meet their readers, new immigrants would meet old-timers and army veterans[,] their friends. Senior adults and even the handicapped would spend their time here, women learn home economy, sewing and participate in Parents' Clubs. ("Community Centers in Israel" 1971)

A proposal to evaluate Community Center operations, written in May 1972, similarly described the ICCC's mission as solving social ills:

The recent recognition of pervasive social problems in Israel society has brought with it persistent demands that something be done about them. The government has committed itself to explore a number of avenues designed to eliminate the causes of these problems and/or to reduce their consequences and/or to offer the victims of these problems a new chance or a new start. High on the list of priorities is the development of forty or more Community Centers in as many cities and towns throughout the land. . . . Each Community Center is expected to develop its own program, geared to unique problems of the locality in which it is located; yet there will be similarities in program due to the similarity in social problems and the similarity in expectations of the local population for service.[37]

These themes are repeated by the agency's national coordinator of Community Organization, Shlomo Segev, in his first report:

The economic growth that has been visited upon Israeli society in the last few years (since the Six Day War) has also reached the development towns and city suburbs. But it has not brought with it the social development expected. On the contrary, the social gap has deepened; the many hopes and dreams of social change have not been realized. Many of the development towns continue to be transit stations on the road to the center of the country . . . those who remain lack the means necessary to contribute to the development of the towns.

Teachers and social workers watched with concern the increase of school dropouts, juvenile delinquency, and girls turning to prostitution. GIs left the towns where they grew up for nearby cities to learn a trade and enjoy the entertainment facilities there. Housing shortages . . . grew.

It was, therefore, necessary to find a solution for this social destitution. The late Zalman Aranne, Minister of Education and Culture, saw in the Community Centers one of the tools with which cultural activities for all ages could be provided. . . .

Segev continued that "self-help"—"full participation of residents in the self management of the Center"—was one of the basic ideas in operating the Centers. The building itself was to be "multistory, restful, furnished and outfitted with great taste, and used to the hilt" (Segev 1973, p. 3).

In May 1973, in the Report to the Second Annual National Conference of the ICCC, Chairman of the Board Elad Peled also wrote about the physical design of the Centers:

The Center building . . . is often a contradiction to the houses surrounding it. Its cultured, spacious, restful atmosphere makes the acute social and cultural problems stand out.

Despite this, when it was decided to build the Centers, it was clear . . . that the Center itself and its programs would belong to the world of a higher level of aspirations, which would serve as an example of what could be the legacy of its visitors. [Hebrew original]

He concluded with a vision of the Center as an all-inclusive, comprehensive coordinating body of educational and cultural services, serving the settlement as a single unit—the only way, he said, to make a great stride forward in the solution of social problems.

The specific programs of the Centers were many and varied. Goldman described some of the activities he saw while visiting a development town Center in 1972, linking the programs to the broader policy statements:

> Only four years ago, in the summer of 1968, I visited [one of the development towns]. . . . You know what the town was like then, politically, socially and economically. How different [it] is in the fall of 1972.
>
> I naturally visited the Community Center. The first program I saw there was a group of 15 to 20 little girls, ages 8 to 12, on the stage of the "air-conditioned" auditorium dancing ballet. How proud some of the citizens of [the development town] must now feel that even their youngsters can study ballet. It is not ballet that is important, but the fact that in this little God-forsaken town, the youngsters of the poor have an equal opportunity to be exposed to today's cultural activities as are the youngsters of the Tel Aviv residents. I could mention many, many things that I saw in [the development town] this time which have given the town greater self confidence, greater pride, and a desire to remain there and develop their town.[38]

The ICCC also undertook programs designed to prevent juvenile delinquency, prostitution, and drugs. JDC-Israel wrote about the

> crash program to activate Community Centers in the depressed urban areas and development towns. . . . Such Centers can serve as major tools of social integration. Community centers already exist in Israel. What is new is the concept of a community center as a dynamic instrument of social change, with special emphasis on attracting disadvantaged youth.

Housing density is linked to success in school, despite the findings of the Katz and Gurevitch (1972) study: "It was recently estimated that 250,000 children in Israel live in overcrowded housing conditions which do not give them the minimum of privacy and quiet essential to their progress in school and thus their success in the future." The new Community Center buildings "include libraries so that children from crowded homes can study at the Center under the watchful eyes of a tutor."[39] Wrote Harold Trobe, executive director of JDC-Israel: "What we are aiming for is that kids from the poorer neighborhoods will be welcomed, in fact invited, to parties and other activities in the 'better' neighborhoods, and the other way around. This will not happen unless the educational level becomes more equalized."[40]

There are a few indications that developing a conception of the Center's purpose and its programs was an ongoing process. During the first several months of 1971, the Public Council for Community Organization held a series of discussions on the nature of the Community Center in Israel. The group, attended by representatives of the ministries of Education and Welfare, concluded that there was a need to define the purpose of the Center and to distinguish among different kinds of Centers in operation under the aegis of various agencies.[41]

Goldman's letter suggests some of the organizational issues involved:

Our contribution in the field of Community Centers would be welcome[d] by those in power not just because of the funds but because of the professionalism and the access to professionals which we can provide. To my mind there is an additional crucial consideration.

Today, the Community Centers program is understood by some in the Ministry of Education and not understood, and perhaps deliberately misunderstood, by others. As long as the source of funds for this program is only the Ministry of Education, some of the officials of that Ministry, because of departmental pressures, would like to convert the Centers Program into another Ministry of Education department.

The late Minister Aranne in conceiving the idea of setting up a "Government Corporation" understood fully the significance of developing an independent voluntary organization so that a creative Community Center program would be developed without the restrictions of the usual governmental bureaucratic regulations.

If JDC were to come in at this time with a program of some dimension, small to start with but with a plan for greater involvement in the future, there is no question in my mind but that this would affect the entire future of the Centers Program in Israel. If the Minister and Director General of the Ministry of Education knew that in addition to their funds outside financing would be possible, even for a limited period of time, they would view the whole Community Centers program differently.[42]

The first American center director to consult to the ICCC and its Centers for a longer term reported the following observations on Center programs at a meeting with JDC staff in early 1973. He, too, touches here on issues of organizational identity as they relate to broader social problems:

As we met and were trying to define a little more what the Community Centers are to do, I think there was agreement that in some ways there are parallels between the Community Center in Israel today and the Settlement House in the States of some years ago. One of the roles of the Center is to get into the community, get into the very fabric of the community and try to deal with some of the concerns of community life, in terms of motivating the kids as far as education goes—that there is a future in it, to try to help parents define their role in the family and thus deal with the cultural gaps that exist with children who are into the Israel scene and parents whose life styles may be of another culture. A couple of the Centers began doing this, and they are meeting with success. *The Center is more than just a happy house for basketball, clubs and batik. It must help build the community and work with the entire family.*

At the same time, he wrote:

Also at that meeting we agreed on the importance of the Center having a gymnasium. Israel will be hitting the health bug in the years ahead, like other Western countries. In America today you have great difficulty driving down the street because of the joggers everywhere, everybody is doing exercises and attempting to be in good condition and good shape.

His is also an early report on some Centers' success in establishing an identity:

At Yahud [a development town], the women of Savyon [a small, fashionable, and well-to-do town] come for the slimnastic classes. When I was there I found some of the Savyon kids in the theater group. No one says, of course, "Hey, I'm from Savyon and you're from Yahud and we gotta integrate, man, and we gotta do our thing together." But there's an attractive show they're putting on, they've got a very good choreographer and kids are coming in from everywhere.

I don't know if they are going to socially integrate, but there are relationships that are developing. In some of the development towns the Center is seen as the place for the North African, the Rumanian and the Grizini [sic—Soviet Georgian]. Many of the directors have a beautiful sense of mission in this concept of respect for cultural differences and yet building a sense of community.

Generally, our Centers have a positive status in development towns. In Jerusalem, the Centers have a real fascinating mix of people. At the Lown Center it's amazing—the skin pigmentation, the hair, the language, it's a real mixture. And the Center staff sees a chance of making a contribution to the country. That's what excites me.[43]

The ICCC and the Yom Kippur War:
October 1973–Summer 1974

Black Panther protest activity petered out after its heyday in 1971 and 1972. Hopes were high that the Katz Commission's report, submitted in November 1972, would effectively address—even solve—problems of juvenile delinquency and the "newly discovered" social gap. The Community Centers took the report's recommendations seriously: they hired street-gang workers and sent their senior staff to training sessions in combatting the use of drugs.

The impetus of this new attention to social problems was interrupted and then diverted by the suddenness of the October 1973 war. Israel sustained the largest per capita ratio of losses of any of her previous four wars, and while not vanquished militarily, the country suffered socially and psychologically. The total lack of preparation for an attack and questionable administrative practices leading up to the war precipitated a degree of public dissent from government policies unprecedented in Israel's history. This led, politically, to the downfall of Golda Meir's government in the short run and to the routing of the Labor Party, dominant since the founding period, in the longer run. Immigration from the West, which had risen to new heights after the 1967 War, plummeted; emigration of Israelis swelled. Of the summers of 1974 and 1975 it was rumored that there were more Israeli citizens outside the country's borders than remained within. The popular joke in circulation at the time asked the last one leaving to turn off the lights.

The Community Centers during the war faced their first crisis. Most of the directors—all men—were drafted. Many of the Centers remained open and operated "crisis programs" under the direction of the librarians, community organizers, adult education or arts coordinators—the female personnel. Some buildings were requisitioned by the Civil Guard or the army for various operations. Programs were run in cooperation with them: patrols of high school students were sent out to inspect bomb shelters; others recruited sandwiches and balaklava helmets from local housewives and distributed them at nearby crossroads to troops en route to the front. Centers' telephone lines were made available to field-based telephones. As the war wore on, some Centers mounted letter-writing campaigns to maintain contact with drafted residents. Teenagers who had been awaiting induction into the army volunteered to fill in on agricultural work at nearby *kibbutzim*, and Center staff coordinated transportation and assignments.

Schools remained closed, and some Centers were able to run programs to keep children off the streets during normal school hours (although many mothers kept their children at home throughout the war). Parents were "relieved to know that their children were engaged in constructive activities, particularly inside buildings with excellent air raid shelters," noted Zipori afterward. "It was especially useful for families where the male parent was mobilized and the mother had her hands full with all the additional chores that she was now forced to carry out. Since the Centers are located in areas with large concentrations of families with many children and low income, this program was of particular importance and a real service."[44]

The war served to consolidate the Centers internally: there was a feeling within the organization that they had proved themselves, that they had "arrived" at last. When it was over, the ICCC congratulated itself on a job well done. Their internal reports and JDC-Israel's press releases described the war as a sort of rite of passage into the society of social institutions—which the Centers passed with flying colors. "The Centers played a key role during the actual war period," Zipori reported, in a second JDC press release (n.d.) which claimed that the Community Centers provided "vital home front services" and "proved a godsend, beyond all previous expectations." Zipori also said:

> The Centers proved they were an integral part of the community, that they were fully adaptable and could be counted on in time of emergency. By carrying out the thousand-and-one small but essential tasks for individual families, they gained the confidence of the entire community and made many new friends. Steps are now being taken to attract them to the Centers during peacetime as well since this will help to integrate them much faster into the social fabric of the country.

In the same press release, Goldman noted another outcome. The war had "hastened a desirable process among the country's Community Centers. It pressed them into becoming multi-service centers, providing a wide variety of community services in addition to the recreational and educational activities which had been their primary endeavor until now."

A supermarket of services: 1974–77

The multiservice idea, popular in American social work circles in the late 1960s, came into its own in Israel as the crisis period receded. The Katz Commission had laid the groundwork by recommending comprehensive revisions of the social service structure, coordination of the various youth-serving agencies, and a "super-agency" of welfare services. The idea of coordinating multiple services fell on already fertile ground in the ICCC, whose programs crossed departmental and ministerial budgetary lines and whose original goals had included upgrading the level of local services.

The idea found its early organizational expression in the conception of the Community Center as a "supermarket of ideas and programs for all ages, at all levels" ("Jerusalem Community Centers" 1974, ICCC Annual Report 1975). Pozner recalled that when her committee began to invent the model Community Center, they tried to design a building that would be "a functional supermarket" in meeting the maximum number of desires. It would contain space for performances and sports practices, for different clubs or classes, and for a "members' lounge" (Lavi 1979). The phrase evolved into "a supermarket of classes." As the multiservice center concept came into vogue, the "supermarket of classes" became a "supermarket of services" oriented toward different subgroups of the population. Coordination of these services became a major issue.

At the time the Katz Commission made its recommendations in 1972, public attention was focused on such problems as the duplication of social services and bureaucratic runaround and red tape. This focus was generated largely by new immigrants from the West, who suggested the need for coordinated provision of information as well as the coordination of services themselves. One proposal recommended that the Community Centers be the coordinators of immigrant services: "Designed to be sensitive to, and to serve, the specific needs of their localities, the autonomous nature of the Centers gives the residents, including new immigrants, a sense of belongingness and a proprietary interest in the Center which enhances their participation." Given its mandate and resources, the proposal continues, the Center is uniquely suited to be the agency to coordinate "all of the information needed by new immigrants," "as many as possible of the services" needed, "informal educational activities," and the fostering of friendships and "good intergroup relations."[45]

While implementation of the Katz Commission's recommendations was diverted by the 1973 war (and deflected afterward by political and other considerations), the idea of coordinated services took root, and the Centers' war experiences were assimilated into this conceptual context. Thus, one JDC staff member wrote that "just as the pressure of [wartime] events forced the Centers to move to new levels of achievement, the presentation to them of a master plan which emphasizes services to the entire community will be very productive."[46]

Zipori called the Community Center "the integrator of welfare services" at the local level. As examples of the administrative complexity of some services, he noted the five national-level agencies responsible for juvenile delinquents—Police, Army (Gadna Branch), Welfare,

Labor, and Education and Culture's Youth Department—and the seven responsible for various services for the elderly—Welfare, Health, National Insurance, Medical Clinics, JDC, ICCC, and the Elder-Care Agency (sponsored jointly by JDC, Welfare, and Health). Added to these were the Local Councils and their own departments paralleling the national ministries. The Center, he wrote, can and should cut across all these entities as their common local agent, adapting its service provision to local need, rather than forcing local need to conform to agency structures. The effort demands maximal coordination, not only for efficiency but also for effectiveness, he noted.[47]

In an interview, Zipori was more direct in his comments: "The integration of services through the Community Centers would avoid the inflexibility of the local welfare and education departments, which are bound by policy of their Ministries or the mayors who appoint them" (quoted in the *Jerusalem Post* 1/6/77).

The scope of social services also broadened during this period. Initial child-oriented programs such as "Head Start" or "Home Start" grew into comprehensive "Early Childhood Education Services." At the request of the ministries of Welfare and Education toward the end of 1972, JDC took on the development of day-care centers.[48] The ICCC Centers, already receiving funding and professional guidance from JDC, were obvious places to house these day-care centers. The first such program opened in Dimona in October 1973, enabling "underprivileged families to send 30 children for daytime care while the mothers partake in a wide variety of activities at the Center," including home economics, sewing, home decorating, and child psychology. A multiservice center necessitated multiuse space, and JDC commissioned "a unique set of furniture which can be completely folded each day, closed into a space no larger than six square meters, and placed unobtrusively in a corner, thus freeing the room for other afternoon and evening activities."[49] JDC expanded its university-based, postgraduate Schwartz Program to Train Community Center Directors and Senior Staff to include directors of early childhood education programs.

These programs received a boost from a different angle, the "laundry club." Because of the high initial cost of a washing machine and the additional 100 percent-of-value customs duty levied, few poor families could afford their purchase. Laundromats were not available. Many of the families in the development towns and city slums had young children. Since the average family had five children, handwashing laundry took up a large amount of a mother's time. Borrowing an idea tried earlier, two or three Centers arranged laundromats on a small scale, but with a difference: while the machines washed, the women were to socialize over a cup of tea. Socializing was to give way to classes on knitting and lectures on health. When women said they could not come because they had small children on hand, the "supermarket" expanded to offer child drop-off rooms with toys and babysitters. As they added cribs, the idea of a day-care center grew. The 1973 war added impetus to this effort: since schools were not in session, children were presumably at home under foot, and mothers could not accomplish their usual marketing and other tasks. The Centers introduced "central babysitting," where a parent could drop off children to run errands.

Another project also reinforced the Early Childhood Education service. After the 1973 war, public attention to the idea that parent-child interaction in the preschool years was necessary for proper development increased. The idea of "toy libraries" was developed, and many Centers adopted it. The libraries stocked educational games and toys, which children could use on the premises under the librarian's supervision. Parents were involved in training sessions designed to improve constructive child-oriented time and could borrow games for home use. Sometimes greater parental involvement in the school and classroom grew out of this activity. The ultimate objective of the toy library was to improve the quality of local schooling to a level comparable to urban schools.

By August 1974, the ICCC's goals had expanded further:

One of the goals of the Community Center is caring for special groups in the community in order to turn them into "consumers" of its services and to make them happier and more ordinary. Among the special groups are: disabled soldiers, work accident victims, the blind, the chairbound, rehabilitated ex-convicts, predelinquents, drug addicts or reformed drug addicts, school dropouts, non-Jewish community members, tourists, students from nearby universities, etc.[50]

At the same time, the task of the Community Centers was seen as bridging "the gap between [Jews of Asian-African origins] and their fellow Jews whose roots are in the modern Western tradition." The former, "because of the handicaps imposed upon them by life in the countries from which they came, were wholly unprepared from the standpoint of education, training and the mental and social outlook for life in a modern industrial society. . . ." The goal statement continues:

In keeping with this concept, the Community Centers have set as their goals the raising of the quality of life in the communities, removing the walls that separate the various ethnic groups from one another, dissipating the feeling of non-belonging that persists among the people who came from the culturally impoverished areas, motivating people to do for themselves things that will improve their condition, and encouraging collective action in shaping a community in which the people can take pride.

These goals are translated programmatically . . . into efforts:

(1) To secure better housing conditions for the people.
(2) To fight illiteracy.
(3) To provide cultural programs that broaden the horizons and stretch the mind.
(4) To involve housewives in programs that will make them more competent in running a household.
(5) To teach mothers what they must do to meet the intellectual and psychological needs of their children.
(6) To help children with learning difficulties overcome their handicaps.
(7) To induce children who should be working or studying, and who are doing neither, to return to some educational framework or to enter a working framework.
(8) To promote for the benefit of infants from severely retarded backgrounds day-care centers where they can be stimulated to engage in activities essential for their physical, mental, and emotional growth.
(9) To inculcate within each ethnic group a pride in its culture as well as an appreciation of the culture of other groups.
(10) To provide opportunities for people of different origins to meet in a natural and relaxed atmosphere and to learn how much they have in common despite their differences.

(11) To encourage the formation of interest groups with a social, recreational, or artistic base.

(12) To motivate people to try their hand in the plastic or performing arts in the hopes that it will lead to activities that will permanently enrich their lives and to encourage the development of local leadership.[51]

Debates about the multiservice nature of the Center, at their height in 1975–76, cooled by the following year. Arnulf Pins, JDC's first full-time consultant to the ICCC and a social worker by training, in effect called the debate unnecessary and moribund, writing in the ICCC's 1975–76 Annual Report:

> Lately it has become popular to describe the Community Center as a multi-service agency or to urge that it become one.
>
> The issue of whether the Community Center in Israel is or should become a multi-service agency is not a real question or a productive debate.
>
> The purposes of the Community Center and its methods of programming *naturally* lead to the emergence of a multi-service agency. It is not a question of a plan or a decision. The Center has no choice, it will become a multi-service Center unless it changes its purpose and method of work.[52]

The first non-labor government: 1977–80

Menahem Begin's Likud Party, in the opposition for thirty years and constituting an opposing faction of the pre-state underground before that, swept the elections in 1977. He rode in on the support of the Asian-African Jews, who believed his campaign pledge to reorient government policies to their benefit, eliminating the social gap once and for all. It was a victory of urban, petit bourgeois, laissez-faire center liberalism over agricultural, antiurban, centrally planned, socialist labor—of the "downtrodden's hero" over the "Establishment." The elation of victory was short-lived. By 1980, most were disappointed in Begin's lack of follow-through, although he succeeded in rallying his disaffected supporters to win reelection in 1981.

Nevertheless, he seemed to begin on the right track. In 1977, shortly after his election, Begin announced a dramatic urban renewal plan, in conjunction with world Jewry, to infuse money into the towns and slums for social as well as physical rehabilitation. Project Renewal, budgeted at $60 million, was to be carried out locally, where possible, by the Community Center staffs who were so familiar with local conditions.

In Begin's coalition, the Ministry of Education and Culture passed into the hands of the National Religious Party for the first time in the state's history. The question arose as to whether the ICCC would now have to establish "religious" Community Centers alongside its "secular" ones, similar to the parallel organization of religious and secular schools in the state. Zipori resisted this pressure, but it did focus attention on the role of the Community Center in inculcating Jewish religious values among its members and participants.

In 1978, two rabbis were invited to address ICCC field supervisory staff on the potential role of the Centers in disseminating and inculcating Jewish values and traditions. The summary of that meeting states: "The Centers can help in the development of the individual's internal meaning, and in developing a new page in the subject of Jewish heritage, in closing gaps, and in creating a framework for the realization of the spiritual experience that is in Judaism. . . . " As a result of the discussion, the protocol continues, "it was decided to devote a full day to a discussion on the 'how': how to begin the activity, where, who could be turned on (to the idea), and which Centers to involve in such a project. . . ."[53] JDC-Israel's director wrote: "There seems to be some misconception . . . that Community Centers are not conveyors of Jewish identity and that they are primarily interested in recreation and social activities. It will be important for us to begin to look at the Community Centers and their 'Jewish activity.'"[54]

Zipori hired a national coordinator of Jewish Programs. He also hired a national coordinator of Camping Programs, for camping as a recreational/social/educational experience had become a major ICCC project. "It is accepted in the Western world that camping is an integral part of the activities of the community center," wrote the first coordinator.[55]

The ICCC entered into its second joint venture with Amidar (the Government Immigrants Housing Corporation) to fund and promote community organizers through the Centers. The goals of the project were:

(1) To help families and groups in the community organize to improve the quality of their lives, through the acquisition

of habits of cleanliness, the design of living quarters, the development of self-help skills in house maintenance—paint, plaster, fencing, general repairs, etc.

(2) To help families and groups improve their residence conditions and to organize their free time through striking social and cultural roots in their places of residence by referring them to Center activities. . . .

(3) To develop good neighborly relations. . . .

(4) To help residents personally solve their problems through house councils and voluntarism. . . .

(5) To encourage citizen participation. . . .[56]

THE SECOND DECADE AND BEYOND

In 1979 the corporation marked the completion of its first decade of operations. It opened its hundredth Community Center in 1980.

As a group and as a political movement, the Black Panthers, who seemingly played a central role in crystallizing a social problem and moving it onto the public agenda, ended not long after their birth in late 1969 to early 1970, due to internal power struggles among contending leaders. Three have since been elected to the Knesset at various times and for various terms; one became head of the Jerusalem Neighborhood Committee; one became director of army preparation programs for the Jerusalem Municipality Youth, Sport and Social Activities division; others have pursued various public and commercial occupations.

Ten years after its founding, the ICCC continued to restate and refine its identity and purpose. The newly appointed director of research and evaluation for the ICCC wrote, in her first interim report, that a necessary prerequisite for planning and setting policy was "the crystallization of a consensus on the general objectives of the Community Center and on principles of its activities."[57]

At a national convention in January 1979, the following concepts were recorded in an open discussion among Center directors about the nature of the Centers:

- The Center must be the warning light signaling [the existence of] local problems in comprehensive service delivery.

- The Center must be a catalyst, an umbrella organization.
- The Center's function is to educate for democracy.

One director asked what the goal of the Center was. Zipori answered: "improving the quality of life—values, spirituality, attitudes, and so forth."[58]

Six months later, at a session the ICCC's executive committee held with the Minister of Education and Culture, Zipori elaborated on the purpose of the Center: "Improving the quality of life by community development in the towns and neighborhoods through a comprehensive approach to all age groups with their needs in the areas of culture, art, education, social activity, and community activity, intended for the individual, the family, the group, and the community." In discussing plans for the coming decade, he noted that the pressure to build new Centers was exceedingly strong. "How do we determine [where to build]?" he asked. "The question recurs whether we are a service to the poor. What is the requisite [population] size? Whom do we assist?"[59]

Many staff maintained a commitment to an organizational identity expressed in ideals ascribed to the ICCC. As one Center director wrote in resigning his post:

We all came to the ICCC from different personal and educational backgrounds, but it seems to me that the work, the shared discussions, and the readiness to work in distant settlements and poverty neighborhoods have turned us into brothers and partners in an important social idea. I feel today that I belong to a group . . . where societal values and willingness to help one's fellow man inform its activities more than the chase after personal gain. . . .[60]

The struggle to formulate an identity linked to solving social problems continued to be impacted by sociopolitical events. Observations and events suggested that the social situation had not changed much. Writing in 1978, Eliezer Jaffe, head of Jerusalem's Welfare Department at the time of the Black Panther riots, expressed the opinion that Egyptian President Anwar Sadat's visit to Jerusalem had, once again, diverted attention from internal matters to foreign affairs. "The danger," he wrote, "lies in the fact that inattention to the internal social problems 'discovered' here in recent years may eventually undermine the kind of life we would like to enjoy in peacetime" (*Jerusalem Post*, 11/6/78).

The Begin government canceled a large part of the government subsidization of public transportation and basic food items such as bread, oil, and dairy products. Inflation rose to 133 percent in 1980; food prices rose by 152 percent overall, 165 percent for vegetables and fruit. Israeli currency was floated: one U.S. dollar bought 10 Israeli lirot in July 1977 and IL100 less than four years later. "The poor get poorer," the *Jerusalem Post* editorialized (1/16/81), bearing the weight of higher food costs, lower real wages, and higher taxes, under the "anti-social" effects of the government's economic policy on income distribution. "The social gap continued to widen last year, as it has for several years now," wrote the *Post*'s Shlomo Ma'oz (1/16/81) in reporting the Central Bureau of Statistics latest figures.

In 1979 there were riots and demonstrations in Tel Aviv and Jerusalem to protest cancelations of food subsidies. In November a group called "Ohel," a successor to the Black Panthers, organized what they called "milk riots" in Jerusalem. Some months later, on June 8, 1980, Ohel once again organized young couples from a Jerusalem slum in a "tent city" demonstration against the continued unavailability of housing. The aim of their struggle was "an equal society, where people won't be discriminated against for the music they like or the color of their skin," as one Ohel leader told *Jerusalem Post* reporter Robert Rosenberg (*Jerusalem Post*, 6/8/80). One thing was different from the Black Panther demonstrations, according to Rosenberg: one of Ohel's demands was for Community Center facilities.

In December 1979 Rosenberg had predicted unrest the coming summer, writing:

For almost 30 years, Israel has awaited the children of the ma'abarot [transit camps]—the original slums of the country—hoping that the second generation of North African and Asian immigrants would break out of the poverty of their parents.

But many of the children of the Moroccans, the Kurds, the Iraqis, and the Yemenites are still trapped in slums and frustration. It matters little whether their complaints about poor housing, ineffective education, limited career opportunities and little ethnic representation on government bodies are real or imagined, for the anger is there, in self-image and in the crowded flats of the Katamonim, Musrara or Shmuel Hanavi [Jerusalem slum neighborhoods].

He continued: "Project Renewal is as much about the re-education of the slum quarter population as it is about the rehabilitation of the buildings those residents live in" (*Jerusalem Post*, 12/19/79).

Eleven months later, commenting on a recent riot in Jerusalem's Musrara quarter, Rosenberg wrote:

> Some people may be prompted to offer a contribution towards [building] a new community centre. [But they] . . . would be wrong. What is needed is some tough . . . thinking about what has been wrought in Musrara. Hopeless, frustrated, . . . the children of Musrara are the children of every slum quarter in the country. . . . It doesn't matter whether the Ashkenazi establishment intended the Sephardi to be the laborers of the Jewish state. It worked out that way, and those who are paranoid cannot be convinced otherwise. (*Jerusalem Post*, 11/20/80)

"Ideology is what we are short of now," Zipori had written in 1976, "and by answering these questions [of values] we are beginning to formulate one." In the same report, JDC's Pins wrote that other agencies with financial and personnel resources were proposing new functions for the Centers, leading to a feeling among local Centers and in the national movement "of lacking clear direction or of having lost control. . . . The goals and methods of any agency should be constantly redefined in the process of trying to realize them."[61]

The ICCC "is in a crisis now," said Dan Ronnen, Minister Aranne's former assistant, in an interview in October 1980. "The push of ideas which brought it up to now has come to a dead end and can't carry it further. It must establish its ideological concept now."

Despite internal struggles to establish its identity, the agency seemingly succeeded in creating a public image. In several public demonstrations after 1980, residents of development towns and city slums where no Community Centers had been built called on the government to build them there as well. ICCC Community Centers had become a sought-after entity. In 1986 the Center for Education and Culture of the General Labor Federation (the Histadrut) announced that it would open a network of thirty-two "clubhouses" (*mo'adonim*) throughout the country, with an emphasis on the development areas. The list of proposed programs and activities echoes those offered by the ICCC, without once using their name or the phrase "Community Center": bringing ideational, educational, and artistic messages through plays, entertainment shows, independent productions, symposia, evenings of discussions, public trials, films, evenings of song and dance, celebrations of important dates in Israeli and Histadrut history. The announcement noted that these clubs constituted the "sole cultural factor" in the more remote settlements (*Ma'ariv* 6/26/86)—the same claim that the ICCC had made fifteen years earlier.

Tensions between the two broadest Jewish ethnic groups continued. The massive immigration of Jews from the former Soviet Union at the end of the 1980s seemed once again to highlight ethnic disparities and tensions between development town residents and city and kibbutz dwellers. In 1990 newly homeless Israelis of Eastern origin, largely from city slums, set up tents in Jerusalem opposite the Knesset building to protest their displacement from apartments by landlords who could get more money renting to newly immigrated Soviet Jews. The "sense of apartness and of second-class status remains," noted reporter Clyde Haberman (*New York Times*, 4/15/92). He quoted a joke told by a resident of Yeruham, a development town three hours' drive to the south, illustrating the sense of social distance: "You need a visa to go from Yeruham to Tel Aviv." And he cited recent research that showed persisting disparities between Westerners and Easterners in educational attainment, income levels, and occupational distribution. Unemployment in one development town ranged from 16 percent to 30 percent at the end of the 1980s (*Jerusalem Post International Edition*, 9/15/90, p. 9). Independent Member of Knesset and former Black Panther Charlie Biton, interviewed in 1990, said about then-current protesters: "You think that our [1970s] demonstrations were violent, just wait and see what happens if no solution is found for the homeless tent dwellers" (Hutman 1990).

By 1987 there were 143 ICCC Community Centers (Yanay 1989). After Labor was voted out of the government in 1977, the directorate of the ICCC and key positions within the agency became political appointments, and by 1992 only one of the agency's original professional staff was left. The agency continues its work to integrate development town and city neighborhood residents into Israeli society.

Their programs reflect demographic changes and changing perceptions of social problems over the decade. For instance, as tensions between observant and nonreligious Jews grew, in some neighborhoods even between devout Jews and "merely" observant ones, the Community Centers became embroiled in efforts to mediate the disputes. The Mekor Baruch neighborhood of Jerusalem is one example. Once a place where religious Eastern Jews and nonreligious Western Jews lived together peacefully, the increasing presence of devout Hasidic Jews (of eastern European heritage) created problems that required police intervention to protect the Community Center. The Center was seen by the devout as the instigator of local troubles—although its director saw his role and that of the Center as bridging among the different ethnic and religious groups (*Ma'ariv*, 7/8/83, p. 22).

Labor continued in the opposition through the 1980s. The Likud coalition included various religious parties, and they continued to hold the Education and Culture portfolio. Those who watched the agency and occasionally consulted to it mourned the loss of the social reform vision that Zipori had brought to its founding, which the directors he had hired had carried. One agency observer expressed hope, late in the summer of 1992, that under the new political leadership of Yitzhak Rabin and a Labor-led coalition government elected that year, a new director would be appointed and the ICCC and its mission would be revived. The feeling was that there was still work to be done, and there was still hope, and faith, that the ICCC was the agency to do it.

NOTES

1. The history of community centers is a fascinating one, combining not only settlement house history in the United States and England, but also the pre-World War I playground and community school movements, the postwar recreation movement, the professionalization of city planning (Clarence Perry's "neighborhood unit" of the 1920s, for instance) and social work and the development of centralized philanthropic drives (e.g., Community Chests and eventually, the United Way), and the memorial halls of the 1940s. It intersects as well in various ways with the Progressives and their antimachine politics Reform movement (Yanow 1976).

2. One of the more remarkable examples of this public discourse on the nature of Israeli identity was published after the (June 1967) Six Day War. Entitled *Si'ah Lohamim* (the conversation of combatants), it reported conversations following the war among kibbutz members ages 25 to 35 about death, but also about the relationship between national pride and "the tragedy of Zionism" (p. 11, English trans.). The conversations were initially recorded, edited, and mimeographed; but what started as an internal Kibbutz Movement dialogue attracted so much attention, as it passed from one person to another, that the mimeographed text was reprinted several times in Hebrew (Tel Aviv: Young Members of the Kibbutz Movement, October 1967) and published in English translation (*The Seventh Day*, New York: Scribner's, 1970). This spawned yet another publication of conversations under the title *Among young people: Talks in the kibbutz* (*Bein ze'irim*, Tel Aviv: Kibbutz Movement and Am Oved, 1969) exploring intersections among Jewish, Israeli, and kibbutz identities. The literary form of conversations between interviewers and respondents was repeated by Amos Oz, one of the editors of the first book, in his *In the land of Israel* (New York: Harcourt, Brace, Jovanovich, 1983), which further explores questions of Israeli society and identity. Reflections on the nature of the Jewish people and their relation to a state characterize early Zionist writings. See Herzberg (1960) for a representative selection.

3. "*Kibbutz u'mizug galuyot,*" in Hebrew—the ingathering and admixture of exiles. This formulation has been challenged in recent years in terms of the identity of Israeli Arabs as non-Jewish citizens of a Jewish state—a formulation that had not occurred to many people earlier. See the essays of Oz (1983) and the novels of Shamas (1988) and Grossman (1988) for examples of the debate. That the central political symbols of the state—the flag, the emblem, the anthem—are built on Jewish elements (the star of David, the menorah, the longing for a return to Zion) that exclude non-Jewish Israelis is only now being publicly discussed (see, e.g., Clyde Haberman, "The Arabs in Zion: What symbols for them?" *New York Times*, 6/1/95, national edition, p. A3).

4. The following discussion is based on interviews with Harman and Ronnen. I was unable to interview Zipori, who died in 1983.

5. Navon later became president of Israel, serving from 1978 to 1983.

6. The phrase "the second Israel" came in the late 1960s to refer to Israelis of non-Western heritage. More will be said about this below.

7. Called Rafi—the Israel Labor List—and headed by former Prime Minister David Ben-Gurion, it split from Mapai, Israel's Labor Party, in 1965. Ben-Gurion had resigned in June 1963 from the government. As a rift grew between the two parties and their leaders, Aranne stayed with the leadership group of Mapai. Zipori and Aranne's relationship was apparently caught in this rift, as Zipori followed Ben-Gurion. Interestingly for our tale here, Rafi cultivated an Easterner constituency (Peled 1982: 88).

8. Israel is physically about the size of New Jersey and had a total population then of about 2.5 million.

9. The following section is based on my interview with Pozner and on Lavi's interview with her (1979).

10. Initiated by Aranne, this restructured secondary education through the establishment of "junior high schools" on the American model which, by absorbing students from various backgrounds, were intended to pull the "disadvantaged" up to the level of their urban cohort. Peled (1982) gives a political analysis of Aranne's Reform effort, in light of the Labor Party politics, structural issues, and ethnic ideas of the time. In the context of Pozner's statement about Israel's sudden awakening to the existence of ethnic disparities, it is interesting to read Peled's speculation about why Aranne had not raised the ethnic issue prior to the Reform effort in 1965, given that he became minister in 1955. He answers: "[L]ike his party and most of his colleagues, Aranne was for many years 'ethnic-blind.' For him the unity of the nation, the melting-pot orientation, the pioneer image were the leading educational values" (p. 105).

11. If my reasoning about the correct dating of this report is right; see Chapter 1, note 1.

12. Israel's victories in June 1967 added geographic buffers in strategic areas: the Golan Heights at the border with Syria, the West Bank at the border with Jordan, the Sinai desert at the border with Egypt. Prior to this, for example, Israeli settlers in the northeast lived under nearly constant sniping by Syrian riflemen overlooking their farmlands. The additional land buffers created a feeling in Israel of physical security that had not been known since the state's founding twenty years earlier (or even before). This point about newfound physical and economic security is discussed further in Iris and Shama (1972).

13. Macarov (1974) makes this latter point.

14. The initial "back to the land" philosophy reflects the Zionist ideology that argued that Jews could correct their position in the world and combat anti-Semitism only by inverting the occupational pyramid that had stuck them in the role of middlemen (because of European laws passed over a thousand years that restricted their occupations and ability to own land). They could then once again become landholders and workers. For more on the expression of Judaism and Zionism in land patterns, see Altman and Rosenbaum (1973), Cohen (1977), and Yanoov (1974). Some development towns were established on the sites of preexisting towns that had been occupied by Palestinian Arabs who left during Israel's War of Independence in 1948. Others were built from scratch, some on the outskirts of cities, some on or adjacent to the sites of temporary tent villages (*ma'abarot*) that had been set up after the war to house immigrants. For more on the design, planning, social structure, and image of the towns, see Ben-Ari and Bilu (1987), Berler (1970), Cohen (1970), Kirschenbaum (1974), Lichfield (1970), Shachar (1970), Spiegel (1966).

15. According to the Central Bureau of Statistics, development towns were losing population at the rate of 7.1 per 1,000 in 1970 and 8.9 per 1,000 in 1975. Cited in the *Jerusalem Post* (1/26/81).

16. Military service was, and is, mandatory for all Jewish Israeli citizens. Beginning at age 18, men have served between two and three years, women, 18 months to two years, depending on the state of military alert. Men and some women also serve reserve duty up to a hundred days each year. Immigrants who are older have their service period adjusted according to their age. Deferments are possible for higher education in medicine and engineering, for example, as well as for religious study. Religious women are exempt from serving; many do an alternative service (e.g., as school teachers or social workers). Some religious men serve, others claim an exemption. Even today, when it is more common for young people to refuse service in the occupied territories as a political protest, the army is still seen as the major educator, socializer, and unifying societal experience. Druze men typically serve, but they volunteer. For other Arab citizens, both Muslim and Christian, military service is a contested issue. Some serve as a mark of citizenship; others do not, because they are not allowed to serve by the military authorities, or because they choose to honor their ties with other Arab noncitizens. It is one of the issues of current concern in evolving Palestinian independence.

17. The gap descriptions ignore, by and large, the rural agricultural sector. Kibbutz and moshav collectives have succeeded and failed, economically and socially, independent—to a great extent—of the geographic or ethnic origins of their members, in the long run. There are American-European kibbutzim which have been in the red for years (such as Gezer and Gesher Haziv); there are Yemenite moshavim that turned a profit only in the late 1970s to early 1980s; and there are other collectives, including "Eastern" ones, that have been independent of central movement aid for a decade and more. One researcher captured the link between the gap and geography and ethnicity, although still omitting the rural sector: "income gap is even a function of geography, reflecting the clustering of the various ethnic groups in Israel's different types of urban communities" (Greenberg 1979, p. 132).

18. A distinction can be made between "immigration" policies and "immigrant" policies. The former refers to policies with respect to those desiring to immigrate; the latter, to the treatment of immigrants after they have arrived (e.g., with respect to housing, language and other training, medical care, employment counseling). In Israel the latter is called "absorption" policy and in the government is the responsibility of the Ministry of Immigrant Absorption (although there are other agencies involved in the funding of these activities—a matter of debate in Israeli politics). In the United States this distinction was just beginning to be heard in the summer of 1994 (see, e.g., Urban Institute 1994).

19. Data in the following discussion are drawn from *Facts about Israel* (1977: 61–96).

20. In the post-statehood period of 1948–51, 687,000 immigrants more than doubled Israel's pre-state population of 452,000. These people came from British internment camps on Cypress (Europeans escaping Hitler) (25,000); displaced person camps in Germany, Austria, Italy (70,000); and various other countries: Poland (103,732), Bulgaria (30,000), Yemen (47,000), Romania (118,940), Libya (30,500), Iraq (121,500). About 48,000 newcomers were settled on 345 new *kibbutzim* and *moshavim*, communal agricultural settlements; some 130,000 were housed in abandoned Arab property in areas later designated as development towns (e.g., Ramla, Lod, Bet She'an); 250,000 were housed

in 113 transit camps (*ma'abarot*—settlements of tents later converted to tin or wood shacks).

Another wave of immigrants followed in 1955–56: from Morocco and Tunisia following independence there; from Poland following an expulsion of Jews from the Communist Party; from Hungary after the revolution (8,680); from Egypt after the Sinai Campaign (14,000)—165,000 in total. The next wave came between 1961 and 1964, bringing 215,056 people from eastern Europe and northern Africa, including 7,700 from Algeria.

21. Shokeid (1980, esp. p. 218) discusses the incorporation of traditional communal positions, of which the office of rabbi is one, into civil service patterns that the new state inherited from British and Ottoman laws and customs.

22. Television might have helped bridge this sociocultural isolation, as it has elsewhere, but it was introduced in Israel only in 1966–67, after social patterns had been established. Even then it was expensive to begin with, and carried a 100 percent of value luxury tax, making it unaffordable for most development town and city slum residents until well into the 1980s.

23. The following data represent some of the indicators that were amassed, especially after the Katz Commission's report was delivered, in support of an argument about deprivation and the social gap. For more extensive data and analysis, see, e.g., Liron (1973) or the report of the Prime Minister's Commission for Children and Youth in Distress (1973), known as the Katz Commission. Smooha (1978) discusses disparities of political and economic power, taking educational achievement, occupational distribution, and material well-being as his indicators.

24. Data are from the Central Bureau of Statistics, reported in the *Jerusalem Post* (1/26/81). The assumed preference underlying the question followed the western European/American model of parents sleeping in one room and children in different rooms with sexes separated. Among immigrants from Asia and Africa, the accustomed and apparently desired density was higher. There was no separation of eating, sleeping, and living areas. Different activities were accommodated, often simultaneously, in the same room. At night, several children would sleep together in the same bed; parents and children often slept in the same room.

Seen through Western eyes, this represented extreme backwardness, poverty, or both. Because of their ignorance of Western customs, including flush toilets and apartment buildings, the most rural of the Asian-African immigrants came to be called "primitives" with intoned disdain and disgust. By 1972, these immigrants had adopted Western custom to such an extent that they called the newly arrived Soviet Georgians *primitivim* for themselves hanging chickens in apartment hallways or washing clothes in toilets.

Whether the Asian-Africans considered three and more persons per room intolerable density in 1957 is, today, moot. At the time, no one asked. It was not raised in academic circles, by planners, or in policy arenas until the late 1970s. With increased awareness in the 1980s, the question of desired densities became sometimes the subject of historical reconstruction and conjecture, with all the limitations of those exercises. Social research for the

Ministry of Housing in the mid-1970s did, however, raise the question, concluding that Asian-Africans often felt lonely at the lower densities considered desirable by Westerners, since they expressed preferences for housing conditions of higher densities.

25. This would support an argument that feelings about housing density and crowding are socially constructed concepts. Iris and Shama (1972) and Smooha (1972) discuss these changes at greater length.

26. Gertrude Conrad, *Jerusalem Post* (2/15/71). The army does not draft men and women who are illiterate or who have criminal records, two characteristics of this population group. At the time, street-gang workers were trying to convince the army to change this policy. The army did experiment in the 1970s with drafting juvenile delinquents; the outcomes were mixed and the experiment was subsequently dropped. See Smooha (1972) or Iris and Shama (1972) for further history on the Black Panthers.

27. JDC-Israel report to the Geneva office, 11/9/72.

28. It is summarized in English in Prime Minister's Commission for Children and Youth in Distress (1973).

29. "*Kahal l'kehila, v'shikun l'shkhuna*"—in transliteration.

30. Report of visit by JDC executive, October 18–27, 1970.

31. This section draws on the files containing memoranda, letters, reports, and other materials of the JDC-Israel in Jerusalem, which played a key role in supporting the early development of the ICCC.

32. From the mid-1970s through most of the 1980s, there was rapid devaluation of Israeli currency. In 1969 US$1 was equal to IL3.5; April 1981 exchange rates were US$1 to IL85. The sheqel has since replaced the lira as the unit of currency (1 sheqel replacing 10 lirot). Zipori (1972, p. 14) made the following comparison: when they started calculating building costs, the average cost of public sector construction was IL400 per square meter. Six years later, in 1972, the average cost was IL1,000 per square meter. And costs were higher the farther one went from the center of the country, which is where most of the ICCC facilities were located.

33. Letter to L. Horwitz, Director, AJ-JDC, Geneva, 10/11/72.

34. JDC-Israel is the Jerusalem-based operation of the American Jewish Joint Distribution Committee, an international grant-making aid agency concentrating on social services. As will be seen below, it played a significant role in supporting and advising the ICCC.

35. Letter to Asher Tarmon, director, World Federation of Jewish Community Centers, New York, 5/26/71 (Hebrew).

36. JDC-Israel proposal for projects to support Israel's Community Centers, written at the end of 1971; emphasis added.

37. Frank M. Loewenberg, "Proposal for Parallel Demonstration Projects," letter to Zipori, 5/21/72.

38. Letters to Mrs. B. S. and Mr. E. C., 9/29/72.

39. JDC-Geneva public relations department, 11/9/72.

40. Letter to S. S., 11/20/72.

41. Meeting protocol, 7/15/71.

42. Letter to S. S., JDC-Geneva, 7/19/71.

43. Written record of comments by Bill (William) Kahn, 7/5/73.

44. Quoted in JDC press release, n.d.

45. JDC proposal, 6/20/72. One month later, an interministerial meeting was held to arrange the coordination of all agencies offering community organization services (protocol, 7/19/72).

46. File memo on community centers, 11/29/73.

47. File memo, n.d.

48. In this it drew on its experience in Muslim countries with financial support from the Central British Fund for Refugee Relief. File memo, 11/9/72.

49. JDC press release, 1/13/74.

50. Memo, "Caring for Special Groups in the Community," August 1974.

51. "Community Centers in Israel: Growth, Program and Needs," February 1974, pp. 4–6. The paragraph is edited here into a list for clarity.

52. ICCC Annual Report 1975–76, pp. 9, 13. Emphasis added.

53. Protocol, 9/17/78.

54. Internal memo, 9/27/79.

55. ICCC Annual Report 1976–77, p. 44.

56. Protocol, 9/3/78.

57. ICCC Newsletter No. 32, June 1979.

58. Protocol, 2/5/79.

59. Protocol, 7/13/79.

60. Letter in files, 9/6/79.

61. ICCC Annual Report 1975–76, pp. 7, 9, 14.

4

Symbolic Relationships:
Re-Reading Chapter 3

The story you have just read is a seemingly objective, factual account of the events that led up to and formed a context for the creation of a new public agency—the Israel Corporation of Community Centers— designed to fulfill a particular social mandate. How well was the enabling legislation implemented? The agency accomplished several tasks: it raised private funds; negotiated ministerial budgets and their administrators; designed, constructed, and furnished new buildings and renovated existing ones; hired and trained staff; developed programs; sought clients; and so forth. In that respect, its implementation was spectacularly successful. By many objective measures—numbers of personnel, amount of program activities, budget size, physical plant, fund-raising—the ICCC could be judged a success. In terms of public acclaim, the agency succeeded in establishing an organizational image such that people from neighborhoods without Community Centers demonstrated in the streets, demanding that the government build Centers for them too.

But measured in terms of explicitly stated goals and purposes, its success is less clear. The social gap was no less evident in 1980 or 1990 than it had been in 1970: disparities of income, educational achievement, housing density, occupational distribution, and so forth were still as severe after ten and twenty years of Community Center operations. The publicly stated goals were many: as the societal context changed, the ICCC added new layers to prior goal statements, without displacing earlier goals. The case is a good example of what Weiss and Rein (1969) called "broad-aim programs"—difficult to evaluate given their broad mixture of social goals.

And yet, no complaints were heard that the ICCC had not fulfilled its mission. On the contrary: the ICCC Community Center had become an item in demand, as evidenced by the demonstrators' call for government to build them in places that had none.

In this case, desired outcomes depended as much on the actions of people designated as clients as on those of agency administrators and staff. That is, the intended outcomes required that intended clients change their behavior: they needed to come to the Center and take part in its programs. Moreover, continued implementation success also depended on the perceptions of more distant, policy-relevant publics. These included legislators who had to reapprove allocations, heads of other ministries and departments and local social service agencies who were potential competitors for public funds, and members of the public who were altruistically interested in government's and their tax dollar's role in improving the lot of citizens who were less well off.

This suggests a view of implementation as a process of communicating policy and agency concepts, not just from legislators to administrators (that is, from one part of the government to another at a single level) and not even just from chief executives to street-level bureaucrats (from the center or top of an agency to its periphery or bottom), but to clients, potential clients, cognate and competitive agencies, constituents, and other policy-relevant publics near and far. What is being communicated is not solely "legislative intent," if we could even clearly establish what that is for any piece of legislation. What is being communicated are the societal meanings (values, beliefs, feelings) concerning the subject of the policy, meanings that have developed over time (and from prior generations of the policy issue if it is not a new one) and which are carried in various ways in various parts of the "culture" of the policy issue. They are carried in the policy's *language*, but also in the language of the debate about its legislation and in discussions surrounding its implementation. They are carried in the *objects* that the implementing agency creates and uses in its operations: agency buildings, programs, manuals, logos. And they are carried in the agency's *acts*, in its daily, weekly, monthly, annual operations.

Clearly, a new agency has to establish itself, and it will undertake all manner of activities to do so that an older, established agency need not. But older agencies also need to engage in the same communicative processes, to convey existing purposes as well as those of new programs. Fundamentally, both newer and older agencies convey

messages about government's responses and responsibilities to con-
stituencies. And both work with their enabling legislation to convey
to citizens (and sometimes to noncitizens, including, at times, foreigners on other shores) the identity of the polity in question.

The next three chapters explore three of the different ways in
which meanings were communicated through symbolic representation: through specific forms of language, objects, and acts. Each chapter identifies a number of the interpretations that were intended by
agency founders and administrators and some of the other "readings"
of these—interpretations—that were made. Each one retells the ICCC
story from a different conceptual point of view that highlights particular aspects of the case. In all of them, the implementation process is
seen as a process of communicating policy meanings, but often doing
so tacitly, through the use of agency symbols. Since the ICCC was
created to address problems of development town residents, part of
what was being communicated were ideas about Israeli identity and
the place in it of immigrants settled in development towns—although
these, too, were communicated tacitly, through symbols, in large part
because of a societal ethnic and class "blindness." One thread of
meaning that I find running through the different symbolic forms
argues for one sort of analysis: an analysis of silenced voices, which
I attempt to make heard. The silenced theme is the existence and
shape of ethnicity in Israeli society and how it relates to national
identity.

In exploring the ways in which meanings are communicated to
and interpreted by multiple audiences, in which clients (and others)
play a more active role as constructors of meaning themselves, analytic
texts struggle with the move away from the single, authorial voice of
the realist tale toward a more multivocal voice. In the chapters that
follow, I continue to be present as the single voice weaving a story,
even as I bring in the voices and interpretations of others who made
one sense or another of legislators' and administrators' intended
meanings. Even in highlighting these various "readers" and their
authored and constructed "texts," the researcher's—my—"I" remains
behind the scenes. These continue to be second-level constructs, my
representations of participants' interpretations—although the ethnographic methods used argue for them as experience-*nearer* than other
forms of research.

5

Symbolic Language: Agency Names, Organizational Metaphors, and Administrative Practice

"When I use a word," Humpty Dumpty said, "it means just what I choose it to mean—neither more nor less."

"The question is," said Alice, "whether you *can* make words mean so many different things."

"The question is," said Humpty Dumpty, "which is to be master—that's all."

—Lewis Carroll, *Alice's Adventures in Wonderland and Through the Looking Glass*

Analysts of policy implementation commonly observe that policy language is often vague and ambiguous when it comes to stipulating precisely which actions implementors should take in order to enact the policies and achieve policy goals. This ambiguity of policy language is blamed for many implementation difficulties. Authors writing from this point of view see the logical solution to implementation difficulties as eliminating the ambiguities in policy language.[1]

This recommendation is untenable on several counts. First, legislative language is often intentionally ambiguous in order to resolve contending positions and get a bill passed. Recent work in policy analysis (e.g., Feldman 1989, Palumbo 1991, Stone 1988) suggests that ambiguity is a commonplace of human life which cannot be eliminated. Ambiguity, in fact, may at times be used strategically in the political and policy worlds to accommodate multiple and conflicting values and meanings. Like metaphors, which cognitive linguists argue cannot be replaced by literal language because metaphoric reasoning inheres in the way humans think (e.g., Lakoff and Johnson 1980, D. F. Miller 1985), ambiguity is part and parcel of the human experience and its modes of expression and communication.

Second, recommendations that ambiguities be eliminated assume that implementors and others know about policy issues exclusively from the language of the adopted legislation; whereas in fact, elements of the prelegislative debate are carried in many ways, and implementors and members of the public are not ignorant of them.[2] Values, beliefs, and feelings existing prior to current policy legislation may well be known by and influence implementors. Implementation of the Prohibition amendment, for example, took place in the context of beliefs about religious affiliation and social status and their symbolic representation in attitudes toward drinking. These beliefs antedated the Repeal movement by as much as a hundred years (Gusfield 1963).

Third, the recommendation is based on the notion that words are "univocal"—that they have or can be made to have only one meaning, and that meaning can be established without respect to time and place. This is the position argued by some analytic philosophers. It is discredited by other philosophers, by anthropologists (such as Victor Turner 1974, who argued for "multivocality"), and by interpretive social scientists (see the essays in Rabinow and Sullivan 1979, for example). If language is innately multivocal, then it is also innately potentially ambiguous, and we cannot rely exclusively on the literal language of policies to determine what our goals are for evaluation purposes[3] or to communicate to implementors how to proceed or to clients and other policy-relevant publics how to respond. How, then, are policy meanings transmitted to these and other stakeholders when policy language and goals are ambiguous? How do they learn about new and revised policies, how do they learn to support or challenge them, how do they learn to act with respect to them?

This chapter focuses on ways in which language created during the various stages of the policy process may symbolically transmit policy meanings. This is illustrated in several parts of the ICCC story: in Minister Aranne's choice of an agency name, in the choice of a Hebrew word for "community center," and in a particular organizational metaphor that enabled the agency to define and shape its otherwise ambiguous identity. Since much of this argument depends on recent theories about metaphors, I will begin with a discussion of metaphor, using the concept in D. F. Miller's (1982, 1985) broad sense as a category encompassing seven kinds, including analogy.[4]

The analysis of metaphors has, especially in the past decade, expanded beyond the realm of metaphor as a literary device—a figure of speech—to examine its role in cognition and reasoning—a "figure of thought" (Lakoff 1986) underlying even that language we regard as conventional. Appreciation of the cognitive role of metaphor allows us to attend to the relationship between metaphor and organizational action, which is the concern of this chapter. In retelling the ICCC story from the perspective of its language use, I will weave the stories of its names together with the tale of its organizational metaphor. The case offers an example of the implications for action of a metaphor created by agency members. The focus here is neither on how metaphors structure disciplinary thought nor on political rhetoric, although both subjects are worthy of analytic attention.[5] Rather, our concern is a metaphor that was born publicly and functioned as a figure of thought in directing organizational action, including that action entailed in implementing a policy mandate. Polanyi's (1966) notion of tacit knowledge helps to explain how the organizational metaphor in the case worked epistemologically to channel administrative action.

Much has been written about what metaphors are and how they work.[6] Lakoff and Johnson (1980) offered the view that metaphors are an expression of a culture's basic ideas. Metaphors determine how we see the world that we experience, as well as how we act in that world. This chapter presents a case example that demonstrates that metaphors "are necessary, and not just nice" (Ortony 1975).

METAPHORS AND MEANING

What exactly a metaphor is, and how it works, has long been the subject of debate in circles of philosophy, linguistics, psychology, and literary theory. Much of this debate is captured in Black (1962) and Ortony (1979) and will not be repeated here. Part of the history of the debate, however, is germane to the subject at hand. Metaphor has for a long time been treated as a figure of speech or literary device reflecting imprecise thinking or added on to nonmetaphorical speech as decoration. As far back as Plato and Aristotle, metaphoric language has been contrasted with literal language. According to the theory that prevailed, metaphoric language was the inferior of the two (being less precise, less scientific, appealing to the emotions, and so forth) and could be eliminated, leaving only literal figures. Traditional metaphor analysis has focused on how these ornamental figures of speech work.

Newer developments treat metaphor more as a way of seeing and/or learning, and as such, as an elemental part of language and thought, rather than as decoration that can be eliminated. As Lakoff and Johnson (1987, p. 79) wrote, "Metaphor is not a harmless exercise in naming. It is one of the principal means by which we understand our experience and reason on the basis of that understanding. To the extent that we act on our reasoning, metaphor plays a role in the creation of reality." In this approach metaphors as literary devices constitute a form of the more general human cognitive activity.

Let us define metaphor as the juxtaposition of two superficially unlike elements in a single context, where the separately understood meanings of both interact to create a new perception of each, and especially of the focus of the metaphor. Subjected to analysis, the surface unlikeness yields a set of criteria which both metaphoric vehicle and focus share.[7] Some simple examples might be "The grass is always greener in the other person's yard" or "green with envy" or "the greenhorn fresh off the boat." In each of these examples, what we might take to be our commonsense notions of "green-ness" are brought into three different settings, illuminating both the concept of green (the vehicle) and its focus in new ways.

When we explore the connections between perception and action, metaphors that initially appear to be merely descriptive often acquire a prescriptive aspect. No longer are we only presenting new insights into the situation described by the metaphor (e.g., the fresh and new green-ness of the immigrant). We are also suggesting the possibility of action in response to that situation. In talking about the economic situation, for example, we might say:

> Inflation has *pinned* us *to the wall.*
> Our biggest *enemy* right now is inflation.
> Inflation has *robbed* me of my savings.
> (Lakoff and Johnson 1980, p. 33)

"Inflation," itself an older metaphor which presents the state of the economy as blown up like a balloon, distorted by swelling from some more natural state, is here presented as a street fighter, an enemy seeking to destroy, a robber. Putting monetary swelling in such a context suggests the possibility (indeed, the necessity) of response: one does not turn the other cheek to a fighter; rather, one searches for vulnerable places and plans a counterattack. These metaphors preclude the possibility of a passive response or that inflation might be immune to planning and policy. If, for example, inflation were part of an inevitable cycle, the best defense would not stave it off, nor the best offense rid us of it.

Some of the attributes of metaphors are illustrated in this example. Metaphors direct vision and thinking. While they give new insight into and understanding of some things, they can blind us to other aspects of the situation. By highlighting some aspects and obscuring others, they organize perceptions of reality and suggest appropriate actions in light of those perceptions. Organizational metaphors do this in their contexts: they may suggest a perception and a course of action for administrators and other organizational members to follow.

Metaphors, then, are neither true nor false. "The more important questions," wrote Lakoff and Johnson (1980, p. 158),

> are those of appropriate action. In most cases, what is at issue . . . [are] the perceptions and inferences that follow from it and the actions that are sanctioned by it. . . . We draw inferences, set goals, make commitments, and execute plans, all on the basis of how we in part structure our experience, consciously and unconsciously, by means of metaphor.

Moreover, the knowledge that links metaphoric perception with action is learned and known tacitly, without being made explicit to ourselves or to others. As noted earlier, the concept "inflation" itself is a metaphor which suggests that something has been blown up and thereby distorted from its normal condition. Yet we use and understand it in common parlance (as we use the fighter metaphors) without explicit cognizance of its metaphoric nature. We have made inflation part of our economic reality and developed theories to account for it and strategies to prevent it. "Inflation" is an old, or conventional, metaphor.[8] It is their conventionality, and the tacit knowledge mutually shared and communicated in their use, that mask the power of metaphors to shape action. Their power, that is, lies in their ability to shape action, when we are not in the habit of making explicit the implications for action that are embedded in them.

In addition, metaphors may also give expression to some prior, unarticulated understanding of a situation. In a culture that values governmental planning and policymaking, it would not be unusual to create metaphors for the economy which suggest action rather than passive acceptance. That is, metaphors can be models *of* a situation as well as models *for* it.[9]

Metaphors, then, are not commonly understood according to the literal meanings of their words. To talk of "housing decay," for example, is not to mean literally that the wood is rotting or that the bricks are decomposing. The decay metaphor is understood through implicit, unspoken analysis of its tacitly known meaning in a particular context of reference (in this case, the deterioration of a typically lower-class neighborhood).

On the other hand, metaphorical meaning presupposes an understanding of its literal sense in some context. If we did not know the ordinary meaning of "decay," we could not apply it sensibly to deteriorating houses. In other words, for metaphors to be understood as part of public discourse, rather than private musings, their literal meanings must be part of a shared context—"a set of standard beliefs . . . ([or] current platitudes) that are the common possession of the members of some speech community" (Black 1962, p. 40) or, we might add, thought community.

When the interpretive context changes, the meaning of the metaphor may change as well. In this way, metaphors entertain the possibility for multiple meanings.[10] In the Arabic of some Middle Eastern countries, for example, "green" connotes maturity, ripeness; in which case a "greenhorn" would not carry its American English connotations of new, bumbling, unknowing, and our other green metaphors would acquire new meanings or become altogether senseless. To the extent that we can explicate the organizational contexts in which metaphors have been used, we can attend to potential differences in meaning and interpretation.

This analysis implies an important caution in analyzing the role of metaphors in organizational settings. If metaphors have capacities for multiple meanings, and meanings are dependent on contexts, we cannot assume that an organizational metaphor holds the same meaning for all members of an organization. This opens avenues for research, exploring, for example, whether the entire organization constitutes a single thought community. The exploration of organizational language and its meanings, in the plural, is one way of assessing divisions and unities within an organization.

This approach to the analysis of organizational metaphors, however, also suggests that we cannot eliminate them as though they were mere decorative additions. It implies a caution against the thought that in discovering the meaning(s) of the organizational metaphor, we will be able to get down to the root of an organizational problem and thereby eliminate the "hidden" source that directs organizational action. If metaphor is indeed a figure of thought, reflecting thought (a model "of") as well as shaping it (a model "for"), attempts to eliminate the metaphor may not eliminate the thought. In finding another expression of that thought, we may, as D. F. Miller (1985) notes, be simply substituting one metaphor for another. In ferreting out one metaphor, we might only discover that it stands on the shoulders of another, much as inflation, the enemy, rests on an older convention of a misshapen, bloated economy. What we may discover in analyzing organizational metaphors are complex relationships between thought and action, between shape and reflection, rather than that we are getting to the final core of an issue. Metaphors and their meanings are potentially always evolving: metaphoric analysis of administrative behavior and organizational action should not assume fixed and single meaning.

The arguments presented here rest on an interpretive approach to what constitutes reality, knowledge, and methodology. A positivist, believing in the possibility of discovering a single objective truth, would be more likely to search for a "final" meaning underlying a metaphor. From an interpretive point of view, the possibility of reinterpretation always exists. Moreover, a literal meaning need not necessarily ever have been constructed "beneath" a metaphor.[11]

The story of the ICCC can be retold from the perspectives of various "readers" of agency names and a key organizational metaphor, as these relate to the communication of organizational identity. As a reminder, to distinguish between "community centers" as general institutions and the particular form of the ICCC Community Center, I use capital letters when referring to the latter.

RE-READING THE CASE: CORPORATE NAMES
AND IDENTITIES

"Corporation" is the proper expression of the ICCC's legal status, as an agency of limited liability and a Government Corporation. The term was questioned, however, by the American Jewish Joint Distribution Committee (AJ-JDC), a fund-disbursing agency headquartered in New York which included the ICCC among its recipients. "Association" was seen as more befitting the sense of a nonprofit entity, a semantic distinction made in an exchange of letters and legal opinion in 1977. AJ-JDC requested that the ICCC refer to itself in its English literature as the "Association," because "Corporation" suggested profit, the wrong image for potential American and other donors whom the philanthropy was planning to solicit for Center building funds. After consulting government lawyers, the ICCC refused the request. The lawyers felt the ICCC might be jeopardizing its legal standing in Israel if it referred to itself as other than a "corporation." They reached a compromise. AJ-JDC would refer to the agency as the Israel Association of Community Centers (IACC) in its English-language correspondence and publications for foreign consumption. The agency would refer to itself as the Israel Corporation of Community Centers (ICCC) in its own English-language publications.

To accomplish its goals, the ICCC needed to establish a presence in each development town or city neighborhood site and hire program staff for these sites and for its headquarters. The executive director and the board of directors would have to be able to convey to potential employees what a Community Center was and did. They would have to communicate these meanings to potential clients, as well, in order to create a constituency for their services.

"Community center" was an American concept. As noted in Chapter 3, inspiration for the development of the ICCC idea came, in part, from people with experience in American community centers. After they discussed those experiences with Minister Aranne, he asked Ya'el Pozner to set up a committee to research the idea and make recommendations because—as she told the story—he did not know what a "community center" was.

There was no conceptual equivalent to "community center" either in the Hebrew language or in Israeli society. Although there were entities performing similar functions in Israel (the urban "Y", the

Bet Am on the kibbutz where meetings were held, where members gathered to read the papers, listen to radio, watch movies, etc.) and in overseas Jewish communities other than in the United States, they were known by other names. This meant that unless a potential Center director or staff person had been to community centers in the United States, he or she had little commonsense understanding of what the Community Center was to do or of what his or her task should be. Moreover, since there were other recreational centers for youth, Center staff themselves needed to understand, as well as to communicate to potential clients, how their Center was going to be different: why go to the Community Center instead of to the Labor Youth recreation hall around the corner? This was especially important to the ICCC since other centers were typically sponsored by political parties, while its own mandate was to provide a nonpartisan alternative. This initial ambiguity around the community center concept was not resolved when the Cabinet Committee for Economic Affairs voted to create the ICCC, when the Knesset ratified the committee's recommendation, or when Aranne signed forms establishing the agency.

The nature of the community center concept was not made any less abstract by the name, corporate or local. There were linguistic problems with the direct translation of "community center" into the Hebrew language. "Community center" as a concept was not an indigenous idea, nor was there an equivalent Hebrew language phrase for it other than a direct translation of the English, which did not convey a sense of what a Community Center should be or do. "Community" in Hebrew (*kehilla*) historically meant a self-governing congregation of Jews, a political unit organized to provide civic, educational, and ritual services (something akin to a Christian "parish"). A *kehilla* might have a synagogue, but it had no "center," physical or spiritual. That made "community center" linguistically suggestive of a place for religious worship, rather than for musicals or karate classes. In addition, the literal Hebrew translation (*mercaz kehilati*) was awkward to say and sounded like a translated foreign phrase rather than like an indigenous concept. The phrase made little sense, conceptually or linguistically, in the Israeli context.

There was a further problem with the literal translation. As explained by David Harman, one of Aranne's special assistants, for Aranne and others "community" as a program concept bound up in a term lay in the domain of the Ministry of Welfare, whereas the ICCC was set up under the aegis of the Ministry of Education and Culture. At the time of the ICCC's founding, the Welfare portfolio and the Education and Culture portfolio had long been held by two different political parties, the National Religious Party and Labor, respectively. As a member of the Labor Party, Aranne insisted on a name other than "community." In choosing a name that had no associations with a competing party, he would ensure the agency an identity separate from a competing ministry and party and create a clear address for attributing whatever political kudos might be forthcoming from the new agency's activities.[12]

A variant explanation is offered by the ICCC's data collector and researcher, who understood Aranne's concern to have been that Welfare already had "community centers." And Ralph Goldman wrote (8/31/70), Aranne "refused to use the term 'community center' only because the words . . . had been pre-empted as a term by the Ministry of Social Welfare." In this understanding, political fortunes aside, Aranne wanted a new name for his new project.

The three bureaus within the Ministry of Education and Culture which lent the most support, technical as well as budgetary, to the new enterprise were the departments of Culture, Youth, and Sports. The ICCC's formal name in Hebrew was "The Corporation for Centers of Culture and Sport—for Youth and Adults." The individual centers became known as "Centers for Culture, Youth, and Sports"—a name whose Hebrew acronym is *matnas*, thereby creating a new Hebrew word (*Mercazei Tarbut, No'ar, v'Sport: MaTNaS*, accented on the second syllable; it became *matnassim* in the plural). The central agency eventually became known in Hebrew as the "Corporation of Matnassim." As more and more people used *matnas* to refer to the new Center buildings that were being built throughout the country, it gradually caught on—although often with variant pronunciations, such as "meknas." This alternative was common among Moroccan immigrants and their children, perhaps because it sounded like the Moroccan city Meknes.

But the creation of an identifiable proper name—no other community center is called a matnas; it refers only to ICCC Centers—did not immediately and by itself create an organizational identity. Dan Ronnen, for example, another of Aranne's special assistants, asked in 1980 why the word "Adults" was in the title or why it was necessary to include the tag "for Youth and Adults." He answered his own question: "Essentially, the Centers were merely big Youth Clubs, and they had to prove to themselves that they served other age groups as well."

In an interview in 1979, Pozner discussed changes in the image of the matnassim from centers that dealt with culture, youth, and sports to centers whose programs touched on all subjects and all ages.

"Then, hasn't the term 'matnas' passed its time?" she was asked.

"Certainly," she replied. "That's why we [ICCC staff] call them community centers."

"If so, why don't you change the name?"

"We haven't succeeded in uprooting the name 'matnas,' which has become so fluent in the mouths of so many people that they can't give it up. I would guess that most of those using the name don't even know what it stands for [as an acronym]. The word catches the ear—it has a ring to it." (Lavi 1979)

The word did indeed seem to have earned a place for itself, as seen in the following story told in 1980 by Ronnen. The story captures one view of the organization's external image, one not necessarily in keeping with its internal identity. The board of directors of the Jerusalem Theater, a major up-scale cultural center that sponsored a film series as well as concerts and other performances, had been debating its future course of activity. One member summed up the crossroads they were facing with the question: "Is the Theater going to continue to be a source of excellence, or is it going to be a matnas?" This captures the theater's elitism as much as the matnas's populism.

METAPHORS AND ADMINISTRATIVE ACTION

Though sounding more like a native word, "matnas" was equally as new a concept as "community center," and it carried no more substantive meaning generally than "community center" did. The newness of the "matnas" name addressed, in part, the political need to differentiate among similar centers, but it still did not provide an image of an operational model.

In an early meeting of the board of directors, one of the founders used a phrase that was soon picked up throughout the agency: the Community Center would be "a functional supermarket." The metaphor entered the oral and written practices of the organization. It was spoken in interviews and conversations, it appeared in written documents of the time, and it also figured in discussions at training sessions for directors. The sense of the metaphor, as used by founders, administrators, and staff in interviews and in writing, was that the matnas would be a multifaceted facility providing a wide variety of programs at the local level, programs that supposedly were not already available to residents locally through other agencies or commercially. Pozner recalled in an interview that her early planning committee which had been charged with inventing the model Community Center tried to design a building that would be a "functional supermarket" in that it would meet the largest number possible of residents' wishes. It would contain space for performances and sports, for different clubs or classes, as well as a "members' lounge." (Lavi 1979) The ICCC's 1974–75 annual report refers to the Community Center/matnas as a "supermarket of ideas and programs for all ages, at all levels." The metaphor appears in subsequent years in documents and conversations as a "supermarket of classes" and a "supermarket of services."

The supermarket metaphor gave form to what until then had been a relatively shapeless concept. It provided a focus for other ideas influencing agency development: it articulated a specific context within which matnas building design could be envisioned; it created a sense of what matnas programs should include, in terms of their variety and scope; it included ideas about measures of success; and it suggested appropriate roles for staff and expectations for clients' behavior. Moreover, it did none of this explicitly: the knowledge about all these things was learned and communicated tacitly.

In explicating what "supermarket" can mean analytically, it is possible to see how the metaphor shaped the concept of a matnas.[13] Just as a supermarket offers an endless variety of standardized merchandise all available in one place to a broad range of consumers, the matnas would "meet the maximum number of desires expressed by residents for programmatic activities," in the words of one of the ICCC's brochures. Just as the supermarket as an ideal-typical concept is a large, centrally located, spacious building providing many goods under one roof, the ideal matnas would contain space for performances and for classes, for a library and a coffee bar, for photography and for football.

In analyzing the supermarket metaphor, it is possible to generate concepts or "labels" from supermarket language which accurately describe the ICCC and its activities as they were developed. For example, the matnas would offer a full array of "prepackaged goods": programs, activities, and clubs running the gamut from sports to crafts, from remedial education to music and dance, to be organized by matnas staff and offered "ready-made" to those who would sign up. The metaphor placed a value on the "high turnover of goods": large numbers of local residents participating in a wide variety of activities. Local residents would develop "shopping lists" of what they would like to "buy" in the matnas and communicate this to the director, who would "stock" his shop with program "supplies" from various ministry departments, "advertise" his "wares" in the neighborhood, and wait for "customers" to sign up. New matnas buildings themselves, while not identical, shared such design features common to supermarkets and different from other buildings as a large scale and sense of expansive space. They had high ceilings, large rooms, often two floors, were typically located on or adjacent to the central town plaza, and were markedly distinct from both public and private local architecture.

In addition to shaping thought and action about program offerings and building design, the supermarket metaphor also guided thought and action about administrative practices and staff roles. These expectations could be seen in agency evaluation forms and in ways in which directors and staff talked about their work—although rarely did anyone make the link to the supermarket metaphor explicit. Community Centers were evaluated on their "volume of sales": the higher the attendance and membership rates and the greater the number of programs and activities offered, the more successful the matnas was judged to be. Like a supermarket manager, the matnas director would be on hand in his office for clients/customers to come inside the building to shop for available products and to request others. Matnas staff—sports directors, adult education coordinators, children's activities programmers, librarians, and so forth—were cast in the role of "sales clerks" or "cashiers." They were expected to be available to clients inside the building and to promote the standardized activities of the matnas. But this role expectation and the programmatic implications of the metaphor contradicted the training of one particular unit of professionals hired by the ICCC to perform a key role in the centers: community organizers (COs).

PROFESSIONAL CO PRACTICE IN THE SUPERMARKET

In 1972 the executive director of the ICCC accepted funding to create a unit of community organizers within the agency, hiring an initial dozen COs for placement at the Centers and a division head based at central headquarters.

The professional practice of community organization (CO), one of the divisions of social work practice, is based on the principle that local residents can and should determine and articulate their needs vis-à-vis government agencies (Batten 1971). CO is a process-oriented practice, and the process of developing communities requires a long lead-time to see results. For example, a community organizer might spend more than two years getting town residents to coalesce around the building of a dam. The organizer's field notes might reveal a series of daily meetings with town leaders, teachers, and various committees, all oriented toward building mutual trust and reaching the goal. Progress is typically difficult to see or measure on a weekly or monthly basis; it is often clearer in retrospect, as the coalition gels or after the dam is built. But "being in the street"—being visible, easily accessible, meeting with residents formally and informally in their homes, cafes, neighborhoods, etc.—is a strong part of COs' professional identity.

COs in the ICCC found that they, too, were expected to work in keeping with the supermarket metaphor: to remain inside the matnas building, waiting for clients to come to them, and promoting its standardized programs. But this role expectation clashed with the norms of their professional practice, which required organizers to be in the neighborhoods meeting with residents or calling on them in their homes. "Shopkeepers" and "clerks" do not leave the store, but expecting organizers to remain inside the matnas building, as the supermarket metaphor does, challenged their professional identity, principles, and practices. One point of conflict that was often reported by COs in the early years of the first Amidar contract was that matnas directors did not understand them to be working when they were not physically present in the Center.

CO activities (such as strengthening community ties by organizing neighborhood councils) are not typically oriented toward residents' attendance of concerts and photography courses inside a community center building. Eleven years after the agency's founding, one director—only the second woman to hold that position, and the only one at the time—expressed this idea herself, one of the instances in which ICCC staff invoked supermarket language explicitly to talk about their work: "There's no subject that we can 'push' [sell] only as supermarket 'owners' or 'clerks,'" she said in an interview. "We must also be outside [the building]."

Evaluation measures implicated by the supermarket metaphor—high attendance rates, rapid turnover—also conflicted with elements of CO practice, which are project-oriented rather than "mass productions." The idea of prepackaged, standardized programs was similarly incompatible with the professional CO orientation toward programs developed according to local needs. This, in fact, had been embodied by the ICCC as its first Operating Principle: that programs "will be derived from the needs of the community" in which the matnas is located. Following such a principle, one would expect to find different programs in different communities, rather than common, preformed, centrally distributed programs (as was nonetheless typically the case).

However, the supermarket metaphor emphasized the operational needs of the agency's planning, budgeting, and evaluation divisions for centrally produced and distributed programs—standardized units which could be more easily dispensed and monitored from central headquarters—rather than individually tailored ones developed locally in response to residents' ideas and in accordance with the first principle. As the ICCC's associate director noted, "I must believe that [local matnas staff] arrive at their [proposed program] idea by researching local needs, although I know that usually the idea comes directly from the director or his staff without their having ascertained local needs." His sense was corroborated by an organizer, who said, "There were certain packaged programs that everybody was supposed to be doing, or that's what you were led to believe. . . ." Even when residents requested neighborhood-based extensions, supported by COs as responses to local needs, most matnas directors were initially highly reluctant to accede, even though attendance there might have been quite high. Their reluctance might also be traced to their understanding of supermarkets in the Israeli context, which are regionally oriented rather than neighborhood-based.

These two contrasting models of Community Center practices are summarized in Table 5-1. The different ideas about daily operations, professional roles and effectiveness, presence within the matnas, attitudes toward marketing matnas activities, and program evaluation fostered conflict between community organizers and their colleagues in the Centers and the Center directors, as well as between the CO unit and ICCC executives. The two cultures—the supermarket culture of agency administrators and the culture of the professional practice of the community organizers—clashed. Activities meaningful for the one culture had no meaning for the other culture or conflicted with values held by the other culture. COs often reported, "My director doesn't understand what I'm doing." Directors demanded that COs remain inside matnas buildings; COs argued that they could not accomplish anything that way. Neither group saw the conflict in terms of a clash between metaphoric interpretations reflecting different cultures. Each "read" the metaphor—tacitly—in terms of its own culture and assumed that reading to be the way to understand its meaning.

In the process of negotiating these conflicts, non-COs found a way of interpreting CO activity which fit their interpretation of the supermarket metaphor. The first order of business for COs new to a particular community was to study the community: to survey residents, human service agencies, local government officials, community leaders, and so forth to find out what the local "felt needs" were, as well as to introduce themselves to community members. When it became apparent that residents were not coming to the Centers in the numbers that were anticipated, Center directors and ICCC executives began to see CO neighborhood-based activity as a marketing device. In terms of the supermarket metaphor, the COs came to be seen as "door-to-door salesmen" or "street peddlers" instead of "in-house sales clerks" or "shopkeepers." They were often asked to take a list of programs with them into the neighborhoods to "advertise" and "sell" to residents, while helping residents develop their own "shopping lists." Implicitly invoking the supermarket metaphor, one director described the ICCC's view of the organizer as a "sales agent" of clubs and programs. An organizer said, "Directors took on COs because they think the COs are going to fill up the matnas." And a foundation offered to fund early CO work in order to bring those "unaccustomed to institutional activities" (e.g., school dropouts, returning soldiers, the unemployed) into the Centers.

TABLE 5-1.   Two Understandings of Community Center/Matnas Action

Ramifications of the supermarket metaphor for Community Center action	*Implications of CO practice for Community Center action*
I. *Implications for building design*	
Distinctive, nonvernacular, large-scale, spacious architectural design; central location; two storys; high ceilings; many multipurpose rooms; display areas and cases	Multiple small-scale, neighborhood-based, clubhouse-type buildings; design resembles local residential architecture (small rooms, common materials, low ceilings)
II. *Implications for merchandise*	
Large variety of programs (sports, adult, youth, language, arts, dance, music), centrally designed, "out of a box"	Small number of programs, unique to local context, according to local needs
III. *Implications for administrative, CO, and staff roles*	
Director sits in office, waits for calls, visitors; manages books and paper, talks on telephone	Director goes out to meet residents, social service counterparts ("Management by Walking Around")
Staff (including COs) work inside, "sell" programs to clients who enter the building; or COs peddle Center programs outside the building	COs and other staff do "street work" to determine local needs for programs, evaluate success of CO efforts
IV. *Implications for evaluative measures*	
• Number of programs offered • Number of attendants per program • Number of people coming inside building • Membership figures • Per capita cost of programs • Number of requests for many different programs, classes	Residents take leadership roles in determining Center programs, place demands on Center rather than depending on Center to initiate offerings; evaluate in terms of extent of residents' involvement, initiative, leadership
V. *Implications for client roles*	
Client comes into the building to register for Center-initiated offerings	Client requests activities in local neighborhood, rather than in central building; asks for programs that Center has not initiated but which address client's needs

145

The activity of being-in-the-neighborhood, in other words, while meaning something different to each symbol-sharing group, could be accommodated within the metaphor. On the other hand, while non-COs' reading of organizers' roles made sense to them in terms of the metaphor, it was not a comfortable fit for the COs themselves, for whom selling programs that had not emerged from local expressions of need continued to clash with their professional principles.

Although administrators' success in reinterpreting CO activity in light of the metaphor lessened their estrangement from the organizers, the latter continued to feel as though they were living in an alien, and sometimes hostile, culture. As directors pushed for organizers to conform to the implications of the metaphor, the clash between administrators and organizers deepened. In 1977, the ICCC's executive director froze the budget and activities of the CO division for a year and forbade them to meet for their annual in-service training sessions. He argued that there was too much "process," too much running around in the neighborhood. As the then associate director said, "We need to see projects, activity groups, people *inside* the matnas" (emphasis added). The executive director subsequently terminated the CO division head by not extending his contract. By 1981, only one of the original COs remained in the field (the only one without university-level training); two others had become regional CO supervisors following a national reorganization.

METAPHORS, TACIT KNOWLEDGE, AND ORGANIZATIONAL LEARNING

The ICCC in its founding period needed to frame and shape its organizational identity internally—to design and construct buildings, to formulate programs, to develop staff, to evaluate progress—and its external image—to attract sources of funding, to rally supportive publics, to attract clients. The task was complicated by several facts: policy language carried no explicit instructions concerning buildings and programs or detailed language about operations; moreover, neither the American "community center" nor the newly coined "matnas" represented widely familiar concepts. Into this void the metaphor of Community Center-as-supermarket was introduced and grew, giving form to the ICCC's identity. It suggested a way of thinking about matnas programs, buildings, and staff that allowed the organization to get on with business. It provided a way of developing categories of appropriate and inappropriate action. What worked was what fit the metaphor.

The metaphor juxtaposed the supermarket with the Community Center/matnas. It brought the greater detail of a more familiar concept together with a fuzzier notion, and in the interaction of the two created a way of seeing the matnas and of thinking about what it should be. The metaphor was not taken literally: no one ordered freezer cases instead of desks and chairs. But agency members' understandings of the metaphor depended on a common literal sense of supermarkets.

For more than the first decade of the ICCC's existence, the supermarket metaphor was an active figure of thought. It became an organizational metaphor. It was not the private musing of the founder who first uttered the phrase, nor was it restricted to the domain of the board of directors where it was initially expressed. It was available throughout the organization to members of the board, agency founders and executives, and Center directors and staff, as well as to anyone else who read agency brochures released at that time or who attended discussions at annual meetings.

Although publicly available and commonly held within the organization, the metaphor was not explicitly examined; it was accepted and used throughout the agency, without its attributes or implications being made explicit. Yet it helped, tacitly, to shape the path of a new organization, to focus other ideas influencing the agency's development, and to determine appropriate and inappropriate management and staff behavior. It was introduced in a moment of cognitive (and perhaps aesthetic) insight, and once on the table, it guided thought and action tacitly. Metaphoric language was used, but without making explicit its metaphoric nature. No one said, "I think a Community Center is like a supermarket." Neither did anyone explicitly and analytically play out the metaphor after it was introduced by asking, "In what ways is a matnas like a supermarket?" It was rare to have someone in the organization use the metaphor explicitly to make a point, as did the Center director quoted earlier who contrasted "pushing" programs from inside the matnas as an "owner" or "clerk" with working outside the building. But even while evoking elements of the extended metaphor, she did not explicitly reflect on the fact that she was speaking metaphorically. Rather, the entire phrase "the

Community Center would be a functional supermarket" or the last part of it alone was picked up throughout the organization, outside and beyond the meeting in which it was first used, without anyone saying, "This is a metaphor that can be useful in our thinking and planning." Adoption of the metaphor made it possible for the organization to proceed with its tasks and created criteria for evaluation.

As the phrase was repeatedly used in conversations throughout the organization, aspects of appropriate supermarket behaviors were known and learned, tacitly. The tacit knowledge about how centers were like supermarkets and the implications for Center practices—a piece of cultural organizational learning (Cook and Yanow 1993)—was initially learned in board meetings and other discussions involving organizational members at the time of the metaphor's adoption. It was passed on to the COs primarily in daily interactions with their organizational superiors, the matnas directors. It was learned by new members—Center directors, for example—in hiring interviews, through training programs (e.g., for new directors or CO in-service training sessions), and through conversations with colleagues and others.

It was in these conversations that the behavioral expectations dictated by the metaphor and the actions mandated by norms of CO professional practice came into contact and clashed. While the clash was palpable, the underlying framework of knowledge provided by the metaphor was not. No one said to the community organizers, "You need to be inside the matnas building *because supermarket personnel don't work outside it.*" No one said, "You can't meet residents in their apartments *because shoppers always come into a supermarket.*" A director might have asked, "Where were you yesterday afternoon between four and six o'clock? Why weren't you here in the office?" In replying, "I was meeting the Edri family and their neighbors in Green Street park," the organizer would perhaps open a conversation in which the different expectations could be voiced. But this would have been done without explicit reference to supermarkets. Unlike the conversations about the use of "association" and "corporation," where meanings were made explicit, supermarket knowledge was communicated tacitly.

Other cases have been identified where organizational metaphors were invoked explicitly by members and analysts after several months of organizational action to explain prior events in a metaphoric manner after the fact (Smith and Simmons 1983); or where conflict developed among three subgroups of a single agency, each supporting its own metaphor (Merten and Schwartz 1982). Unlike them, the ICCC's supermarket metaphor came into existence early in the history of the agency without the intervention of external consultants and without explicit design, and it was a single metaphor interpreted differently by two agency divisions. Like the adoption of the matnas name which proceeded over time, the supermarket metaphor caught on. It was accepted throughout the organization without explicit direction to do so by anyone.

The conflict that developed between COs and management was not due to improper behavior on the part of the organizers (the point of view at times of some ICCC administrators); nor was it due to unprofessional practice (the self-doubting view of the organizers themselves, and sometimes of their supervisors in the CO division); nor to mismanagement by Center directors of their staff in any traditional sense (some COs' point of view). It can be explained, rather, in terms of the implications for action of an extended, unexamined organizational metaphor that, while enabling thought and action of one sort, nonetheless ruled out traditional CO thought and action that were incompatible with it. The conflict was played out in everyday organizational life, but the cognitive framework underlying the conflict was never explored because it lay in an unexamined metaphor.

Professionals and administrators within the same organization often clash (see, e.g., Raelin 1986). However, had the ICCC hired MBAs, for example, rather than COs, such clash is less likely to have occurred, since the norms of MBA training and practice are closer to the retailing practices implicit in the supermarket metaphor.[14] Without the supermarket metaphor, there would not necessarily have been the same clear, if unspoken, conceptual model for acceptable staff behavior which the COs were not living up to, and the clash between them and administrators might have been more diffuse or nonexistent. As Bennis (1972, pp. 104–5) noted, "Metaphors have tremendous power . . . to give life and meaning to what was formerly perceived only dimly and imprecisely. What *did* students experience before Erikson's 'identity crisis'?"[15]

It is difficult to know whether the supermarket metaphor determined the solution to the problem of defining the nature of the Community Centers/matnassim, or whether tacit knowledge of the desired solution determined the choice of metaphor. Schon (1979), adopting a medical metaphor in his own analysis, argues that the diagnosis of the organizational problem is made first, determining the selection of a metaphor, and the metaphor-diagnosis then embodies the prescription for subsequent action. The choice of a particular metaphor, however, could just as well devolve from some prior, although tacitly known, and perhaps vague, notion of what the solution should be, and an equally tacit search for a conceptual vehicle to shape that abstraction. It is in this sense that metaphors may be both models of prior but unarticulated understanding and models for subsequent metaphorically articulated understanding.

WHY A SUPERMARKET? SOCIETAL CONTEXTS OF AGENCY AND POLICY MEANINGS

Metaphors are embedded in a cognitive context particular to a time and place. An artifact of the agency's culture, the supermarket metaphor reflected part of the agency's tacitly known values and beliefs. One of these was that its goal was to enable clients to adopt Western, middle-class values and behaviors—although, as will be discussed more fully in Chapter 7, this was a "verboten goal," a policy goal which is not and often cannot be articulated explicitly, because it is not supported by explicit public consensus. The supermarket metaphor gave expression to this verboten goal through a vehicle that itself embodied Western, middle-class values and behaviors—the literal supermarket—and, by extension, through the specific programs offered by the matnas-as-supermarket (e.g., ballet, string quartets, etc.). The metaphor was particularly appropriate to the situation: the supermarket, itself an American concept and called in Hebrew by its English word, had first appeared in Israel a few years prior to the founding of the ICCC. It was perceived as belonging to a higher socioeconomic status in a way that the traditional grocery store and open air market were not. The metaphor fit a social service agenda, itself rooted in the American experience, for establishing programs in lower-class areas that would educate Eastern residents to the Western, middle-class way of life that the supermarket represented. The context required a vehicle that could express these tacitly held values; seeing the Community Center as "a functional department store" or a library or a synagogue or some other metaphor might not have made this possible.

There are, perhaps, objective reasons why none of these possibilities came about. Department stores, for example, were unknown in Israel at that time. But the important thing to note is that the metaphor was created, in a moment of serendipity, by a member of the organization—not by a third party—and it sprang full-blown out of existing organizational values. That is, as a model *of* the situation, the metaphor reflected some preexisting cognition of what was desired in a Community Center, at the same time that it was a model *for* and directed further thought and action once it was expressed and accepted as an organizational metaphor.

Spelling out the supermarket metaphor would have entailed addressing the problems of operationalizing a "broad-aim program" (Weiss and Rein 1969). The metaphor allows a certain operational ambiguity and flexibility: low "turnover" of one product-program need not imply organizational failure; if one program does not "sell" well, the matnas-as-supermarket as a whole is not threatened—the director can "open up shelf space" for other products.[16] There is no conceptual limit to the number of items a Community Center-as-supermarket can offer, unlike a youth center, whose offerings are limited by age suitability, or a sports center, which is limited by program type. The advantage of such ambiguity to the Community Center/supermarket is flexibility; the disadvantage is ever-changing, largely unattainable goals. Both are seen in the list of the ICCC's goals over its first decade of operations, ranging from providing "someplace to go" to "narrowing the social gap" to providing "quality of life." Defining success in terms of attendance rates provides an organizational goal far more concrete and measurable than these broader, more ambiguous social goals.

The ICCC might have spelled out the implications of the metaphor for administrative and CO practice, as has been done here, but we cannot know for certain that this would have eliminated the conflict. Such an argument is based on the assumption that the metaphor caused the conflict between COs and Center directors. This causal relationship might hold if metaphors were only models *for* perception, but as models *of* perception, giving voice to prior cognitions, they are not causes, and eliminating them may only leave the cognition to be expressed in some other form, thereby continuing the conflict through other means. Moreover, making the supermarket metaphor explicit is not the only way the conflict might have been addressed. It is equally plausible that in changing its way of thinking about its work—under a new executive director's different vision, for example—the agency might have given rise to a new metaphor that would have articulated this new cognition, possibly replacing or reinterpreting the supermarket metaphor and its implications for action. Furthermore, one might argue, there are times when metaphors should not be made explicit because doing so might surface for general scrutiny deeply held assumptions that the organization has not chosen to make public or that the polity is not yet prepared to discuss.

Metaphor's epistemological role both enables new insights and blinds us to other relationships that might be germane to the subject at hand. The capacity of metaphors to blind has been seen by many as a pitfall of metaphor and as an argument that metaphors should therefore be eliminated or that unexamined metaphors should be made explicit. While metaphors may blind sight as they highlight some features of organizational life, it is not clear that this pitfall can be eliminated by substituting either literal language or other metaphors. Counter to the view that metaphors are decorations or unclear thought and thus unproblematically interchanged, the view that organizational metaphors are cognitively grounded suggests that they cannot be replaced without changing the way people think about and understand the nature and mission of their organization. Put differently, the replacement metaphor is just as likely to reflect the same understanding of the situation and to have the same or similar blind spots as the one it replaces. The supermarket metaphor illustrates both aspects of the epistemological role of metaphor: the enabling and the limiting. In light of the concerns raised here, the limiting potential of organizational metaphors should not be taken by administrators or policy analysts as a call to eliminate or replace them or to make them and their implications explicit. Metaphors are not *only* word play.

The analysis presented here illustrates the context-specific meaning that an interpretive approach emphasizes. That is, while the metaphoric phrase itself is a visible and accessible artifact—"a functional supermarket" is printed in agency literature, it is not private or hidden knowledge—it rests on and derives its meaning from values and beliefs which are specific to the context of a particular organization in a particular society at a particular point in time. It can only be understood—interpreted—in that context. We would not expect to find "supermarket" used metaphorically in other organizations, although we might find other metaphors playing similar epistemological roles in communicating meanings, shared and not shared, throughout an agency, shaping its internal identity.[17]

In one, perhaps fundamental, sense, all language is symbolic. Letters, written marks on the page, represent sounds. Words stand for things and concepts. Beyond that, however, there are forms of language that not only denote meaning, they connote meanings beyond their specific, immediate referent. Names, category labels, and metaphors are such forms.[18] This chapter begins to suggest the multiplicity of readers and voices involved in the communication and interpretation of policy and agency meanings that is implementation. The language examples we have looked at were largely, but not exclusively used for internal communication of identity. The ICCC also needed to develop an organizational image for external communication. To do so, it also drew on artifacts other than language, including agency buildings, programs, and other objects.

NOTES

1. See, e.g., Edwards (1980), Mazmanian and Sabatier (1983), Nakamura and Smallwood (1980). I have discussed this further in Yanow (1990, pp. 218–20).

2. Baier, March, and Saetren (1986) made a parallel argument.

3. For a discussion of language and evaluation, see Palumbo (1987) or Hallett and Rogers (1994).

4. The other six are metaphor proper, translation, exchange, contradictions, synecdoche, and metonymy.

5. In the social sciences, recent metaphor analysis has focused on matters of both theory and practice. The former concerns metaphor's epistemological role in creating researchers' theoretical categories and concepts: dominant metaphors are seen to underlie the theories of the field and to structure researchers' creation of new knowledge and categories of analysis. We find this concern in sociology (Brown 1976); in political science (Landau 1964, Myrdal 1968, Rayner 1984, Yanow 1987a); and in organizational studies (Bourgeois and Pinder 1983, Keeley 1980, Manning 1979, Morgan 1980, 1983, 1986, Pinder and Bourgeois 1982, Yanow 1987b).

The second focus of analysis has been on the ways in which metaphors used in daily life shape public thought about and action toward the subject of the metaphor. Traditionally, most work on metaphors and general social life has been done by anthropologists studying geographically remote societies (e.g., Fernandez 1972, 1974). Attention to the role of metaphors in directing everyday life in a Western or American context has been undertaken typically in other disciplines. Political science and policy analysis have been concerned with rhetorical devices in public language (such as social policies or politicians' speeches) which categorize political events and direct public perception of them and action in their regard (Bosman 1987, Edelman 1977, Garrison 1981, Howe 1988, D. F. Miller 1985, E. F. Miller 1979, Rein and Schon 1977, Schon 1979, Stone 1988, Titus 1945). And organizational studies has focused on the connection between organizational metaphors and organizational action (Donnellon, Gray, and Bougon 1986, Krefting and Frost 1985, Merten and Schwartz 1982, Pondy 1983, Smith and Simmons 1983, Srivastva and Barrett 1988).

6. The extent of interest in metaphor as a field of analysis may be seen in comparing two bibliographies on the subject. Shibles (1971) included 3,000 annotated entries on the subject of metaphor. Van Noppen, de Knop, and Jongen (1985) cited 4,300 new entries not included in Shibles's work, most of them published between the early 1970s and 1985. Commenting on a set of papers for a symposium on metaphor in 1978, Booth (1978) wrote, "The bibliographies [of these papers] show . . . that the year 1977 produced more titles than the entire history of thought [about metaphor] before 1940."

7. This definition follows Black (1962, 1979) and Lakoff and Johnson (1980). Definitions of metaphor, according to Black (1962), have taken one of three approaches to seeing what they are and how they work: as *substitution*, in which the metaphor takes the place of some equivalent literal formulation; as *comparison*, in which the metaphor, seen as an abbreviated simile, could be filled in to spell out the comparison being made between its two parts; and as *interaction*, in which some unnoticed aspect(s) of the focal object of the metaphor is highlighted through an interaction between the two parts of the metaphor, leading to a new understanding of the metaphor's focus. The definition suggested here is in the latter tradition.

8. Such figures have been called "dead" metaphors, but as Lakoff (1987a) points out, this is a holdover from the view of metaphors as figures of speech rather than of thought. As a figure of speech, metaphor referred only to a novel expression; an analogy that had become commonplace and lost its novelty was considered dead. But, as the inflation metaphor illustrates, even commonsense metaphors do not necessarily lose their ability to direct perception. The original meaning of inflation is still available to us in the context of economic thought, although more often under the rubric of "over-inflation," when economic policy is developed to apply cold compresses to the swelling or to prick a hole in the balloon and let the air out. See Lakoff and Johnson (1980) for further discussion of conventional and "dead" metaphors.

9. Geertz (1973, p. 93) notes that cultural patterns have the dual aspect of giving meaning to "reality" by shaping themselves to that reality—being models *of* it—as well as by shaping that reality to themselves—being models *for* it.

10. This is what Victor Turner (1974) called "multivocality"—the capacity to resonate among many meanings at once, like a chord in music is a resonating of many tones.

11. This difference of approach lies at the heart of the debate over whether metaphors can be eliminated in favor of literal language. Some of the substance of this debate within organizational studies is captured in the exchange between Morgan (1983) and Bourgeois and Pinder (1983).

12. See Yanay (1989) for a discussion of local conflict between the Ministry of Welfare's Local Welfare Boards and the Ministry of Education and Culture's ICCC Community Centers. The conflict at times extended to community organizers fielded by the two agencies.

13. The supermarket ideal denoted here draws on an American model, a point taken up in the last section of the chapter.

14. I thank Steven Maynard-Moody for suggesting this counterfactual.

15. The psychologist Erik Erikson introduced the phrase "identity crisis" to describe what he saw as a developmental transition between late adolescence and early adulthood. It figured prominently in descriptions of U.S. college students in the 1960s and 1970s. See Erikson (1963, ch. 7).

16. I thank Ed Wachtel for this reading.

17. For example, Paul 't Hart (personal communication, April 1994) noted that the supermarket metaphor is unlikely to have emerged in a government agency in Holland through the early 1990s, where people would associate it with "a kind of mindless clientelism, catch-all pathologies, and a lack of substantive policy vision." He observes, however, that this disapproval of a market metaphor in public service may be quickly waning now "with the changing balance between 'hierarchists' and 'individualists' in our public sector and among opinion leaders."

18. On creating categories, see Edelman (1977), Lakoff (1987b), Stone (1988), and Yanow (1996).

6

Symbolic Objects: Organization-scapes, Agency Programs, and Policy Meanings

We shape our buildings, and afterwards
our buildings shape us.
—Winston Churchill

We have seen that the concept of "community center" at the time of the ICCC's creation was unfamiliar to most of the agency founders and staff. Policy language was also operationally vague: although calling for the creation of an agency to implement social, educational, and recreational programs, it did not make specific what these programs were to be, nor did it specify the type of building necessary to house them. Even the names chosen for the corporate entity and its operational bases, while directed both internally and externally, did not immediately crystallize an internal identity or an external image. We have seen that agency founders drew on an organizational metaphor to shape their ideas. But whereas this worked for internal agency purposes, it did not help directly in communicating policy meanings to relevant publics such as potential clients, members of supporting and contending agencies, legislators, voters. To create an organizational image and communicate it to audiences outside the agency, the ICCC needed to draw on other forms of communication.

Objects—physical artifacts such as agency buildings, office decor, uniforms and uniform modes of dressing, award plaques and pins and the like, agency programs, and so on—are one such form. Both organizational and policy meanings may be embodied in and communicated through objects that are their symbolic representation.

They may communicate meanings to external, as well as internal, audiences of various sorts. They may be especially significant when policy language and goals are ambiguous and vague. This chapter explores ways in which one type of symbolic object, "organization-scapes"—agency buildings and built spaces, including their siting, landscaping, materials, decor, furnishings—may embody and represent policy and agency meanings, and then looks briefly at agency programs as another type of symbolic object. In exploring the interpretations made of these buildings and programs by agency founders and executives, center staff, clients, volunteers, donors, and members of the broader public, we encounter several other readers of intended meanings.

This focus on built space draws on one aspect of Burke's (1969/1945) dramaturgical analysis, taken up later by Edelman (1964), as well as on the methods of social geography. Burke identified five elements in analyzing interaction: agent (the actor and his or her role), act, agency (the means of acting), purpose, and scene or setting. The audience is an implied sixth element, what I have been referring to as "readers" to indicate that they play a more active role than a listening or watching "audience" presumes. The focus here, then, is on the settings of policy and agency acts.[1]

READING ORGANIZATION-SCAPES

Buildings convey meanings in two ways. The substance of their design—their materials, scale, siting, landscaping, and relationship to their surroundings—as well as their interior decor may communicate the values of their designers and the clients of the design.[2] Built spaces also act on their users—through such things as their mass, interior proportions and shape, use of light—to produce behavioral, cognitive, or affective responses. Substantive symbolism may act alone to convey meanings, as for example when the use of marble or expensive woods represents wealth or social status. Enacted symbolism, however, relies on design substance to effect responses: whether natural light in an airy space induces meditative or playful feelings and behavior depends on the materials, furnishings, decor, and other design elements present.[3] Passersby, who interact only visually with building materials, siting and landscaping, the scale or mass of the building, typically read the substantive symbolism of the building. Although substantive symbolism may evoke an emotional response in passersby, enacted responses usually depend on the user entering the building and interacting with the interior spaces, furnishings, and decor.[4] In the context of government buildings, this occurs typically through some instrumental activity such as requesting a service or participating in a program. The conveying of policy meanings through agency buildings may be more difficult when the client is only an onlooker.

A second issue is inextricably intertwined with how meanings are conveyed, and that is the nature of the audience for whom the object has meaning. We will turn later to a third set of concerns about whose meaning is being carried and how that meaning is interpreted.

Organizations communicate meanings to both internal and external audiences, conveying both identity and image. Public and private sector organizations share the need to communicate organizational identity to an internal audience of their own executives, managers, and employees. This may be accomplished through the materials of building design and decor: office location, the quantity and quality of furniture and decorations, colors, plant materials, distances of office and parking space from the building's entrance, and so forth. These signal social status within the organization, and are used to situate the individual with respect to superiors, peers, and subordinates for purposes of establishing and maintaining individual identity and evoking appropriate behaviors.[5]

Communication of meaning in this way illustrates many of the aspects of symbols: that they are social conventions; that meanings are public, not private; that they create a unifying identity within a group that shares them and separates that group from others. Meanings are also highly context-specific: while the use of dress, personal effects, and symbols of office to signal status crosses cultures, the meanings of particular symbols do not. It is common in the United States, for instance, to understand the fourteenth-floor office (in a fourteen-story building) as a symbol of high status within the organization, whereas in Ghana, for example, it would signal that the occupant is of relatively low status. There, as in India, executive offices are more typically located on the ground or second through the sixth floors. As Mazumdar (1988, p. III-145) noted with respect to Indian organizations, when there is little, no, or inconsistent electricity and elevators are nonexistent or unpredictable, office space on floors easily accessible by foot is more desirable than a grand view.

This example of context-specific meaning points to what may be the source of manifestations of meaning through built spaces: that their "embodiment" of meaning is literally that—derived from bodily experience. Lakoff and Johnson (1980) note that a considerable part of American English derives from orientational metaphors: up-down, front-back, central-peripheral, and so forth. "Up" is associated with control ("He's at the *height* of his power," p. 15); more of something is "up," as the pile gets taller ("My income *rose* last year," p. 16); and "status is correlated with (social) power and (physical) power is up" ("He has a *lofty* position," p. 16). "These spatial orientations," they write, "arise from the fact that we have bodies of the sort we have and that they function as they do in our physical environment" (p. 14).

We "embody" vertical, erect bodies. Western society values reason and the rational, which we see as the activity of our brains, which are at the topmost position of our bodies. And so we establish "quarters for the *heads*" of our *corpor*ations and *organ*izations—those at the heights of hierarchy (itself part of this conceptual configuration), control, income, and therefore economic, social, and organizational power—at the tops of our buildings.[6] Hindu culture supplies a bodily explanation for the lower location of Indian offices. The Upanishads relate that the center of human consciousness lies just below a hand's span from where the lowest ribs converge. Also, according to the legend, the world (in the form of a lotus blossom) sprang from Vishnu's navel while he slept. For a culture that locates the soul in the center of the body and values it as the source of human activity, it makes less sense for corporate headquarters to be at the heights of buildings. To speak of buildings as the *embodiment* of meaning appears to have a literal as well as a figurative sense.[7]

Matters of personal organizational status and identity are only one sort of meaning that buildings convey. In examining how implementors communicate policy and agency meanings especially in the face of ambiguous policy language, other audiences and facets of agency identity and image are more germane. Government-scapes have a wider variety of external audiences than private sector buildings typically are seen to have. While private sector organizations have an external audience of customers and potential customers as well as competitors and allies in the organization's environment, public agencies communicate their image also to legislators, to other government agencies including Congress and regulators as well as local agencies, to residents in surrounding communities, to policy-relevant publics such as interest groups and potential voters, to possible fund-raisers and donors, as well as to clients and potential clients. Our starting point in this second retelling of the ICCC case is the initial ambiguity around what "community center" was to mean. "Do you know what a community center is?" Aranne asked Pozner, saying that he did not. Pozner's planning committee members saw the Centers as serving one of three purposes: educating the population, changing individual and social values through community development, or providing social services (Zipori 1972, pp. 12–13). These were woven together in early agency goal statements. Later goals included reducing ethnic tensions, combatting juvenile delinquency, the comprehensive coordination of social services, and "providing quality of life."

The ambiguity of these goal statements added to the ambiguity of the enabling legislation's language and that surrounding the name and concept of "community center." Yet the ICCC was faced with the necessity of having to hire staff, draw clientele, attract ministry funds, and raise private donations—all of which required the translation of this ambiguity into more concrete terms for a program whose very concept was unknown and whose goals were not obviously and clearly actionable. To communicate policy meanings, which had now become agency meanings, the ICCC drew on its buildings, among other artifacts, to represent them symbolically.

COMMUNITY CENTER BUILDINGS AND LANDSCAPING: SUBSTANTIVE SYMBOLISM

The typical Community Center was to be "a large building, spacious and comfortable" ("Community Centers in Israel," 1971), centrally located, and easily accessible. Town planning design for the development towns where most ICCC Centers were to be located featured a large, cement-tiled central plaza with plant boxes, sometimes a fountain, and cement park benches, around which were usually clustered municipal office buildings, local shops, the health clinic and other services, the cinema, and banks. Residential buildings were planned to radiate out from this center. Town residents had become neighbors by accident of immigration date, and many of the groups from countries of different origin did not get along with each other. The design of the central plaza was intended to address this (as was the ICCC itself): it was intended to serve the social function of causing town residents to intermingle, thereby breaking down barriers between strangers.

Central siting for the Community Centers in these towns meant locating them near these central plazas. Since the Centers were planned six years after the completion of the last development town, such siting was not always easy. In some cases a cement-tiled area was added on to the central town plaza, and the Center was built there. The lower-class city neighborhoods where Centers were also built had also been planned around central park and service cores, where sometimes land was still available centrally to accommodate the addition of a Community Center.

One Community Center built in this fashion stood on the pathway between the central plaza, a public garden, and the open air market. Standing in the plaza, one could see the top of the two-story building over the roofs of the other buildings, all single story, in the square. The long, wide, tiled expanse leading up to its broad, glass-paneled entrance (see Figure 6-1), its two floors, and its unusual stone construction materials set the Center apart from its surroundings and accorded it a stature different from any other building in town. Only the Workers Council (Histadrut) building also had two floors, but at half the width of the Community Center, without the surrounding open space, and with a small, treed front yard, iron gate, cement-block frontage wall, and short exterior access pathway, it had a quieter, less eye-catching appearance (see Figure 6-2).

By virtue of its size, scale, materials, and surrounding exterior space, this particular Center is also markedly different from the town's residential structures. In this it is typical of other ICCC Community Centers. Housing in this town was built in five stages and reflects public housing styles of those periods. The earliest are single-level, cement-brick structures of about 1,200 square feet of floor space divided in half, each unit containing three small rooms and a kitchenette (56 square meters per unit; Figure 6-3). Built in the early 1950s, these structures were considered temporary housing; by 1981, most had been demolished. Permanent building began in 1956: 263 two-family units similar in design to the first ones were built around the central town core, with added indoor plumbing and a surrounding plot of land for truck farming (Figure 6-4). In 1957–58 thirteen two-floor apart-

Figure 6-1.   Community Center facade. Note the wide expanse and broad glass doors.

Figure 6-2. Workers Council (Histadrut) building.

Figure 6-3. First-phase housing (*ma'abara*, ca. 1950): One 600 sq. ft. unit.

ment buildings clad in sand-colored stucco were added to this central area (Figure 6-5). A subdivision north of the town center was developed in 1963, with three- and four-floor apartment buildings, followed by a similar subdivision to the northwest in 1976 (Figure 6-6). Housing unit sizes grew with each new stage of building: by 1963 an average apartment was 64 square meters (8 more than the earlier size), luxurious at the time and in that location, but small compared to units going up in Tel Aviv by 1973 with 86 and 112 square meters.

Figure 6-4. Second-phase housing (ca. 1956): Two basic units, one expanded, joined by a common wall.

Figure 6-5. Third-phase housing (ca. 1957–58).

Figure 6-6. Fifth-phase housing (ci. 1976).

Size, siting, and building materials are not the only things that set the Community Centers apart from other public and residential buildings. Their interior architectural design and furnishings also marked them as different. The entrance hallway of one typical Center is cavernous, the height of its full two floors, and furnished, as are most Centers, with Scandinavian-style upholstered armchairs and coffee tables (Figure 6-7). The size of the interior cavity overpowers the lightness of the furnishings. The walls were hung at one point with reproductions of colorful paintings by Modigliani, Matisse, Picasso, and others. One of the walls is wood-paneled from floor to ceiling. In a side alcove is a console television (installed at a time when few local people could afford one because of full-value luxury tax duties) and a radio. Adjacent to this area and directly across from the main entrance is a snack bar with an espresso machine and a display case for fresh cakes. A basketball-tennis court behind the building, with built-in cement bleachers and night lighting, is visible from the lounge through the glass rear door. By contrast, the Youth Club sponsored by the Histadrut/Workers Council is a small, single-story, whitewashed cement construction with an adjacent hardtop, marked for basketball, and set off from the street by a chain-link fence (see Figure 6-8).

The Center just described was one of the first built, in 1971. The 104th Center building, opened in November 1980, followed an even grander design. Erected in a suburb of Jerusalem, the Center—like others in city neighborhoods—did not have the central plaza siting of the development town facilities. Its design, however, compensated for siting limitations in attracting attention. Designed by the Mexican sculptor Goeritz, a proponent of "emotional sculpture" (according to Meir Ronnen, 1980, an architecture critic), the building has three stories and five levels. "Its windows and light sources are concealed from exterior view," wrote the critic, explaining that the sculptor-designer pioneered the use of the sharp angle found in this Center's design, a feature I. M. Pei later used in the National Gallery of Art in Washington, D.C. and in Boston's John Hancock Building. Like Pei's Hancock, this "fortress-like" Community Center (Ronnen's assessment, again) was a source of much attention and design controversy. To say that it stands in marked contrast to its surrounds would be an understatement.

Figure 6-7.   Community Center entrance hallway, with snack-bar at back.

Figure 6-8. Workers Council (Histadrut) Youth Club.

INTENDED MEANINGS AND SUBSTANTIVE SYMBOLISM

In an interview one Center staff member said she felt that she and her colleagues were telling their clients: "Here's a building. You fill it with content—and turn it into the center of a community." But a building, together with its siting and furnishings, is not a blank slate. "Ordinary landscapes" (Meinig 1979) embody meanings. They are symbolic of the values of those who designed them—both architects and their clients. When buildings are designed to house agencies implementing governmental policies, we may say that the buildings represent public values as well.[8] These and other meanings may be read in the buildings by agency clients and other relevant publics. From interviews with organizational founders, executives, managers, and other members, their correspondence, and other contemporaneous documents, we may learn what values they intended Center design to convey.

Community Center construction materials—stone, glass, wood—were not used in residential or other public architecture in the development towns. They are more expensive than the local vernacular and represent the availability of financial resources—wealth—

associated with a higher class. Interior design elements—paneling, upholstery, appliances—reaffirm this message. The scale—the massiveness of built space—is also much larger than surrounding buildings. This expansiveness is echoed in the broad plazas that are the approaches to the buildings; it also speaks of the command of resources. To physically take up space is, in many cultures, a sign of power and control.[9] The Community Centers are also typically set off on both sides and in back: they stand alone, without challenge.[10]

The messages of wealth, power, and control are communicated not only through the intrinsic cost of materials and of land and space, but also through opposition or contrast. Most of the Centers are singular constructions in their towns and neighborhoods: no other building looks like them; they stand out. A stranger to town who is familiar with a handful of Centers elsewhere could find the local Community Center within five minutes. No attempt was made to fit the buildings into their natural or built surroundings (as, for example, the architect Safdie did in designing Habitat). This adds a message of "difference" to the other meanings conveyed by the Centers. That these meanings of "difference" and "otherness" were intended by agency founders can be seen in their speeches, correspondence, and reports of the time.

The architecture, landscaping, interior design, and furnishings of the Community Center buildings represent concepts of Western, middle-class Israeli life. Recall Warner's (1959) comment with respect to individuals' homes, quoted in Chapter 1, that decor and so forth "are all symbolic objects . . . which refer to the manners and morals . . . and express the significance of the people and their way of life . . . ," evoking "sentiments about who they are and . . . justifying [a] vision of the [meaning] of their world" (pp. 44–50 passim). The symbolic objects in the Community Centers referred to the "manners and morals" of their founders and their wishes for the development town and urban neighborhood residents where Centers were constructed. Policymakers and agency executives and founders intended the Center buildings to provide local children with an "escape" from what the planners saw as their overcrowded homes, as an early agency document notes. Quoted at length in Chapter 3, it describes the Community Center as presenting to local residents "a pleasant atmosphere of social and cultural well-being which is often *absent from* their impoverished dwellings" ("Community Centers in Israel," 1971, emphasis added).

Central agency administrators and local Center directors felt that residents would come to the Centers if the image conveyed the right message. Some Center staff were explicitly conscious of working with the physical plant to shape it to this image. One Center director said:

> I got a Youth Club [building]. My job was to turn it into a Community Center. You could see [the enterprise] was growing by the number of kids who came to the building; but this didn't do anything for the image of the Center.
>
> People see a nice building [it had been renovated] and very strict discipline (that is, no street gangs are allowed inside, because they are a destructive force). But they ask why we don't have a Center like South-town. In part it's a function of physical plant: [South-town] built a brand new building, with separate and identifiable youth and adult wings. In part it's a function of your starting point: the people who come [to South-town] are of middle-class orientation—if you put up a poster advertising a new club, people read it and come and register. I did that in [North-town] for three seasons, and one [local] person signed up. Our classes are filled by people from outside the neighborhood.
>
> If the building were different, [the locals] would show up. Prestige is a fundamental problem of the neighborhood. There's a basic sense in the neighborhood that it's been neglected. People feel like they were promised things which were never delivered. . . . So if there is some activity elsewhere that they don't have [here], they feel deprived. It's almost irrelevant whether they need the activity or not. They feel that it should be there.

A senior researcher at an independent grant-making agency, familiar with the ICCC, related in an interview:

> The Centers that have lots of activities are those which are built very differently from the way the community's houses are built. The more closely the Community Center resembles the houses, I would predict that it would be less successful. If you put a Community Center in a building that looks like public housing, no one will come there. Look at Jerusalem: the "successful" Community Center is the one built on the American model— with all the varied facilities, a swimming pool, rich programs, and many, many classes. If it has nice armchairs, if it's spacious

and all sorts of ashtrays are floating around—if you tell me that's not the ideal attributed to the middle class, I don't know what is. From the point of view of identifiable symbols, that's it. And it comes to "sell" leisure activities—that is, the patterns and habits of the middle class—nothing else.

The building's message of social "difference" is communicated through physical difference: the contrast with local vernacular in materials, size, scale, mass, furnishings, decor, and so forth. These are summarized in Table 6-1 in terms of the elements in use in the first decade of operations. The message is sent simultaneously through several different mediums. Local residents entering the Center building encounter these marked contrasts with the settings of their everyday activities. These contrasts indicate that the Center building frames an activity that is not ordinary life. Such a setting "focuses constant attention upon the difference . . . ," creating in the participant a "heightened sensitivity" to "connotations . . . [and] authority" (Edelman 1964, p. 96). Removed from the immediacy of the everyday, the resident becomes receptive to the messages suggested by the building's substantive symbols.

DESIRED COGNITIVE, BEHAVIORAL, AND AFFECTIVE RESPONSES: ENACTED SYMBOLISM

The Center director who chose to hang posters by Matisse rather than Andy Warhol, a still life of sunflowers rather than a madonna, used the symbolic meaning of "art display" (even in reproduction) as well as of "oil paintings" to convey a message. It is not just the substantive content of the artwork that is symbolic; the choice to hang things itself is a symbol. The director could have mounted cartoon posters or graphics instead of "oil paintings," or hung local residents' original artwork instead of European reproductions, or left the walls empty— they had been bare for five years. Both content and act are symbolic of Western, middle-class values. By "visiting" the Centers to participate in their activities, local residents would "acquire" the values, beliefs, and feelings which the Center buildings embodied. In this way the substantive symbolism of the buildings would combine with

TABLE 6-1.   Siting, Materials, and Decor: A Story of Contrasts

Community Center	Local residences	Other public buildings
Siting/scale/design:		
1. central location	radiate from center	central and dispersed
2. set apart on four sides	close proximity	adjoining; or small yard
3. massive, oversized scale	in scale	in scale
4. broad entrance plaza	small approach	small or no approach
5. wide entrance doors	in scale	small and in scale
6. oversized entry rooms, halls	small rooms	small interiors
7. renowned architect	no	no
8. American concept	no	no
Materials:		
9. stone facade, with glass	stucco	stucco
10. interior wood paneling	no	no
Decor:		
11. European-style furnishings	less costly	plain, utilitarian furnishings
12. radio, TV	not affordable	not affordable or not appropriate to job
13. "oil" paintings (reproductions)	no	no
14. tennis court, pool	no	no

the symbolism enacted in their use to produce the desired behavioral, moral, and affective responses.

Center design was to teach norms of cleanliness and appropriate behavior to both children and adults. The chairman of the board in 1973 wrote in the annual report that the buildings' "cultured, spacious, restful [internal] atmosphere," in contrast to their surroundings, "would belong to the world of a higher level of expectations, which would serve as an example of what could be the legacy of its visitors." This atmosphere was to be created in part by the substantive symbolism of the space and its furnishings, but the desired behavior could only be effected through the enacted symbolism of space use. "This building—you come in and feel you're *someone*," said one Center staff member, straightening his shoulders and standing tall. "It's sited near the 'villas'[11] and upper class of [the town]. It's filled with activities and lots of people come—not poor people, but the local elites." The communication of intended meanings, in other words, depended on clients' engagement with the space, even if they read its substantive symbolism from a distance.

The ICCC's executive director and other founders and board members anticipated that local residents would share their understanding of the Centers' high social status and would not want to settle for anything less. One of the founders sent the executive director a guide for planning and development standards for another community service agency with the recommendation that a similar guide be adopted for Community Centers. In two letters on the subject, he wrote:

I recognise the dangers involved in the preparation of such a Standards Guide because it might produce *pressures from the local communities for the inclusion of the maximum* in their own Community Center. . . . We could find ways to overcome the psychological problem of [raising and then not meeting the communities'] level of expectation. (8/5/71, 3/14/72; emphasis added)

From a design or aesthetic point of view, the contrast between the Center buildings' size and materials and those of local residences and other public buildings might seem to raise the question of the design appropriateness of the building to its location. But the contrast itself was part of the message being sent to policy-relevant publics. The contrast presented by the Center's scale combined with the values of wealth and status to carry meaning symbolically for local residents. The clothing, automobiles, appliances, and cultural elements of the West, the United States in particular, have long been desired and imitated by residents of non-Western countries, including the former USSR and developing countries. In this case, the American style of the Community Center buildings served to entice local residents to attend, because of the appeal of things American. The building and its trappings tacitly conveyed a social message: if you visit here, you will acquire the social status represented by the edifice and its decor.

MULTIPLE AUDIENCES AND DIVERGENT READINGS

So far we have been focusing on the meanings that agency members intended to convey to clients and potential clients through the design and use of Center buildings. But clients were not the only audience for these messages, nor can we assume that any audience would read the same message that agency members intended to convey, or that if it was read "accurately" it evoked the intended response. To suggest that organization-scapes are "read" by their various audiences is to suggest also the possibility of misreading from the perspective of the intended message. More than that, readers bring their own experiences to the "text," and therefore there are always the possibilities of multiple readings of any organization-scape.

For example, the director who spent part of his budget on oil painting reproductions hung them to decorate the television lounge area, in keeping with the upholstered, living room-style furniture and function of the room. Yet the same act was interpreted differently by two different publics. The director hung the posters close to the ceiling, to teach respect for property and to minimize vandalism and theft since his limited budget would not allow for their replacement. Young local residents who participated in Center programs read this as the director's and the agency's distrust of and dislike for them. On the other hand, women from a nearby upper-class neighborhood who volunteered in the Center interpreted the height as yet another sign of the town's social backwardness, this being considered an inappropriate height at which to display artwork.

While the building's scale might be considered inappropriate from a certain design perspective to its immediate surroundings, it is entirely appropriate to sending a message to external audiences at a farther distance.[12] As Edelman (1964, p. 100) points out, settings address a wider audience than that immediately present to observe the acts therein contained. To more distant Israeli audiences, the buildings' visibility called attention to the fact that government moneys were used to build something in development towns. The expensive materials and the Centers' existence in lower-class areas represented the country's development success and status as a nation. This meaning-creation and communication process acts in ways similar to individual acquisition and ownership of an oil painting, although in this situation it is a group process. It is not just that the possession of a designed building speaks for the status, reputation, and identity of the organization.[13] In the case of public organizations it speaks for the status and identity of the nation as a whole. It is a statement about property ownership and about objects of value which is made to all who would see the building from the outside—external, and more remote, audiences than those who would participate in the agency's activities. This very broadly public statement redounds on the owner of the building—in this case, the public—as a confirmation of their collective good fortune and judgment in this ownership.

John Berger (1972) makes a related argument with respect to individual ownership of oil paintings and ways of seeing. Buying the painting, he says, is equivalent to buying what it represents. In the case of the Community Centers, the connection is more convoluted. In a sense, members of the public, through their tax payments, had built the buildings—an act of acquisition—and could thereby feel that their values represented in the buildings were endorsed. Local residents could not buy Community Centers or their furnishings, but they could participate in Center programs that represented the same values as the furniture. The acts of entering the building and taking part in a program become the symbolic equivalent of buying the building. The message conveyed is twofold: one, the buildings represent government's attention to the needs of its poorer citizens; two, the buildings proclaim that wider publics have responded and are continuing to respond to social problems. As one local Center director said, "People want to think they're doing something." The buildings become symbolic of legislative and democratic processes as well as of policy substance. They speak at once both to local audiences and to broader, though still domestic, publics.

A second distant audience is the wealthy foreign donor. To attract a donor, an agency's fund-raisers must be able to communicate a clear image of what they want supported. The American model that the ICCC Community Center emulated conveyed a meaning that potential American and European donors could easily interpret since it was based on something familiar to them. Founders were aware of the fact that such communication took place. In the letter quoted earlier urging the ICCC's executive director to prepare a guide to planning and development standards (3/14/72), the writer warned that the lack of a book of standards is likely to bring about "a lopsided type of Center . . . but equally important is the fact that if you have proper plans, the contributor might have contributed more funds."

Nearer external audiences included other social service agencies (e.g., the town's Welfare Department, youth clubs), schools, voluntary associations (e.g., various women's organizations), sources of volunteers (such as nearby *kibbutzim* or middle- and upper-class neighborhoods), and residents—the pool of clients and potential clients. While the question of divergent readings is important for all of these, it is crucial with respect to potential clients. Those who had read the intended message and responded to it attended Center programs, became members, and supported its activities. Others did not. It is well known in social work practice that centers such as the *matnassim* attract clients who already aspire to middle-class status and describe themselves as such (see Whyte 1981 on this point), more than they attract those of lower status.

This does not mean that non-upwardly mobile residents "misread" intended meanings. It is possible that they read them "correctly" and chose to behave otherwise, or actively rejected the message, or simply ignored it. This suggests that agency staff's ability to use buildings to dictate a desired and intended human response is limited, as illustrated by the following example.

The Center described earlier with the cavernous entry had some 900 square feet of open floor space directly inside the front entrance furnished with tables and chairs. One set of these stood about five feet from the main doorway, a set of two broad glass doors with side panels also of glass. Soon after the Center opened, a group of middle-aged men of Spanish Moroccan origins came to sit at this table for a daily game of dominoes. They would appear at about 4:15 in the afternoon after working the day shift in the local factory or before going off to the night shift, order tea and cakes, and play, talking and sometimes laughing, watching the comings and goings of Center visitors and passersby outside on their way to the central plaza or the marketplace, keeping to themselves and their game until about six o'clock, when they would move on, homeward or to work. Anyone coming to the Center during these hours had to pass their table to get to the Center's office, library, and other facilities.

This daily game gave a sense of life to an area that otherwise seemed oppressively gray and empty because of its huge space and dark walls. The Center's director enjoyed the idea that his Center was providing a meeting place for a recreational activity. The game contributed to his good reputation in the ICCC: when the executive director dropped in on an occasional site visit, he was impressed by the sense of liveliness and public use, which suggested that the Center was fulfilling its goals. But Center staff discovered that few women were coming between those hours because of the men's presence; they also kept their daughters away during what were prime hours of afternoon recreational activity for children. The men gathering to play dominoes were following the custom of their country of emigration, in which men gathered for afternoon tea in neighborhood cafes to gossip, exchange news, and pass time. The women, in refusing to enter the same space, were also following their custom: those neighborhood hangouts were off limits to women. Even in the direst emergency, a woman would send a child for her husband or brother before she would think to go to his cafe herself.

These customs had not been left behind when people had immigrated. Moreover, each immigrant group in this development town had staked out its own cafe. That the Community Center's entrance had been "adopted" by the Spanish Moroccans meant not only that women and girls would not enter the Center then, but that men from other ethnic groups (including French Moroccans) would also not come into the building during the afternoon hours. This discovery was of great puzzlement to the Center's director, a Czechoslovakian by family origin who lived in another town, although it was well known by the Center's secretaries and librarians, themselves French Moroccan women. They used the small side door in the afternoon to get to their offices.[14]

Differences of interpretation of another sort may be seen in an example drawn from the community organizers (COs). As noted in Chapter 5, the organizers' norms of professional practice required them to circulate among residents in the neighborhoods, apartment buildings, and streets. This meant that an agency activity was taking place outside the Center buildings. Moreover, one element of COs' work had come to be the organization of youth and adult clubs in apartment building shelters, chosen because of their proximity to residents' homes, an important feature for families with many young children from cultures not accustomed to having women socializing away from the home. Center directors and agency executives initially did not see this from the perspective of client service, but rather focused on the fact that this meant that some staff were not working inside the buildings and that clients would not be entering the Centers for activities. The problem was partly one of organizational identity and image: for an agency in its early years still working to establish itself, apartment shelters were not identified with its mission, and directors feared that their input of budgetary and staff resources would not be recognized as an ICCC effort. Moreover, the physical image of the shelters—small, dark, of common materials, unfinished and unfurnished—was not in keeping with that of the Centers.

But in light of the preceding analysis another component of the problem emerges. If buildings' meanings are in part communicated through their use, then the shelters—which did not physically embody the meanings associated with the Centers—could not convey these meanings. In this case, since the transmission of Western, middle-class values was "built in" to the buildings the agency had created, it could not be assured of accomplishing its goals if clients were not interacting with those spatial artifacts.

AGENCY PROGRAMS: SUBSTANTIVE AND ENACTED SYMBOLISM

Policy language no more specified what types of programs the Centers were to offer than it had the shape or design of the buildings. And yet agency executives and Center staff were able to create programs that also embodied the unspoken, inexplicit, yet tacitly known values, beliefs, and feelings that underlay the policy, and many local residents, clients and potential clients, and more distant policy-relevant publics were able to read these meanings in the programs. As with the elements of the organization-scapes, programs also conveyed meaning through their substance as well as in their enactment.

Center programs, clubs, and activities represented an array of societal values. Most of the programs offered in the first decade of the ICCC's operations symbolized the Western, middle-class values that were embodied also in the Centers' organization-scapes. Program offerings varied by Center size (as measured more by population served than by physical plant, although there was usually some relationship between the two). For example, one rather small Center offered, in 1980, classes in exercise, ballet, ceramics, shepherd's flute (*halil*), enamel work, and woodworking. A much larger Center offered, in the same year, classes in ladies hairstyling, exercise for women, Weight Watchers, guitar, English (on three levels of mastery), drawing, medieval religious poetry, sewing, ballet, drama, folk dance (beginners and advanced), drums, ceramics, basketball, in addition to a concert series of ballet and chamber music (held in a nearby town's concert hall), a Mandolin Orchestra, and a theater series that included I. B. Singer's *Yentl* put on by the Cameri Theater, Federico García Lorca's *Blood Wedding* performed by the Tsavta Theater, and a Habima Theater production.[15]

The meaning of a program might be clearly perceptible to some, and opaque, differently understood, or nonexistent to others. Programs served to attract some people to the Centers and keep others away. Sometimes, interpretations were based on program names, as in the following example from a Center director. ICCC headquarters proposed to fund a set of activities around the wintertime Chanuka holiday.

> They wanted to call it "Chanuka Program" instead of "Winter Camp." We said, "If you call it 'Chanuka Program,' no one will come." They said, "No, no, only 'Chanuka Program.'" We said, "Okay, let's ask the neighborhood." They [local residents] said, "What's 'Chanuka Program'? Is it a camp?" They [ICCC staff] said, "Okay, we'll call it a camp."

The program activity would have been the same in either event, but the naming of it was key in communicating meaning. Here is an example of the interrelationship of language and objects.

Ballet classes were a perennial favorite in the Community Centers, attracting a constant flow of little girls. We may understand their meanings for the ICCC's founders by focusing on an excerpt from a letter written by one of them (quoted more fully in Chapter 3) on September 29, 1972:

> How proud some of the citizens [of this development town] must now feel that *even their* youngsters can study ballet. . . . It

is not ballet that is important, but the fact that in this little God-forsaken town, the youngsters of the poor have an equal opportunity to be exposed to today's cultural activities as are the youngsters of the Tel Aviv residents. (emphasis added)

This understanding was seemingly shared by Community Center clients. One young Jerusalem resident, Tunisian by birth with a B.A. in English literature, who worked full-time as a secretary, enrolled her two daughters in her neighborhood Community Center's ballet classes. She complained that the high cost put such classes out of reach of many of her friends and neighbors, but she added that she was thankful that the class gave her girls a chance to acquire what urban Ashkenazi children had. Elsewhere, a development town's high school Youth Council organized by the Center was discussing a program that entailed inviting a Youth Council from Tel Aviv. One of the teenagers remarked: "They're so much better than we are. How can we possibly host them?"

ICCC staff were aware of the meanings that some Center actions carried to clients and potential clients. One of the agency's Ten Operating Principles, for example, was that clients were to pay for classes and other programs—some amount, at least, and in kind if not in currency. "If it doesn't cost anything, then that's how it looks and that's how the people take it," said one staffer. "If it costs something, then they look at it in a different light."

Some staff were also aware that programs might carry multiple meanings, some of which might conflict with the meanings they wanted residents or others to read. One such program was a literacy and high school equivalence curriculum for adults. One Center director documented the tenfold increase in program enrollments resulting after he had succeeded in "breaking through the wall of that image the residents have of [the program]." He used the same phrase— "break through the wall of their image"—to describe what he had to do to overcome the Ministry of Education's resistance to his operating the program locally, in a development town, rather than at its usual urban base some distance away.

The meanings conveyed by programs are not static. They may change as general societal values change or in response to other influences. The game of tennis provides one example. In 1973 one Center offered tennis lessons among their other sports classes; only one high school junior signed up. Tennis was seen at the time as an elite "Anglo" sport; it had no audience within Israel and no local appeal. In 1974 the Center director renovated the court, adding night lighting, and hired an instructor trained and licensed by the renowned Wingate Sports Training Institute. No more than a handful of youngsters registered.

Between 1975 and 1978 a professional tennis trainer who had immigrated from South Africa started coaching youngsters at the Tel Aviv Country Club. He entered them in international competitions and they placed well. One boy was seeded in the top fifty in the international juniors ranking. Israeli news coverage reported the prize moneys. A national tennis court and stadium were built outside Tel Aviv. By 1980 the same Center had more requests for tennis classes than it could handle.

Center activities communicated meanings not only between Center staff and local residents, but also at times among different groups of residents. The example of the Spanish Moroccan domino players in the Center's entrance hall is a case in point, where the adoption of the space by one community group conveyed a message to others in the community, both men and women, about the accessibility of the space. Although Center staff were for a long while ignorant of the meanings residents attached to this activity, residents saw it as happening under the Center's aegis. This reading was reinforced by the evident delight taken in the domino game by the visiting ICCC executive director, who made his approval known in conversations with the house and snack bar manager, himself a French Moroccan by origin.

SYMBOLIC OBJECTS AND POLICY MEANINGS

Organization-scapes, agency programs, and other objects communicate meanings, even when these meanings are not expressed explicitly in policy language or in implementing agencies' goal statements. These meanings were communicated through both substance and enactment: substantively, through the design elements of the building, for example—their expensive materials, European furnishings, lighted tennis courts and swimming pools, wood paneling, use of space in height and width, in exterior entry plazas and interior rooms;

in enactment, through entrance into the Centers to attend its programs and other forms of artifactual interaction (engagement with the space, participation in the programs and activities). In both cases, meaning was conveyed through opposition, rather than similarity, to the commonplace surroundings and everyday activities. By contrast, for example, nineteenth-century New England factories and schools communicated meaning through the use of similarity, rather than opposition. They were built to resemble churches, and they brought church behavior into their settings—quiet, order, and deference to authority (Smith 1979).

The policy the ICCC was created to implement, as seen through the values, beliefs, and feelings embodied in its objects, suggests a motif of proffered and desired upward social mobility of a particular ethnic and geographic color. Specifically, it came to teach the values of and reinforce beliefs in Western and urban culture, providing Eastern-origin development town and neighborhood residents with the socio-cultural means to "acquire," symbolically, a higher status, although they were and could become neither Western nor urban.[16] Western and urban values were considered desirable by policymakers, imple-mentors, upwardly mobile residents, and more distant policy-relevant publics because they were perceived as being of higher social status and closer to the center of power. In the Israeli context, the ICCC's building design and many of its programs symbolized these values.[17] Ballet classes and string quartet concerts, for example, were, at the time of the ICCC's founding, the Israeli equivalent of what Cadillacs, swimming pools, and color televisions once were in the United States as symbols of social status. Attendance at these events and the acquisi-tion of social and cultural skills associated with society's upper strata are symbolic surrogates for the possession of material goods, and they carry the illusion of acquiring this status.

This goal of turning Eastern development town residents into urban, higher-status Westerners was not stated in explicit language either in the legislative act that created the ICCC or in agency docu-ments and discussions. Yet it was known tacitly and communicated by way of the organization-scape and other artifacts. "Even when a building does mean," wrote Goodman and Elgin (1988, p. 43), "that may have nothing to do with its architecture." The building, they indicate, may come to stand for an activity associated with it—"a costly county courthouse may symbolize extravagance." While for

Goodman's philosophy of aesthetics "to mean in such a way is not thereby to function as an architectural work" (p. 649), from the point of view of government organization-scapes, such associational meaning is precisely the sort that civic spaces may come to represent and exactly how they may play a role in the implementation of policies. This is the enacted symbolism of buildings, which combines with the aesthetic components of substantive symbolism to attempt to produce desired behavioral, cognitive, and affective responses in various audiences. Organization-scapes and other objects also convey the political culture contemporaneous with their design—not in the sense of the political attitudes of individuals, but in the sense of "habits of mind and practice" (Goodsell 1988, p. 8) of the collective, what in Chapter 1 I called the artifacts of culture together with their underlying values, beliefs, and feelings.

One of the ways in which some symbolic objects do this is by removing us from the mundane activities of everyday life. When citizens and government representatives interact in such organization-scapes, in their difference from the practices of normal, everyday life, the citizen feels the presence of government and its messages—sent symbolically, not explicitly. The ICCC's Community Centers were one such space that, through their contrast with the vernacular, removed the participant from ordinary life and communicated policy meanings that were not made explicit in policy or agency language.

Center activities were not mundane in two respects: by virtue of the nature of the activity (a performance, a club meeting) and by virtue of the scale and mass of building design. The entrance cavity of the early Center and the odd angles of the 104th Center would always set them apart from the everyday, and continually act on even the most regular visitor to produce feelings of otherness and difference. Even weekly church attendance, for example, does not diminish the ceremonial—the not-everyday—nature of the space.

Objects communicate policy values even when these values are not expressed explicitly in policy language or agency goal statements. Through them ambiguities of language are made more concrete. It is the inability—for political and other reasons—to express values explicitly that may underlie such ambiguity, which at times is intentional ambiguity.

When Winston Churchill spoke of the mutually reinforcing interaction of people and their buildings, he was pointing to the ways in which we tell ourselves through built spaces who we are as a society, what we value, believe, and feel, and perhaps, how our built spaces report back to us the messages we read in our bodies. Governmental power is, in part, power to frame and communicate meaning. In contemporary American society, for example, we value private enterprise, and these values of and belief in capitalism are conveyed through corporate spaces—look at our cities' skylines, for instance— as well as civic spaces. Agency buildings contribute to the expressive process whereby through our public policies, we tell ourselves—as well as more distant audiences—who we are as a polity, in terms of our identity, our self-image. In our interactions with them, our buildings shape us, conveying the societal beliefs of the culture that has fostered them as well as our affective responses to the organization-scapes through which policy and other civic beliefs and values are communicated.

NOTES

1. Goffman (1959) also developed a dramaturgical analysis. These points are nicely summarized in Feldman (1994). See also Lasswell (1979) on government buildings and their symbolism and Mosse (1975) on the Third Reich's architecture and meaning for other examples of settings. References to other works in social geography may be found in the next several notes.

2. There is more problem in the client-designer relationship than indicated in this sentence. See, e.g., Mazumdar (1984). Much of the work on the meaning of built space has been developed in the context of the meaning of homes: the relations between individuals and their dwellings (e.g., Rullo 1987). Sadalla (1987), e.g., notes: "houses . . . function to symbolize and display the self." (See also Cooper 1976, Rapoport 1976, Sopher 1979.) Some look at the towns or neighborhoods people inhabit (Perkins 1988) and the meanings ascribed to them that people fight to defend against change. This theme is well developed in social geography (e.g., Rapoport 1982, Zeisel 1981). Processes by which meanings are ascribed to public buildings, whether by architects or public policies or by their implementors, constituents, clients, or other stakeholders, have been less developed (see Craig 1984, Edelman 1964, 1995, Goodsell 1988, Lasswell 1979 for examples of such analyses). As a subfield of organizational studies, it has received some attention in terms of organizational climate, the status significance of the corner office, etc. (Steele 1981), or organizational culture (see the essays in Gagliardi 1990). Goodman (1985) develops an argument for how buildings mean aesthetically,

and work has also been done in semiotic analysis of cities and their signs (see, e.g., Gottdiener and Lagopoulos 1986, Preziosi 1971).

3. Goodsell (1988) refers to these two aspects of the social meaning of space as "expressive" and "behavioral."

4. This principle of artifactual interaction obtains also with "open" spaces such as plazas or groves of trees that carry meaning in a particular culture.

5. Most of the organizational literature analyzing the meanings of buildings and their materials has looked exclusively at an internal audience (e.g., much of Berg and Kreiner 1990, Ciborra and Lanzara 1990, Doxtater 1990, Hatch 1990, Larsen and Schultz 1990, Mazumdar 1988, Rosen, Orlikowski, and Schmahmann 1990, Steele 1981). Much of this work is based on Hall's (1962, 1959) and Goffman's (1959) work on nonverbal communication and various analyses of the meanings of "home" (e.g., Cooper 1976, Rapoport 1976, Sopher 1979) and the built environment (Rapoport 1982, Zeisel 1981). Hall, for example, wrote in 1962 (p. 21): "Because of the deep influence of space over interpersonal relations, it now seems pretty clear that no one should build a building for an organization without studying the organizational culture and determining its needs." It has taken thirty years for that reasonable suggestion to begin to be accepted.

6. Lakoff and Johnson (1980) note further that rational is up, emotional is down; as in, "The discussion *fell to the emotional level* but I *raised* it *back up to the rational* plane" (p. 17). Since women are associated with emotions and men with reason, this adds another layer to structural explanations for why women are more prevalent at lower organizational levels and why they hit a glass ceiling on their way up.

7. The observation about office location in Ghana was made during a class discussion of the meanings of the fourteenth-floor office by a Ghanaian student, who said she was having difficulty understanding her American classmates' association of height with the heavens and God and human social status. In Ashanti culture, she said, Gods are in the earth as well, and libations are poured to them on the ground. She further noted that only poorer Ghanaians lived in the hills—unlike wealthier Americans who live in the Oakland, California hills and elsewhere—because hill residents had to walk longer distances from the downtown markets, carrying heavy bundles on their heads. This prompted an American student who had served with the Peace Corps in Sierra Leone to recall that volunteers excavating an archaeological site there had found ceramic figures buried in the ground and assumed them to be ancient artifacts rather than the contemporary offerings to the ground-based Gods that they were. I thank Maami Dugbartey and Luana Kiger for their observations, which underscore the contextual specificity of symbolic meanings.

8. Goodsell (1988, p. 10) makes a similar point about public buildings representing regime values.

9. This, too, is a reflection of bodily experience, where in many cultures height and broad shoulders in a man are signs of physical power and financial or social stature.

10. Analyses of gender and class relations in the workplace make related points. Many women, and men feeling depressed or powerless, tend to sit and carry themselves with rounded shoulders and dropped head—hence, being "in a slump." Confident, powerful people expand their shoulders and chests and use their arms to take up more space—in the extreme, we speak of such a person as a "stuffed shirt" or "full of himself." It is those in power—man to woman, superiors to subordinates—who touch their opposites but are not touched by them in return, like the building that is set apart from its neighbors. See, e.g., the analyses in Hearn et al. (1990). This extends the relationship between bodily experience and interpretations of organizational and other "ordinary" landscapes.

11. This word is used in Hebrew to mean single-family detached homes, as distinct from the apartments or small kibbutz "rooms" and moshav "houses" most Israelis live in.

12. This discussion of the appropriateness of a setting to the message desired to convey is related to Burke's (1969, pp. 3, 6–7) discussion of the appropriateness of acts to settings.

13. Berg and Kreiner (1990, p. 56) have also noted this in respect of designed corporate headquarters buildings.

14. After this discovery, the director attempted to move the men either into the side alcove off the main entrance hall or into another room near by. Closed off from their view of passersby and from their own informal visibility and accessibility, they quickly stopped coming. Faced with the loss of their presence and with objections from the snack bar manager (himself a French Moroccan who also oversaw the rest of the physical plant), the director relented. Things soon reverted to the status quo ante.

15. These three theater groups are repertory groups based in Tel Aviv, who take their productions to other parts of the country.

16. Edelman (1964) argues that such actions pacify quiescent publics, a point I engage in Chapter 8.

17. It is not uncommon for Western objects such as American blue jeans and music groups to become valued in other countries. For an analysis in the context of eastern European countries, see Bar-Haim (1987).

7

Symbolic Acts: Rituals and Myths, Verboten Goals, and Silences in Policy Discourse

In Chapters 5 and 6 we looked at some of the ways in which various kinds of symbolic language and symbolic objects may communicate policy and agency meanings to and among multiple "readers" of those entities. But although it may be analytically neat to separate them, language and objects do not always work alone. They are often mutually influencing and mutually interactive, and they do this also through human acts, the subject of this chapter.

Policy and agency acts—debating, negotiating, legislating, managing, programming, leading, and so on—usually entail language or objects, or both. Policy documents, annual reports, correspondence: these are objects that entail the use of language, and the ways in which both objects and language are used is the action context that is also interpreted. Nonverbal communication also falls into this category of symbolic acts: choice of dress, posture, gesture, tone of voice, and so forth at the individual level have their organizational or institutional counterparts in rituals and myths enacted by groups. In these, meanings are rarely stated explicitly. An outsider needs to know the group "from within" in order to understand the tacit knowledge that is being communicated symbolically.

As with language and objects, we are interested here in meanings symbolized in collective acts rather than in individual, private acts and meanings. As the word "ritual" suggests, the kinds of acts that are symbolic at the group level are often regularized, repeated actions. It has become common to look at such actions under the analytic labels of "ceremonies," "rites," "rituals," "play."[1] These are found in organizational life in award ceremonies, holiday celebrations, retirement dinners, training programs, and so forth, where printed and oral language is often combined with objects to communicate agency meanings.

I include myths in this group because, as I will discuss in more detail below, myths are not just stories or fairy tales. From an anthropological approach rather than a literary one, myths may be seen as explanations constructed in the face of puzzling parts of their organizational or policy contexts. Humans create myths as an act of mediating contradictions. It is the importance of their creation and enactment that leads me to treat myths as symbolic acts, rather than as symbolic language. Their meanings rely, perhaps more than other parts of human life, on tacit knowledge. Rituals are the more visible and accessible enactments of myths, and they preserve and propagate the values, beliefs, and feelings embedded in those myths (Lakoff and Johnson 1980), drawing on language and/or on objects to do so.[2]

Postmodernist and feminist thought suggests that what is not said, the silences in discourse, based often on assumed and implicit norms, are as deserving of analytic attention as what is said. One situation in which we often create or encounter silence is when we are faced with accommodating in daily life the mandates of two (or more) irreconcilable values. In the face of such incommensurables, we often create myths, which hold competing values in a tension of temporary resolution and direct our attention elsewhere. While the discussion is applicable to myth analysis in general, our concern here is with the realm of public policies and their related administrative practices. We find incommensurable values particularly in policies of a social nature, as well as in the realm of administrative actions in the implementation of these policies. We would thus expect to find both policy myths and organizational myths in the ICCC case.

The chapter begins with a definition and discussion of myth and then turns to a third retelling of the ICCC story. Three organizational myths are explored as they appear in ritual acts and in their relationship to incommensurable values and "verboten goals," those goals which cannot be made explicit because they lack the social consensus that would support their public discussion. The chapter concludes with an examination of policy implementation and public silences.

A CONSIDERATION OF MYTH

In most political and organizational analysis, myths have been understood to be stories or fictions, at least in contemporary U.S. culture (see, e.g., Elder and Cobb 1983, p. 54). This may be in no small part because what we typically learn as "myths" are the tales of gods and goddesses—Greek, Roman, Norse—interacting among themselves or with mortals as they go about creating fire, thunder, winter and spring, and the "opposite" sex. Such tales have been widely read in the elementary and secondary school curricula in the United States. Or we learn what "myths" are from the biblical stories of worldmaking in Genesis—Adam and Eve, Noah and the flood, the Tower of Babel—that are taught in religious school. These tales of origin are told in story form: they have settings, actors, plots, conflicts, and resolutions. They are treated as fictions: made-up moral tales that entertain, that perhaps teach wrong and right, and that are assumed not to have taken place in reality.

Such stories have their counterparts in American political myths. The story of George Washington and the cherry tree, young Abraham Lincoln walking miles and miles to school and doing his homework with little light in a drafty log cabin, Horatio Alger going West to make his fortune from nothing are three examples. These also are entertaining tales that teach young people and new citizens the American values of truth-telling, diligence, and sacrifice for later gain. But emphasizing the storied aspect of myths diverts attention from the fact that plot-rich myths are but a subset of the genre. It diverts attention from the situations under which myths are created and from the existence of nonfictional myths. In looking for fictions we may miss the myths that characterize policy issues and organizational action, myths that do not always have plot lines and transparent morals. These become more evident when we take an anthropological approach to the field, rather than a literary one.

Myth analysis has traditionally focused on the ancients, or on so-called "prescientific" peoples engaged in myth-making activities, or on comparative studies of religions. Although some have contended that myth-making is an activity that characterizes the prescientific mind (e.g., Cassirer 1946), there is growing recognition that myth-making is also an activity undertaken by rational, modern, Western society. Recent writings have attended to the role in American political life of myths of the Independence era (Nimmo and Combs 1980), the Thanksgiving myth (Robertson 1980), the "Emma Lazarus myth" (Boston Sunday Globe 1981), as well as Western myths of modern administrative practice (Ingersoll and Adams 1986, 1992, Westerlund and Sjostrand 1979).

Reviewing studies of traditional myths, Cohen (1969) found that myth analysts attributed to myths seven types of purpose: explanation; creative expression; manifestation of the unconscious; socialization; legitimation of social institutions; symbolic and/or ritual-istic expression; and the reconciliation of conflicting principles.[3] Draw-ing on this classification and on traditional theories of myth-making (e.g., Honko 1972, Thompson 1955), I propose the following definition of myth for use in the context of policy and organizational analysis: *a myth is a narrative created and believed by a group of people which diverts attention from a puzzling part of their reality*. This definition includes the following elements.

First, policy and organizational myths are stated in a narrative form. To say that is to comment on the structure of the language they use. Myths are not propositions of logic, nor are they the arguments of rhetoric. Their language is not explicitly persuasive. Myths are matter-of-fact statements, but they are "immune to factual attack" (Cuthbertson 1975, p. 157). Policy and organizational myths need not necessarily be fables or fictions entailing heroes or villains and discernable plot lines. In retelling the ICCC case from this point of view, we find organizational myths of rational goal-setting, of organi-zational flexibility, and of uniqueness, and an unnamed policy myth— none of which has the structure of a story (with heroes and heroic action) or of a persuasive argument.

Second, myths are social constructions rooted in a particular time and place, in a particular culture. Myths are produced in response to the needs of the moment (Cuthbertson 1975, Tudor 1972). That is, they are not necessarily universal.[4] The myths analyzed in the ICCC case are particular to the agency at a particular time; they may or may not be found in other organizational settings or in the same organization at a different time. This means that myths may be transi-tory: a newly created myth may replace an existing one. This is not to suggest that such replacement is easily accomplished. Beliefs are often held tenaciously, as demonstrated in the recurrent revivals in the United States of the debate dating from the 1925 Scopes trial over teaching evolution versus creationism in schools.

To say they are social constructions means that policy and organi-zational myths are public, not individual or private. Yet they are not an explicitly conscious, intentional creation. Myths are *constructed* explanations, not *authored* ones. No one says, "Let's sit down and make a myth." They evolve in much the same socially constructed way that the rules of society do, over time, drawing on societal knowledge known tacitly.[5]

Third, myths are believed. The explanations they provide, the concepts they express, are reality for those who subscribe to them. "When in doubt, the transmitted myth can deliver you from skepticism—you *know*. For the believer the myth expresses what *exists* . . ." (Westerlund and Sjostrand 1979, p. 3).

Fourth, policy and organizational myths are typically found when a policy entails incommensurable values—two or more equally valued but incompatible principles embodied within a single policy issue or agency policy or practice. Incommensurable values may produce *verboten goals*: goals that are known (sometimes tacitly) and shared, and yet for which explicit, consensual collective public support is lacking, typically, because such support underlies an incommensurable goal or principle. Were these verboten goals to be spoken and discussed publicly, public turmoil would result—when the general public or members of the organization (depending on the context) are not prepared for such public dissent. It is this latter condition that gives rise to myths, which mask tensions between or among incommensurable values.

In the face of such conflicting values, we construct a myth which allows us to believe, however temporarily, that the conflict has been reconciled. The construction is not done explicitly, nor is it done necessarily with the intention to deceive or manipulate. Rather, it is a product of tacit knowledge, created tacitly and communicated tacitly. Our knowledge of the contradiction masked by the myth is tacitly known. The suspension of conflict works as long as the group maintains its belief in the myth. The contradiction, and the myth's role in temporarily resolving it, are only revealed explicitly when analytic focus on the myth yields up the competing values that underlie it. If the myth is publicly identified and labeled as such, the suspension may dissolve, the conflict may (re)appear, and the myth's power to mask the irreconcilable differences may be lost. But unless there is public support for public discussion of the contradictory values, a new myth is likely to be constructed that will, once again, suspend the conflict and maintain the verboten nature of the policy or organizational goal.

One way of holding irreconcilable contradictions in a tension is to provide a solution that "block[s] further inquiry" (Cohen 1969), deflecting continued attention away from the incompatible, yet equally valued principles. Cohen cites a Talmudic legend that wonderfully illustrates the point. The Biblical creation story opens in Hebrew with the word B'reshit—"In the beginning," the first letter of which, the bet, is written ב , looking much like a bracket. The Talmud asks, "Why was the world created with the letter bet?" and it answers: " 'Bet' is blocked on three sides and open only on one; therefore, one has no right to demand knowledge of what is above, what is below, what is before, only of what comes after, from the day on which the world is created" (Bialik and Rabinitsky 1939; remembering that Hebrew reads from right to left, before is to the right of the letter bet and after is to the left.) Myths similarly direct attention toward what can be known, away from continued analysis of that which is contradictory and puzzling. This is a likely explanation for why many of the plot-oriented ancient myths are origin-stories: they are designed to explain what we do not know and cannot know absolutely, to block further inquiry and redirect our attention, to enable us to temporarily suspend doubt especially in the face of contradictory information.[6]

This does not mean that policy or organizational myths are explicit explanations of puzzles. Typically, they do not explain anything in an explicit way. It is not only that we often know "more than we can tell" (Polanyi 1966, p. 4). We can also at times communicate what we know without telling it explicitly. Myths are one way in which we do this: they allow us to communicate knowledge about policy and organizational matters without making the knowledge explicit—thereby maintaining silences in public discourse.

This discussion suggests the epistemological properties of myths, as well as some of their cognitive, moral, and affective aspects. Myths provide a way of knowing about the world. They compel emotional as well as intellectual belief, they socialize and moralize, and they thereby prompt action. Myths validate and authorize not only belief, but also the customs, ceremonies, rituals, and rites that enact them; they create, alter, and are created by these enactments (Cuthbertson 1975, Patai 1972). Moreover, myths legitimate the social, political, and economic order as it is vested in existing institutions.

Since policy and organizational myths are believed in and are not subject to factual disproof, they are difficult to perceive. Myths are protected by their believers, because they have been created at points of tension or uneasiness to mask those very sensitivities. Since myths shut off further inquiry, they are difficult to discern and fathom. As they redirect attention, it is hard to see through or beyond them, adding further to public silences.

AGENCY GOALS IN THE FOUNDING DECADE

We begin our story this time by recapitulating the explicit initial goal history of the ICCC, in order to illustrate the verboten and tacit nature of its policy and agency goals and myths.

1969–1970: Recall that the agency's formal Hebrew name, the "Israel Corporation of Centers of Culture and Sports—for Youth and Adults," reflected two of its original goals: (1) to provide public, non-partisan facilities to support recreational activities for residents of the development towns where Centers were located; (2) to provide programs for both youth and adults under the same roof. This concept of providing recreational and cultural activities to people of all ages drew on the then-current idea of the "constructive" use of "leisure" time. This goal became conflated with a second set of emerging issues: the desire to stem out-migration from the development towns and overcrowding of the metropolitan centers. In thinking about these issues, agency planning committee members thought of the Centers as fulfilling educational goals, social change goals, and social service improvement goals.

1970–1973: Increased public awareness of societal problems, specifically the lack of "absorption" of Eastern Jews into the social, educational, political, and other areas of Israeli life, added to the early issues. Part of the new awareness reflected Western Jews' perceptions of "difference" between themselves and Eastern Jews and their construction of "S'faradi" identity. Some saw in these perceptions discrimination on the basis of skin color. Others saw the difference as inherent in the behavior of people who came from less developed countries, who were not accustomed to indoor plumbing or to sharing common spaces in apartment buildings, and whose other lifestyle expressions ranged from greater numbers of children per family to different accents, cuisine, and ways of dress. In this telling of the ICCC story, we encounter the notion of ethnicity within Israel head on.

The ICCC added to its goals a fulfillment of certain parts of the Katz Commission report that called for changes in existing patterns of formal and nonformal education, recreational facilities, and other social services. The goals of integrating populations, narrowing the gap, and combatting juvenile delinquency and drug use were added to the earlier agency goal of providing leisure time facilities and programs. The implication of these new goals was that in their achievement—by creating Center buildings and programs that development town and city neighborhood residents could physically enter and partake of—the ICCC would integrate these residents into Israeli society and narrow the social gap between Eastern and Western Jews, if not eliminate it altogether.

1973–77: In filling a variety of home-front needs during the war and its aftermath, the Centers established themselves as multiservice Centers. The executive director now called the Community Center "the integrator of welfare services" at the local level. To their existing programs the Centers added day-care, elder-care, delinquency programs, "laundry clubs" (offering adult education and child care while making washers and dryers available), toy libraries (combining parenting classes with child care and recreation)—all of them programs that crossed ministerial and departmental lines, requiring the coordination of effort to provide comprehensive services.

1977–1980: Project Renewal, initiated by Prime Minister Menahem Begin under his new government, added a new layer to the goals of the Community Centers, joining the other new goal of inculcating Jewish religious values among Jewish participants. When asked at the ICCC's national convention in January 1979 what the goals of the agency were, Zipori answered: "improving the quality of life—values, spirituality, attitudes, and so forth."

INCOMMENSURABLE VALUES, VERBOTEN GOALS, AND ORGANIZATIONAL AND POLICY MYTHS

In examining the ICCC's changing goals, we do not find myths in the form of fictional tales explaining organizational or other origins. We do, however, find several points where incommensurable values produced "verboten goals" that in turn gave rise to organizational and policy myths, as these goals could be neither fulfilled nor publicly discussed. These myths emerge from an analysis of organizational rituals. The organizational myths could be called "the myth of uniqueness," "the myth of rational goal-setting," and "the myth of flexibility." They are linked to a central policy myth.

The policy myth and the myth of organizational uniqueness

The ICCC was charged with solving major societal problems. Yet, several analyses, including major parts of the Katz Commission report, had indicated that these problems would be resolved through economic means—providing employment opportunities, tax incentives, credit options, larger housing, and a minimum guaranteed income—none of which were within the purview of the ICCC and its resources. One organizational myth arose out of this contradiction, in response to the central policy myth underlying the creation of the ICCC.

The ICCC undertaking was based on the policy myth that its actions could close the so-called "social gap." That the gap was only "social" in nature was itself a broader societal myth that diverted attention from its economic and ethnic character and its geographic basis in development towns and urban neighborhoods. The situation is not unlike the "other America" that Harrington (1963) identified in the United States. Like the poverty that he found which had been ignored, the "ethnicity" of the Israeli Jewish population is something which until recently has not been publicly and explicitly explored. It is in the connection between unspeakable ethnicity and agency practice that we find the policy myth, a myth that runs to the heart of national identity and purpose, as well as the first organizational myth.

The ICCC presented itself as a new and unique institution. The agency argued, for example, against purchasing professional supervision from other organizations on the basis of "the Community Center's unique message . . . which distinguishes it among other agencies. . . ." The bases given for this uniqueness claim included the agency's provision of services to all age groups; its nonpartisan nature; its foundation on principles of participatory planning; the voluntary, public nature of its boards; the multiservice nature of the Centers' programs; the Centers' multifunctional physical space.

In point of fact, community centers as a general type of institution were not new to Israel or to their clientele, nor were ICCC Centers unique with respect to these claims. Although the matnas was a new institution, there were a few "community centers" by other names around the country in 1969: the Jerusalem YM-YWHA, Bet Rothschild and others in Haifa, the kibbutz prototype (the *Bet Am*), and so forth. As they pointed out to Ya'el Pozner, Israelis who emigrated from Casablanca had had a community center there; there were centers in Jewish communities in Iran; similar entities existed in Poland, Romania, and elsewhere (Patai 1980). The Israeli predecessors included some that were nonpartisan, some whose facilities were multifunctional, and some whose programs included a variety of activity types for a wide age range. It is true that the ICCC was an innovation in the development towns and that the agency pioneered the ideas of participatory planning and public boards. However, these have always been only partial or marginal bases for the ICCC's claim to uniqueness.

Any agency would claim to be unique when faced with establishing itself in a field of existing agencies performing similar activities. The ICCC Centers needed their own unique name and identity to set them apart from others so it would be more difficult to eliminate them through budget cuts and absorb them into a competitor. But there were other factors that *were* unique to the ICCC, on which it could have based such a claim. The ICCC might have claimed uniqueness as the first and only publicly funded national institution to provide recreational facilities and programs to entire communities. Or it could have based a claim on its mission as the first government agency to implement an expressly social mandate. It did neither. Why should an agency lay a claim to uniqueness based on elements that were not unique, especially when other criteria were available?[7]

The other criteria entailed "verboten goals," and to invoke them would have involved making those goals subjects of public discourse. This phrase is related to Harold Garfinkel's notion of a "publicly unmentionable goal" (discussed by Edelman 1977, p. 39). But it is not only that such goals cannot be *mentioned* in public, which suggests an individual uttering something in conversation. Rather, the point is that they are not part of the explicit public agenda, they are neither speakable nor discussable, because there is no public consensus supporting them. That is what makes them verboten: there is a cultural prohibition against talking about them. Public discourse is silent on their subject, and the prohibition itself is culturally verboten: publicly neither speakable nor discussable. The emphasis is on collective and public, rather than private, practices. Indeed, verboten goals may be the subject of private conversations out of "public" hearing. In fact, it would not have been uncommon for an Ashkenazi to express in private the personal opinion that S'faradim should meld into the mainstream culture. What characterizes verboten goals is that their discussion is not part of the explicit public agenda.[8]

Explicit discussion of these goals and subjects would bring to light contradictions and conflict that would be more disruptive than what the society was prepared to handle at that time. Claiming uniqueness on the basis of implementing a unique, government-mandated social policy would have focused explicit attention on the nature of that policy. There was no consensus behind publicly declaring the Ashkenazi population and its values as the superior group to which all others must be educated. This would have required explicit attention to the notion of "ethnicity," which was studiously ignored through the first thirty years of the state's existence (Avruch 1987, Goldberg 1987). It also would have focused explicit attention on the meaning of the metaphor of immigrant "absorption"—absorbed into what?—and challenged the accepted notion that all immigrants would be blended into a single identity (much like the American melting pot concept). To say that the ICCC's goal was to erase the Levant from S'faradi peoples and imbue them with the values and behavioral repertoire of middle-class Ashkenazi culture would raise, explicitly, a set of issues which existed in the realm of private, not public, communication. Doing so would have brought onto the public agenda a volatile subject which the public was not yet ready to discuss, publicly and explicitly.[9]

On the other hand, to proclaim that a policy or program will "narrow the gap" is a goal which all strata of society can support: those at the lower end of the gap who wish to close it by assimilating, as well as those at the upper end who are guided by the metaphor that immigrants will be "absorbed" under the presumption that they will do the "absorbing." "Absorption" suggests both that the values, beliefs, and feelings of the absorbing group will not be changed, and that the result will be a single, homogeneous layer. Israel was founded on socialist principles opposed to social stratification. "Narrowing the gap" is a publicly discussable goal in this context.

The ICCC needed an organizational "myth of uniqueness" based on the not-unique to establish itself organizationally while drawing attention away from its social mandate. The uniqueness myth was necessary to stop further questioning as to the nature of the agency and whether this new institution could tackle society's verboten goal of "absorbing" S'faradim into Ashkenazim. In laying claims to uniqueness based on the not-unique, the ICCC anticipated charges that it was duplicating services. Meeting these charges head on diffused them, at the same time that it diverted attention from what could not be spoken of publicly. This was achieved through the policy myth of the all-doing agency implementing Herculean societal goals.

Both the policy myth and the organizational uniqueness myth took the form of myth discussed earlier. Neither appeared as a rhetorical argument or logical proposition. When elements of either were presented, they came in narrative form: e.g., "the ICCC is a unique agency." In their specific configurations, they are not universal myths, but are particular to a time and place. Both were firmly believed: agency members were committed to the idea that they and the ICCC would solve the social problems surrounding them, as much as they believed in the Community Center's uniqueness.

The myth of rational goal-setting

It might appear from the review of explicit agency goals that the ICCC was changing goals so rapidly that it would be difficult to keep track of them, or that the agency had no goals at all and grabbed whatever new idea came along. Neither situation appears to be the case, looking at agency publications, correspondence, and records of meetings and in talking with personnel. Extensive attention was devoted constantly, in in-service training sessions, individual supervision, agency publications, quarterly and annual meetings, and so forth, to articulating the goals of the ICCC and translating them into programs and objectives.

But something puzzling does emerge from this study. As noted in Chapter 3, at the end of 1979, the ICCC's head of research and planning wrote that the agency's goals and operating principles were only then beginning the process of "crystallization." Does this mean that there was no clear understanding prior to 1980 of what the agency's goals were? Yet the ICCC behaved during this time very much as though it had clearly understood goals: it hired staff, built buildings, raised funds, created and carried out programs, established an identity and an image.

Moreover, every year for at least its first period of operations, at the annual meeting, with all Center directors and some other staff in attendance, the executive director would ask: "What are our goals and objectives?" From an instrumental perspective, given the full attention devoted to that question in other settings, one might wonder why it was necessary to ask the question at all, let alone repetitively, and why in a public forum such as the annual meeting.

Furthermore, in taking on the coordination of Project Renewal, the ICCC was venturing further beyond its explicit mandate to provide social, educational, cultural, and recreational facilities and programs to development town residents. Housing or neighborhood redevelopment had never been included before. What was there about the nature of policy or organizational goals that allowed the ICCC to accede to this request and to implement Project Renewal in those sites where Community Centers were already in operation without arousing the criticism of evaluators or the public? Not only did it not arouse criticism, the ICCC became a desirable entity demanded by neighborhood residents, as we have seen.

These actions embody the organizational "myth of rational goal-setting." The succession of goals moved from the early ideas of providing "someplace to go" in development towns and building nonpartisan facilities for recreational activities for achieving social integration, filling increased leisure time, and retarding the exodus from development towns; to the middle group of narrowing the social gap, advancing weak communities, reducing ethnic tensions, combatting juvenile delinquency and drug use; to the later goals of providing multiservice Centers and comprehensive coordination of social services; ending with providing quality of life. But this is not the story of an agency that has achieved its goals and needs to replace them or else cease to exist (Sills 1961). The social gap was no narrower in 1980 than it had been in 1970, to judge from reports on income levels, employment, social status, and the image and reputations of the development towns. Ethnic tensions and crowded housing conditions were as severe in 1991 as they were in the 1970s—witness the residents of urban neighborhoods staging tent city demonstrations in the capital after losing their apartments to new Russian immigrants.[10]

An explanation may lie in the difficulties of implementing such diffuse goals as achieving social integration, advancing weak communities, narrowing social gaps, and providing quality of life, while also demonstrating successful implementation of these goals. Sustaining an organization over a lengthy period when one cannot point to progress in attaining its goals can be difficult. It is not only personnel who need to be exhorted to continue in the name of the goals; skeptical publics also need reassurance (Edelman 1964). In focusing attention on the ritual of setting goals, deriving objectives from them and a plan of operations from the objectives, attention is deflected from the goals themselves and their questionable attainment to the process of setting goals rationally.

The annual attention to the need to determine goals and to the mechanics and processes of goal-setting had the quality of a ritual in the regularity of its repetition. The ritual of asking "What are our goals?" underscored the belief that agency activities are goal-oriented. As the Polaris missile system's managers projected the image of success through the use of formal Management Information Systems tools such as PERT (Sapolsky 1972), so the ICCC created the aura of success by appearing to pursue goals rationally. The ritual of identifying what their goals are and discussing them at the annual meeting was communicating to members and stakeholders that the organization is a modern, rational organization and that it is doing its work properly, even if it is difficult to demonstrate accomplishment of those goals. The ritual enacts the myth of rational goal-setting.

Not only does the appearance of rational, goal-oriented behavior grant the agency legitimacy and public support; it also creates a buffer between the goal-setting activity and the actual technical operations of the Community Centers, which serves to put the latter beyond the public's inspection. As long as the public sees the agency acting to set and pursue goals, as it does in the annual ritual, the public believes that agency programs are goal-oriented.[11] As Manning (1977) wrote:

> Complex, industrialized societies have committed themselves to a public posture of rationality, and the rational myth legitimates organizations and institutions within this society. It is not surprising that organizations of central symbolic importance should call upon the legitimating powers of the myth of rationality to justify both their existence and actions.[12]

The myth is narrative in form: it is enacted as a matter of fact, without argument. It is a social construction—not the intentional creation of an individual but the evolving property of the group. Its specific expression—in the form of annual discussions—is particular to this organization, although the myth is commonly found in other organizations with similarly broad goals.[13] The discussions are believed—they are taken by organizational members to be bona fide deliberations about the goals of the organization. And the myth reconciles temporarily the tension between two incommensurables: the value of maintaining organizational existence, which requires (among other things) that the agency demonstrate success in achieving its goals; and the value of the stated goals themselves, which cannot be demonstrably achieved by this agency with its limited resources, through no fault of its own commission. By directing attention to the processes of goal-setting, the myth diverts attention from the conflict between members' desires to achieve explicit agency goals and the impossibility of their doing so.

The myth of organizational flexibility

Together with the "myth of rational goal-setting," the "myth of organizational flexibility" worked to deflect attention from the unattainability of the agency's social goals. Both myths allowed the agency to continue on in face of this difficulty.

Staff were excited at discovering a new organizational goal—of finding that the provision of leisure time activities could also address the new problem of out-migration or the newer problem of social integration. The excitement of these discoveries deflected attention from the relative ineffectiveness of Center programs in solving these massive social problems. When questioned why they asked about goals every year, organizational members answered that continual examination of agency goals was a positive undertaking. They said:

> It keeps us from bureaucratizing or stagnating.
>
> It's a sort of zero-based planning where we continually reexamine our premises.
>
> After all, if the Community Center is a tool for social change, and society is constantly changing, then we should continuously raise the question of what are our goals.

Such flexibility—a willingness to change in light of a new situation—also entails an ambiguity. Centers will always be adding new programs. The "myth of flexibility" makes traditional forms of evaluation impossible, since evaluative criteria are always changing. This myth is also presented as a matter of fact (e.g., our goals change because society changes), rather than as a rhetorical argument. It is a construction made by agency members as a group, and it is believed. The belief is enacted in the same ritual of goal-setting: recurring attention to the mechanics of goal-setting underscores the "reality" of the myth of flexibility. That is, the continuous discussion of goals raises the possibility that goals will indeed be changed. In this way agency members enact over and over the "fact" that the agency's goals are adaptable to society's changing needs. The myth deflects attention from the conflict between the need to show goal attainment and the difficulty of evaluating performance against constantly changing criteria.

SILENCES IN PUBLIC DISCOURSE

Policy and organizational myths, then, are the nonfictional, socially constructed beliefs of a group, which, at least temporarily, divert attention from incommensurable values that they (are believed to) reconcile, temporarily, in practice if not in concept. Such myths are constructed tacitly: they embody a tacit knowledge of the incommensurable values, and this knowledge is communicated and shared tacitly through regular enactment of the rituals and interaction with other organizational artifacts and daily activities that support the myths.

"Myth" is widely used today in a pejorative sense, implying fictitiousness, purposeful deception, lie, false belief. This attitude may derive from the belief in rational scientism developed by the positivists and logical positivists of the nineteenth and early twentieth centuries. Their legacy may also have contributed to the assumption prevalent in traditional anthropology that myth-making is an activity belonging to prescientific or primitive peoples, a stage that civilized people outgrow. Popular understanding of myths as hero-stories about gods and how the world came to be compounds this view. From a modern vantage point, belief in such tales is a false belief, and their perpetration can only be for purposes of intentional deception. Myth is seen as belonging to the realm of religion or of fairy tale, both of which have been replaced in modern times by science, both physical and social. Hence, many believe that myths do not—or should not—exist for us today.[14]

But policy and organizational myths are very much part of contemporary life with their inherent contradictions and incommensurable values. They allow us to maintain public silences about those contradictions. To label something as "myth" is to assume the stance of critic, the nonbeliever for whom the myth no longer resolves contradictory principles. Only when the reality of Haitian boat people tossed about on the Atlantic blatantly contradicted the belief in the United States as a haven for refugees did the *Boston Globe* (11/1/1981) chide the public for its "Emma Lazarus myth." When a myth is labeled as such, the contradictions that had been contained and communicated tacitly are made explicit, and the myth ceases to divert attention from them. At that point, public silence is replaced, however briefly, by public discourse or by the construction of a new a myth that diverts attention and discussion once more. Throughout the 1980s in the United States, facing growing numbers of immigrants, both legal and illegal, and a stumbling economy, many editorial cartoonists rewrote Emma Lazarus's poem at the base of the Statue of Liberty—suggesting at the time that we were becoming more explicit in our public discourse on the limits of our national identity as a haven for refugees. That suggestion has since materialized in the early 1990s, as more and more efforts to limit and control immigration are coming onto the public and legislative agendas. How the tension between incommensurable views of immigration will be resolved—whether we will revise our national identity or construct a new myth to suspend the incommensurables again, however temporarily—remains to be seen.

Lasswell (1952) postulated that an existing political myth is more likely to be supported if its adherents are indulged rather than deprived. That is, a myth's believers will more probably begin to challenge it if their security (in the form of power, wealth, respect, or other) is threatened; if they see that a different myth brings greater value to its adherents; if believers in a contending myth are rewarded. We see this in the case of the ICCC. The challenge to the policy myth that immigrants were being absorbed came from the S'faradim, residents of development towns and urban neighborhoods, who were deprived—of status, income, adequate housing, education, etc.—relative to others. What was not challenged then or subsequently was the policy myth that the ICCC could mitigate this deprivation. The demonstrations in the 1980s calling on the government to erect Community Centers in "deprived" neighborhoods illustrate the extent to which having a Community Center itself became a symbol of recognition and reassurance.

Explicit public attention to Jewish ethnicity began to grow in the early 1980s. It was shunted aside by the *intifada*, the Palestinian uprising in Gaza and the West Bank. But immigration from the former Soviet Union and Ethiopia brought more newcomers in 1990 than any year since 1951. One result appears to be the return of the subject of ethnicity and the status and treatment of Westerner versus Easterner to the forefront of public discourse. The analysis presented here suggests that the S'faradim of the neighborhoods and development towns can be expected once again to challenge myths masking verboten goals. We can only wait to see whether this time the myth of the ICCC as the answer to social integration will be dissipated, or not.

This discussion raises further questions about evaluating policy implementation in light of policy intent (Palumbo and Calista 1990). Assuming "intent to implement as written" becomes problematic when what is written constitutes publicly speakable goals, whereas agencies may also be implementing verboten goals. Blaming implementation problems on ambiguous language posits the norm that policy ends should be stated explicitly. Yet verboten goals are no less real because they cannot be stated explicitly. Governments must, at times, accommodate conflicting values. Adapting Arnold's (1935, p. 131) comment on the courts and criminal trials, we may say that the legislation and implementation of public policies "bring into sharp relief various deep-seated popular moral ideals [of justice, while appearing] as an efficient means of enforcement and working order." And further (p. 49):

> An official admission by [an] . . . institution that it was moving in all directions at once in order to satisfy the conflicting emotional values of the people which it served would be unthinkable. . . . The success of the law as a unifying force depends on making emotionally significant the idea of a government . . . which is rational and scientific.

So it is with public agencies implementing verboten goals.

If value conflict in public policy relates to matters of group status or status-based power in a society based on egalitarian principles, then we might expect some of the policy's goals to be verboten. In those cases, policy language is more likely to be ambiguous or vague, and we are more likely to find policy or organizational myths which deflect attention from that which is publicly undiscussable. The issue here is not so much explicit *versus* ambiguous language as it is policy wording that allows for multiple interpretations. Explicitly worded policy may still mask goals whose explicit public discussion is verboten. And verboten goals may still be known and understood by policy legislators and stakeholders. Such understanding is made through tacit communication by way of policy and agency symbols.

In this view, implementation success or failure may ride on the construction of meaningful, believable myths or other symbols and their associated ambiguities, rather than on the direct pursuit and achievement of explicit policy goals. This is the moral of the ICCC case, the Polaris missile case (Sapolsky 1972), the Farm Bill (Moseley 1990), the Japan External Trade Organization (Nakamura 1990), and the Kansas Department of Health and Environment's administrative reorganization (Maynard-Moody and Stull 1987). It is likely that it is operative in other cases as well.

This analysis supports the argument that the policy process is not exclusively about instrumental behaviors. Another very real part of it is its expressiveness, a public play about the allocation and validation of symbols of status as much as the reallocation of tangible resources subject to administrative controls. Arnold (1935, p. 13) continued: "If the results are more important than the moral lessons which are to be taught by the process—we move the settlement of the dispute into a less symbolic atmosphere." This analysis of the ICCC case suggests that the arenas of policy legislation and implementation are also symbolic settings in which public expressions of identity (a form of moral lesson, perhaps) are as important as the instrumental results, where the tension of incommensurable values may require silences in explicit public discourse about policy issues, and where such silences are supported by policy myths as well as by the organizational myths of their implementing agencies.

NOTES

1. Basil Bernstein (1977), for example, defines ritual as "a relatively rigid pattern of acts, specific to a situation, which construct a framework of meaning over and beyond the specific situational meanings" (p. 54). On the subject of myths, ceremonies, rituals, play, and so forth in organizational and governmental life, see also Floden and Weiner (1978), D. Handelman (1976), Harris and Sutton (1986), Meyer and Rowan (1983), Robertson (1980), Trice and Beyer (1993, pp. 107–27), Westerlund and Sjostrand (1979). There has been considerable attention given to elections and television as contexts for rituals and ceremonies. See, e.g., Edelman (1988) and Nimmo and Combs (1980). Seeing "play" in organizational life as one way in which tacitly known meanings are communicated has led to a reexamination of the roles of humor, jokes, gossip, and so forth (see D. Handelman, 1976, e.g.), as well as to a critical assessment of the absence of emotion and sexuality in academic studies of worklife and to attempts to suppress them in practice (see, e.g., Hearn et al. 1990).

2. See, e.g., White (1986) and Martin (1990). Of all the literature on myths in organizations, the work of Ingersoll and Adams (1992) comes closest to capturing the sense of myth and tacit knowledge that I present here, in their treatment of the managerial "meta-myth" that, they argue, underlies and informs much organizational action today. They use "meta-myth" to denote tacit knowledge. The difference between their approach and mine is not only definitional: theirs is more literary, mine more informed by anthropological understandings. There is nothing "mythic," as that would be understood by anthropologists or scholars of religion, in their treatment of the rational thought patterns that pervade much of contemporary life. From the perspective outlined here, that pattern of explanatory activity would be mythic if it diverted attention from incommensurable values in administrative practice—something Ingersoll and Adams might indeed have found, although they did not make this explicit.

3. See Thompson (1955) and Honko (1972) for other classifications of myth types.

4. Joseph Campbell maintained in several publications (e.g., 1972, 1979) and on the public television series with Bill Moyers that myths are universal. He was referring to myths of origin and other story-type myths and not to the policy and organizational myths under discussion here. Yet even with respect to tribal origin myths, there is debate about his conclusions (see, e.g., Doniger 1992). My argument that myths are social constructions parallels part of Nimmo and Combs's (1980) definition of myths.

5. See, e.g., Berger and Luckmann's (1966, Part II) explanation for how societal rules come into being.

6. Others have also seen myths as ways of temporarily resolving conflicting values. Robertson (1980, p. 346) wrote: "Myths are the mechanism by which people believe contradictory things simultaneously." Westerlund and Sjostrand (1979, p. 31) noted that myths "make for peace and quiet so

that they [people] can work." Cuthbertson (1975, p. 158): Myths "function to bridge tensions. . . ." Arnold (1937, pp. 356 ff) wrote that institutional creeds, which he also called myths, express contradictory ideals, allowing the contradictions to coexist.

7. Martin et al. (1983) call this claim to uniqueness based on the not unique "the uniqueness paradox." Interestingly, they found that such claims are widespread among organizations. The present analysis differs from their study in examining the societal context of agency myth-making, linking one organization's uniqueness myth to the myth of the policy it was created to implement.

8. Bar-On (1989) describes the psychological effects of such collective unspeakability in his analysis of children of Nazis. He notes the "societal dimensions" of the postwar "atmosphere of collective silence" in Germany that made his interviewees' dilemmas "unmentionable issues" (pp. 328–29). Interestingly, he also links the matter of collective silence to the question of establishing a national identity, in this case, the "heated disagreement in Germany about what belongs in the collective memory" (p. 328).

9. See also Westerlund and Sjostrand's (1979, p. 40) "taboo aims" which are like verboten goals. Ingersoll and Adams (1986) also talk about myths as tacit, "undiscussed and, perhaps, undiscussable" (p. 365).

Edelman (1977, p. 39) claims that we accomplish such goals by focusing on popular ones. As an example, he presents vagrancy laws as society's control mechanism for people made poor and unemployed by a disintegrating economic system, who might violate the law. As "vagrants" they are labeled "criminals" and thereby controlled under the general rubric of "crime control," a publicly discussable goal. This view, says Edelman, is more comfortable for people to live with than to face the complex realities of the economic system. He is, in other words, suggesting that we deal with the incommensurability of two values by creating a way of deflecting attention from them, which is the process I have discussed as myth-making. Now that "vagrants" have been relabeled "homeless," we have forced ourselves to "see" the economic system—but in many places we have passed laws making homelessness a crime, thereby continuing our "blindness" and collective public silence by means of a different conceptual framework, metaphor, and myth.

10. The *Jerusalem Post* reported on these demonstrations from August 1990 through June 1991.

11. Meyer et al. (1977) noted a similar process with respect to public schools, which must appear to carry out societally mandated "rules" in order to garner public support and legitimacy. The technical aspects of schooling— curriculum and teaching—are less important in shaping the public's belief. (Their professionalization has also removed them from the public's purview.) As a result, the organizational structures of schools are decoupled from the technology of schooling.

12. In acting in accordance with societal expectations for a modern, rational organization, the ICCC was following what Ingersoll and Adams (1992) have called the rational, managerial "meta-myth." But I am suggesting here that the agency was also doing more than that. Their actions were

intended not only to conform with accepted practices, but also to persuade others that they were doing so. Like the persuasive actions of Polaris missile designers noted by Sapolsky (1972), these actions had another layer not noted by Ingersoll and Adams in their analysis.

13. Ingersoll and Adams (1986, 1992) argue that the "rational technical myth system" characterizes American culture in general. See also Westerlund and Sjostrand (1979, pp. 36–42) on the myth of rational goals.

14. Indeed, Ingersoll and Adams's (1986) search of the management literature for articles using "myth" in the title found that of 85 such, only 6 percent suggested myth as a serious analytic tool.

8

Reading Public Policy "Texts" as Identity Stories: The ICCC and Israeli Ethnicity

What might it mean to say that the ICCC had successfully implemented its policy mandate? That is the question most traditional implementation studies would begin with. They would then examine the piece of legislature by which the agency was created (concluding, no doubt, that goals were vague, policy language was ambiguous, and the agency could not have succeeded under circumstances such as these, although other indicators show that, in many residents' and others' eyes, the ICCC and its *matnassim* were a great success). In purely administrative or organizational terms, absent the policy context, the question would be: Has this organization achieved its goals? But such questions themselves come out of a particular way of understanding human action. They are based on the assumption that there is or should be an explicitly stated mandate or set of goals and that there is only that mandate, and none other, that is operative. With the exception of recent policy evaluation literature, "a success at what, in whose eyes?" has less often been asked.[1] The evaluative standpoint of legislative and/or executive intent has been implied, unspoken, and assumed.

Positivist-based theories and analyses, especially those characteristic of administrative and organizational studies with their executive and managerial bent, also assume and thereby underscore this certainty with respect to the univocal meaning of policy and agency actions. Interpretive analysis, by contrast, is equally fierce in its certainty that multifold and even incommensurable meaning is far more characteristic of human endeavor than such univocality. Yet it is not just that policy and agency language, objects, and acts become texts for (re)interpretation by policy and agency actors in a general sense. They may also serve as texts of a particular sort: texts in which the values, beliefs, and/or feelings of their society or polity context are reflected. This may be particularly true of implementation "texts," since implementing agencies, by virtue of their role in the schema of public policymaking, are caught up in the playing out of contending visions of the ideal polity. Policy issues may in this light be seen as contests between two or more visions of the desired, ideal identity of a polis.

Questions of identity are often answered by pointing to what we are not. Since shared meanings of cultural artifacts reinforce distinctions between "us" and "them," policy contests viewed interpretively may be seen as vehicles for the expression of group identity as well as individual identity as manifested in and through group membership (as in "I belong to and find my identity through *this* group which supports this policy, not *that* one"). Membership in a group entails not only a statement of "who I am" but also the simultaneous expression of "who I am not," by juxtaposition with and opposition to the competing group(s). Expressions of those visions at times come down to lifestyle issues. For example, what we call collectively in the United States "the American dream" is often an expression of the tone and substance of national identity. Debates over homeownership carried out in the context of housing policies play out ideas central to American national identity.[2] Luker (1984) suggests that this sort of expression of identity is being played out in U.S. pro- and anti-abortion debates, each position giving its members an opportunity to act out their individual identities through an affiliation with others who have chosen the same lifestyle (of motherhood-housewife or career primacy, in her analysis), thereby making public statements about their values, beliefs, and feelings. The battle, then, is not only about abortion.

The public policy arena becomes, in such cases, a forum for public acknowledgment and validation of one position over opposing others. With the final legislation of a policy, the battle has seemingly been won. But it is not final: the contest is carried into implementation in the multiple, tacitly known meanings that flourished in the issue culture during policy design and live on in policy and agency artifacts during implementation, affecting agency staff and other readers' interpretations, and potentially encumbering—or at times, facilitating—the implementation process. In this way the policymaking and implementation of Prohibition and Repeal, for example, may be seen as a battle for public validation, dominance, status, and hence, identity of two social groups within the American population (Gusfield 1963).[3]

READING ETHNICITY IN THE ICCC CASE

In the ICCC case successful implementation depended in part on convincing policy audiences, including funding sources, that the agency's identity and image, as expressed symbolically through its artifacts, matched the image of their expectations. That the ICCC did so successfully may be seen, among other actions, in the public demonstrations calling for *matnassim* and in the Histadrut's imitation of them in its own plans for a community center network. On the other hand, the ICCC did not "narrow the [social] gap," and yet implementation was not judged to have failed.[4] The absence of complaints from either policy "targets" or other concerned publics about the ICCC's failure to achieve its explicitly stated mandate seems to require explanation.

A theory that sees only instrumental action cannot readily account for this. It is difficult to establish a single genesis, a single purpose, or a single intent for the ICCC enterprise. The case traces a cross-fertilization of people and ideas, coming together under the accomplished guidance of Minister Zalman Aranne in legislative actions and Executive Director Hayim Zipori in bureaucratic-administrative ones. The idea for the Community Center came from many people: from Ralph Goldman and his visitors, from two of Aranne's assistants, from the field research conducted by Zipori and Ya'el Pozner. The sources were heavily American: Goldman and JDC-Israel brought professional experiences in U.S. community centers; Aranne's two assistants drew on their educational experiences in the United States; and the supermarket metaphor that guided much of agency development was largely an American concept. Agency goals developed and shifted and became more multilayered as new social problems and agendas emerged. Aranne was said to have seen in the Centers "one of the tools with which cultural activities for all ages could be provided" (Segev 1973, p. 3); JDC-Israel saw them "as major tools of social integration" (file); the first national coordinator of Camping Programs saw them as providing camping as "an integral part of the activities of the Community Center," accepted as such "in the

Western world" (ICCC Annual Report 1976–77, p. 44); and so forth. And so we see the construction of an idea over time, drawing on and intertwining preexisting notions and new ones: the public's growing awareness of the development towns and their residents and associated social problems, reflected in Aranne's concern and attendant actions; residents' sense of having "no place to go"; American experiences of immigrant-oriented settlement houses and community centers; Israeli city and kibbutz models of Ys and social clubs based on eastern European experiences.

Despite its failure to implement a major part of its explicit mandate and internal debates concerning the nature of its goals, the ICCC established itself as a desirable entity. This suggests that it did succeed in implementing something. To explain this we need to see that what the agency achieved could not be measured in terms of explicitly stated mandates and goals. We also need to drop the assumption that implementation processes enact legislative language alone. Administrative activities may indeed begin with the passage of a bill, but the substance of legislation often has a prior history in legislative debates and societal dispositions, and these carry over into the administrative phase. The transmission of this knowledge is often done symbolically through policy language or agency artifacts that embody those prior concepts, and it is these prior concepts that may constitute (part of) what is being implemented. The ICCC successfully implemented a mandate that was tacitly known and communicated through various symbolic representations that were read in various ways. Shared, though tacit, knowledge of the value, belief, and feeling abstractions that were embodied in policy and agency artifacts guided agency actions as well as many interpretations of those actions. Some of these readings coincided with intended legislative and agency meanings, or were complementary to them; others were not.

How might we explain public acclaim for the ICCC, given that the gap was no narrower after many years of operation? What was being implemented through the creation of the ICCC and its programs were tacitly known parts of the enabling policy which reflected earlier and ongoing debates about Israeli identity. The agency's external image and internal identity were to help lower-class, Eastern-origin, development town and urban neighborhood residents—the "targets" of the policy by which the agency was legislated—attain a "higher level of aspirations" (in the words of one agency founder) by seeing examples of this status (the Center and its programs) and by being socialized to it by entering into the building and participating in its programs. In order to implement this mandate, agency staff and potential clients had to be convinced of the following logic:

(1) That clients should desire a higher level of aspirations—that is, a Western lifestyle.

(2) That Community Center buildings and ballet and other programs were symbols of such a level and lifestyle.

(3) That clients' physical presence inside the Community Center building and participation in classes and concerts would acquire for them the desired status associated with this level and lifestyle.

By engaging or interacting with the symbol, clients see themselves and are seen as possessing what the symbol means.[5]

It could be argued that it was inappropriate to expect one agency to narrow a gap that had deep historic, ethnic, and economic roots; or that providing recreational activities locally would not integrate the two populations. Since the gap was expressed in disparities of educational attainment, housing density, job structure, income levels, etc., how would ballet classes and traveling string quartets narrow it? The logic works as an analogy: architectural design and decor, ballet and Beethoven stand in for Western, middle-class values and status; presence and participation stand in for the acquisition of those values and status or for being Western. Readers of these analogies are not only legislators, implementors, and (potential) clients. Readers also include members of the general public who are assuaged through the enactment of these analogies that their accepted values and way of life are valued and desired by others. They are reassured that their cultural beliefs, feelings, and practices will be upheld and maintained. This is communicated through both the substantive symbolism of ballet and the enacted symbolism of others entering Center buildings. Clients are also reassured through the enacted symbolism of government's responding to Black Panther and other demonstrations, that both the action and the substance of their claims on government are legitimate, that their expectations are justified, and that their aspirations may some day be achieved.

These ideas were transmitted, tacitly, in public discussions within a society of which legislators, the ICCC's founders and board of directors, and its clients and other relevant publics were a part, as the ICCC established and communicated its image and identity. The disjunction between what the ICCC accomplished and its explicit mandate, rather than indicating an unhealthy or failing organization, points to expressive meanings encompassing instrumental action which often require tacit, rather than explicit, communication and interpretation. This does not necessarily reflect an intent to deceive or a conspiracy of silence. Human knowledge includes a tacit dimension. These processes depend on interpretation—by agency executives and staff, by legislative and executive governmental bodies, by relevant publics, by policy "targets" who are potential clients and who may choose whether or not to attend center programs; and, in addition to these and other actors, by policy analysts, evaluators, and researchers.

Agency acts included all sorts of symbols of centralized power: a comprehensive policy; coordination of services; a budget inflexible to local innovation; "universal" class issues overtaking particularistic leisure concerns. All these signaled that individual and local concerns were being overridden in favor of national concerns (see Schon 1971, pp. 146–47), whereas explicit policy and agency statements indicated that the ICCC was designed to improve the well-being of individuals and communities. This tension was manifested in the disagreements between community organizers and Center directors with their respective local and central concerns, and to some extent within directors themselves, located as they were at the nexus of those two incommensurable drives.

The coexisting and sometimes contradictory notions about Community Centers survived through policy design and legislative action into implementation design and enactment—the design of a new agency with all its administrative apparatus. Mixed in with these substantive ideas was the intent to involve local residents in planning the Centers—a kind of self-determination (replaying, perhaps, the self-determination of the state's originating socialist-Zionist ideology). Mapped onto that was a contradictory paternalism conceptually inherent in bringing state budgets and administrative apparatus to plan and execute national policy ("We had, therefore, to teach the community members . . ."—Ralph Goldman, quoted in Lavi 1979). Largely a benign paternalism in its intent, it nevertheless guided agency planning without leaving room conceptually to consider that those same strongly held values, beliefs, and feelings that were meaningful to policy and agency designers and administrators might not be equally meaningful to residents (as potential and then actual clients) or might carry for them some other meaning entirely.

ICCC programs addressed the expressive dimensions of policy: feelings about living in development towns, beliefs in the possibility of social advancement, values placed on things Western (not only jeans and kitchen appliances but Western dance and music). The ICCC explicitly and intentionally juxtaposed "Community Center culture" against "cafe culture" (what Israelis also called Eastern or Oriental or Levantine culture), expecting that the implications of the contrast would be clear: that it would underscore a shared, though tacit knowledge that one lifestyle was more desirable, thereby convincing Easterners to abandon theirs for the Western one symbolized by Community Center artifacts. This analysis links agency action to its societal context: the subject of ethnicity in Jewish Israel, the questions of social status that ethnicity entails, and the role of a social agency that is charged explicitly or tacitly with an ethnicity-related agenda.

In Israel's case, and specifically in the case of the ICCC, ethnicity matters are directly related to immigrant policy. The language used in Israel to talk about this subject is "absorption" (*klitah*, in Hebrew): the Ministry of Immigrant Absorption, immigrant housing in "absorption centers," and so on. But what precisely does it mean to "absorb" immigrants? The English word expresses the connotation of the Hebrew, "to take in": immigrants will be "taken in" to a preexisting sociocultural identity, they will be "absorbed" into a "sponge" of given shape and character. Water absorbed by a sponge cannot be differentiated from the sponge; the sponge retains its shape. Similarly, new immigrants will be merged into the preexisting sociocultural, undifferentiated mass. It is related to the American notion of a melting pot into which all varieties are thrown, out of which emerges a consolidated whole. Although unspoken in Israeli public discourse, it is understood that the "sponge" is Western. Its lifestyle would absorb all others without leaving drops. So, for example, it has not been uncommon to hear Israelis say that in another generation or two, all population problems will disappear because the rate of "intermarriage"—between Easterners and Westerners—is increasing, the unspoken assumption being that Ashkenazi culture would dominate in the intermarried household. This is as close as public discourse has usually come to expressing explicitly that which is shared knowledge known tacitly: that the Eastern partner's culture will disappear into the Westerner's.[6]

One way of understanding the ICCC Community Centers is to see them as a means of inculcating those at the margin into Israel's civil religion (Leibman and Don-Yehiya 1983, Bellah 1980). It was explicit and clear that policy "targets" were on the margin geographically. They were residents of rural area development towns and of city neighborhoods, in both cases on the geographic periphery at a physical distance from the urban and kibbutz sociocultural centers. As noted in Chapter 3, being a development town resident connoted a social class as well as an economic class: being unemployed, on welfare, illiterate in Hebrew, uneducated beyond a few years of grammar school, having evaded or been denied army service (because of lack of education or drug use), being a "family with many children" (a classification for National Income Support consisting of having four or more children—the ceiling was lowered from five to four in the mid-1970s). High school, paramilitary youth movements, and army service were central institutions for acculturating the next generation into the civil religion, and development town residents were largely absent from all three. The ethnic component of development town identity—ethnic stigmas attached to Jews of non-European heritage—added another layer to the negative development town image. Although city neighborhood residents might have more easily escaped the geographic marginalization, they were of the same Eastern ethnic background. Both groups were excluded from other elements of the state's civil religion by virtue of their ethnicity.

The ICCC policy and program had meaning beyond the social, cultural, and recreational activities that it was established to provide, meaning that was not spelled out because the subject of ethnicity itself was not acknowledged. The ICCC was implementing an ethnic policy that was known tacitly. In this sense, the policy was a statement about civil religion, about national identity and values, and the ICCC could be seen as an acculturating institution of this civil religion. Conflicting views of the civil religion did not arise until Menahem Begin and his party moved out of the opposition in 1977, at which time urban, petit bourgeois activity acquired greater status, the kibbutz movement began to lose increasing numbers of members and entered

major economic difficulties, and observant Judaism of all varieties—
from ultra-observant to Reform and Conservative Judaism, heretofore
nonexistent in Israel—took a larger place in national values and identity. Religious observance and the place of the Community Centers
in fostering religious values became contested issues in the ICCC
because of its role in expressing and communicating national identity.

Goldberg (1987), analyzing the changing meanings of ethnicity
in anthropological discourse in general, as well as in Israel, makes a
point that underscores the analysis presented here. In reviewing social
science research on Israeli ethnicity in the 1950s, he notes that what is
striking is its relative absence from this literature as a term, "ethnicity"
being referred to by other variable names (e.g., "country of origin,"
"cultural background"). "The trend," he writes, "was to play down
the importance of ethnic differences, . . . focus . . . on institution-
building . . . and the process of absorbing immigrants into the existing, and developing, social structure . . ." (p. 42). The term "ethnic"
implied problematic situations and, hence, was avoided.

When in the late 1960s ethnic discourse became more explicit
(with the discovery of the "social gap"), the term still retained its
problematic connotation. Writes Goldberg: "There was an *unexamined*
premise that ethnic influence in Israeli society was something that
had to be neutralized" (p. 43, emphasis added), a premise that he
noted continued into the 1980s. In discourse in the field of education,
this public silence was quite clear:

> . . . the euphemism, *te'unei tipuah* (those in need of care/nurtur-
> ing) [i.e., disadvantaged, in American parlance] . . . [entailed]
> *no explicit mention* of a specific ethnic group, nor of the general
> category, *edot ha-mizrah*—the Eastern (Oriental) Jewish commu-
> nities. However, it was *tacitly understood* that the education prob-
> lems referred to were those in the urban neighborhoods and
> development towns with a high percentage of children from
> Middle Eastern backgrounds. (Goldberg 1987, p. 43, emphasis
> added)

The disinclination to address explicitly the ethnic nature of the ICCC's
agenda in public discourse about its role, goals, mandate, programs,
and so forth is attributed to the general societal focus on institution

building. And yet it was tacit knowledge, known and shared at all levels of stakeholders and policy-relevant publics connected with the ICCC, much as it was in Goldberg's research context of social science and educational research, policies, and programs.

This silence in public discourse extended not only to academic and policy-relevant research, but also to policies themselves and to agencies implementing ethnic-related policies, such as the ICCC. Yet while academic and policy research proceeded to engage ethnicity more explicitly, even with a problem-oriented focus, for the ICCC (and, most likely, for other agencies as well) ethnicity remained a verboten area of public discourse. The ICCC represented an attempt to continue to build the state and its institutions, including its national identity, by removing ethnic impediments to the absorption of a major immigrant population into the dominant national identity, without being able to name the ethnic component of either that population or the absorbing identity or to make any of that effort part of public discourse.

Others argue that programs like the ICCC's are intended to distract local residents' attention from their real problems. Poverty, inadequate housing, unemployment, lack of job-related skills, poor education, and so forth are national problems which the Community Centers have not been given the tools to solve.[7] One veteran Center director called "the entire Community Center undertaking shamanism or witch-doctor medicine designed to create the perception of something being done. What's *really* needed," he said, "are clean streets, window panes in the schools, good teachers, preparation for matriculation, and university educations." Edelman (1964) similarly argues that political symbols pacify and encourage quiescence.

But development town residents know these are real problems; they work with them or around them every day, and are not blinded to them by Community Center programs. In fact, those most burdened with these problems typically do not attend Center programs, making it harder to argue that such programs pacify them. Drawing on reader-response theory once again, we find in it a caution against assuming that meaning-making through symbolic means is done only by those with the resources to create policy and organizational symbols. Local residents, as suggested in the preceding chapters, do not automatically and passively accept others' meanings. Seeing them as active creators and interpreters of meaning, as an interpretive analysis does, is a democratic move that endows them with a sort of power, if not with its material form.[8]

On the other hand, the enactment of legislation may enable more remote publics to feel that they are doing something about these problems and quiet *them* rather than policy recipients. This is part of the situation that creates verboten goals: until there is agreement in the polity to discuss these and other issues publicly, knowledge of and communication about them will continue to be tacit, through the linked vehicles of purposefully ambiguous policy language and agencies' artifactual symbols.

What was unique about the ICCC by comparison with other community center-like institutions is that, unlike others that were partisan or that limited their service in some other way, the ICCC's Centers were promoted by the government at the national level to address one or more issues of social policy without representing a party line. They were not to be idle meeting places for people after work, simply to pass time in pleasant company—a general perception of the kind of community center that was the *Bet Am* on the kibbutz. Rather, a social purpose was to be attained through such gathering in an ICCC Center—the absorption of immigrants. And the Center was to be part of a nationwide chain, not an isolated building in a single municipality such as the Jerusalem Y or Haifa's Bet Rothschild. The policy and organizational story of the ICCC, then, is a story about the formation of national identity out of immigrants from a wide variety of cultural, economic, and religious backgrounds, in a newly created, developing state. It is also, therefore, a story about what "ethnicity" means in the Israeli context. The ICCC, although not created to engage these issues directly and explicitly, entered into a social service context for which these formed the backdrop.

There have been a few signs lately that parts of this situation in Israel are changing. With the fall of the Berlin Wall, Jewish Israelis of European origin—those not identified explicitly in Hebrew as "ethnics" (that is, as members of an *edah*, a "tribe")—began to speak more directly about their ethnicity and explore their roots, often traveling back to the German, Polish, or Russian villages from which their ancestors came. Looked at in retrospect, the notion of "ethnicity" has been such a strong subject of silence in public discourse, not spoken of since prior to the creation of the state in 1948, yet it is one of the elements (if not the central one) that marks residents of the development towns and urban neighborhoods as "Other." Making the concept of ethnicity explicit might extend societal value to those from non-European backgrounds, enabling a reexamination of immigrant "absorption" and social policies and programs like the ICCC. Then, the Community Centers might provide a wider variety of educational, recreational, and cultural programs that will either cease to be symbolic of ethnicity-based identities or will change in meaning in other ways.

NOTES

1. Those in policy evaluation who have raised these and other relevant questions include Guba and Lincoln (1987) and Palumbo (1987b).

2. This is also noted by De Neufville and Barton (1987), who trace homeownership to Jeffersonian ideals. In discussing homeownership as a myth, however, they call on policy analysts to make myths explicit in order to improve them and make "creative, conscious use of them," a position I reject in seeing myths as an area of tacit knowledge which, by definition, cannot always be made explicit.

3. See also Geertz's interpretation (1972) of the cockfight in Bali as a text representing Balinese societal values.

4. Moseley (1989) also found in analyzing implementation of the U.S. Food Security Act of 1985 that its explicit goals were not attained—spending targets were overshot, government financial involvement deepened, farmers became more dependent on artificial supports—but that did not detract from its acclaim as a successful federal policy.

5. Bauman (1987, p. 124) argues that unlike in the Soviet-type system, where values were articulated by the state, in the consumer society of the West, "values have been turned into attributes of commodities" and the market has become the verifier of values. In the ICCC, however, it would seem that both state and market processes of value-creation and validation are intertwined; and, I would argue, that is the case for other policies that express national identities.

6. This has its parallels in part of the racial discourse in the United States. A similar point about intermarriage is raised, for example, in an interview with sociologist Kenneth Clark (*New York Times* 5/7/95).

7. See Macarov (1974) on a related point.

8. Schneider and Ingram (1993) make a parallel argument about the democratic values underpinning social constructionist analyses.

9

Interpretive Policy Analysis

Interpretive modes of policy analysis seek to identify both the specific meanings, intended and made, of specific policies and how those meanings are communicated and variously interpreted. Several themes are highlighted by such analytic approaches: the creation and communication of shared as well as incommensurable meanings; the possibility of multiple meanings in policy and organizational actions; the role of tacit knowledge in the communication of values, beliefs, and feelings; and the understanding of public policies as expressive and not only as instrumental solutions to problems. Interpretive analyses are, in short, meaning-focused approaches. This book has explored some of the ways in which policy meanings may be communicated through agency actions, illustrated by examples from a single, extended case study, at the same time that it has identified what some of those specific meanings were for various "readers" in the case. Showing the contrast between intended meanings and interpreted meanings, and giving full weight to the latter as well as to the differences in interpretation, expands the definition of policy analysis and shifts the role of policy analysts. The following sections address the implications for organizational, implementation, and policy analysis.

CULTURAL STUDIES OF ORGANIZATIONS VERSUS ORGANIZATIONAL CULTURE STUDIES

Policy implementation is the social construction of a reality: it is a process of meaning-making through interpretation. Much of this (but not all of it, as I have shown in the preceding chapters) is done by an organization and its leaders and staff. Often, this is an organization in a broad, cross-geographical, federated sense—a large, complex public agency that crosses federal-local or capital-village lines, such as a centrally located department or ministry or division with regional and/or local branches, each of them an organization in its own right as well as part of a larger organization. Administrative activities unfold across these levels, from center to periphery and sometimes back again, and over time, often entailing groups of professionals as well as managers and administrators and other staff. The possibilities for multiple interpretations abound.

The capacity for multiple interpretations both suggests that one should look for multiple interpretive communities and is implicated by their presence. While it may be possible that an organization would have a single culture—a unified interpretive community—it seems likely under such circumstances that one would find multiple cultures within an agency and that some of these might not be harmonious with the "parent culture" (if one exists). In this sense tensions between managers and professionals within the same agency can be explained as different interpretive communities—different cultures—living within the same organization. The ICCC case is, in part, a twice-told tale of two cultures. It is an organizational identity story of "supermarket" administrative styles versus "social change" community organization styles, two different interpretations of what it meant to be a Community Center and to enact the Centers' mandates. And it is a national identity story of "cafe culture" (Easterners) versus "Community Center culture" (Westerners). Each of these "cultures" or "communities of interpretation" had its own set of values and beliefs, types of activity, behavioral norms, career objectives, evaluative measures, and so forth.

Part of the confusion in the organizational cultural literature of the past decade over whether organizations are or have single, unitary cultures or potentially multiple cultures derives from epistemological and ontological confusions over what "organizational culture" means. If we look to the beginnings in the 1980s of recent work in organizational culture (and one can find much earlier beginnings; see Trice and Beyer 1993, pp. 23–29), we can see that the field has been split since its recent inception between those working within a positivist paradigm and those taking an interpretive approach. Positivist approaches (e.g., Deal and Kennedy 1982) have seen "culture" as simply another analytic tool similar in kind to climate (Schneider et al. 1990), strategy (Davis 1982), and so forth. Culture, for such scholars, exists as an objective entity in the world, and one needs to figure out how to quantify it and measure its impact on various aspects of organizational life.[1]

Those working from interpretivist assumptions, on the other hand, have used the concept to mean ways in which people make or find life meaningful, communicate meanings to themselves and others, and express themselves in the world (Kunda 1992 is a good example). More recently, they have begun to change the language with which they conceive of their work, no longer speaking of organizational culture (which seems to reify the concept, to suggest a concreteness and reality that they believe is not there), but, instead, of doing cultural analyses of organizations (Smircich 1995). Ingersoll and Adams (1992), for example, present a cultural study of a public agency which explores tacit knowledge as a key cultural element and uses cultural methods—analyses of meanings—to understand change in that agency.

The case analysis in this book is of the same genre. The mode of analysis is cultural: ethnographic, in part, and using symbol, metaphor, ritual, and myth, among others, as some of the key analytic tools to explore the meanings underlying organizational action with respect to a specific public policy. Crucially, it focuses on meanings to actors in the situation. Seeing organizational action in its policy, polity, and/or societal context opens up the possibility for seeing multiple cultural influences within the organization, as well as for seeing that organizations do not create internal cultures de novo, but draw on cultural materials—values, beliefs, feelings—from the society within which they are constituted.

Part of the confusion in U.S.-based research over whether organizations are or have unitary cultures comes from the cultural construction of business and, within the academy, of organizational studies as the domain of business organizations. Because we have conceived of business and its organizations as "private" enterprise, the work of the "private" sector, we have tended to neglect the fact that the very enabling of this construction is a *public*, societal enactment. Organizations are not islands unto themselves, but we have tended to treat them this way. An exception to this has been the construction of public administration as an academic department and discipline, which has seen more clearly the link between organizational action and governmental or societal activity. Although one might study the ICCC, for example, as a self-contained organizational culture and subculture(s), one would thereby miss much of the meanings underlying agency actions and other artifacts, meanings that derive from its place as a policy-implementing agency in a societal context. By comparison with analyses of private organizations, such a contextualized analysis would be concerned with more than just internal audiences, organizational identity, and social status or the somewhat broader focus on strategic image and external audiences of customers and competitors (e.g., Berg and Kreiner 1990). A contextualized analysis looks beyond intended meanings to include clients' and others' meaning-making in the societal context. As Noschis (1987) wrote about neighborhoods, "the built environment might be symbolically meaningful not only when this appears to have been its designer's explicit intention, but also in cases where the inhabitants' continuous use and taking possession of it have loaded a setting symbolically." This broader perspective of necessity forces implementation and evaluation studies to abandon the exclusive standpoint, implied and assumed, of legislative and executive intent.

To apprehend such meanings, one needs to move beyond the study of organizational cultures as it has been construed in a positivist vein to cultural studies of organizations, whether "public" or "private." Such studies, looking for meanings made by actors in a particular organizational situation of artifacts created to express and convey those meanings, are what I have been calling here interpretive studies or approaches. Such an approach looks past the boundaries of a single organization, thereby opening up questioning around its links to or roles in society. This is broader than the product- or technology-oriented view of an organization's "environment." It allows us to see, for example, how much of what many organizations do may be an enactment of national identity stories as construed in different societies. The organization, whether implementing agency or "private" corporation, from this perspective is seen to move back and forth between meanings in its area of practice and meaning in the surrounding world.[2]

Positivist approaches to organizational culture raise a thorny ethical issue that arises out of their functionalist predispositions and managerial orientations. The problem facing most of the work in organizational theory and behavior is the problem of control: controlling a workforce through structural or behavioral engineering such that "it" will perform as desired. The problem of control is also the problem of implementation: controlling unintended consequences resulting from implementors' actions or inactions. Implementation theories and organizational theories follow parallel courses in prescribing means for achieving control: through incentives (a human relations approach), improved communications flows (a systems approach), professional training or clearer rules and organizational design (a structural or bureaucratic approach), the use or threat of power (a political approach) (Yanow 1987a, b).

Organizational culture arguments from a positivist perspective have promised management an extension of its control over the workforce.[3] As tools of persuasion, symbols are used in advertising campaigns with various rates of success. But at their further extreme, such symbols have been used as tools of mobilization and coercion— as, for example, in Goebbels's public relations efforts for the Third Reich that succeeded in inciting large numbers of people to riot and kill. Positivist approaches to organizational culture have not only suggested that the manipulation of symbols is a reasonable activity for managers and leaders to undertake. They also dehumanize the "targets" or subjects of such symbol-use by inferring that it is appropriate to manipulate them.

In seeing humans as objects, positivist corporate culture analyses have not raised the possibility that the objects might resist such efforts or engage in their own constructions of meaning. No suggestion has been made that cultural manipulation might fail, or that it might adversely affect human feelings and attitudes. These possibilities arise when one undertakes a cultural or interpretive analysis of meanings made by members of an organization. When Kunda (1992) did, he found ensuing feelings of distrust, disillusionment, and so on, and he suggests that the control promise proffered by positivist cultural analysts is not necessarily forthcoming. By focusing on the founding era and first decade of operations of the ICCC, the case as presented here highlights the role of founders and leaders, as Schein (1985, 1993) does. But bringing in "constructed" texts alongside "authored" ones shows the limits of leaders' abilities to determine meaning. Seeing clients, workers, and others as active creators and interpreters of meaning in their own right, rather than just as passive recipients of others' meanings, calls further into question the promise of control, as it moves us toward a more democratic and humane theory of organizational action, highlighting the antidemocratic aspects of the approach it seeks to supplant.

IMPLEMENTORY ACTIONS AS INTERPRETATION AND AS TEXT

Implementation as a subject of study was born out of an intellectual heritage that saw the administrative phase of the policy process as one of routine, technical administrative practice. Sharkansky (1970), for example, wrote: "it is the administrator who generally implements the *precise* statute that is enacted by the legislature . . ." (p. 8; emphasis added). But not only are statutes not precise; the philosophical grounding of interpretive analysis holds that statutes cannot be made precise because language cannot always be made precise (even absent political reasons for such imprecision). Administrators interpret legislative language, because human action is more interpretive than robotically technical. (For that matter, even the technical application of rules requires interpretations, of language, if nothing else.) Furthermore, language is not the only source of such meaning-making: artifactual objects and acts also communicate meanings and are also interpreted. Moreover, administrators are not the only actors in an implementation scenario who engage in interpretation and meaning-making. Clients, potential clients, and other policy-relevant publics near and far also read (or do not read) meanings in policy and agency artifacts, and their interpretations may bear on the success or failure of implementation.

Most implementation analyses have been framed in terms of legislative intent, comparing agency outputs or outcomes to the intentions of the enabling legislation that put the agency or its programs in place. In order to measure the degree to which outcomes match intentions, intentions must be capable of being made explicit and must, in fact, be made explicit. Indeed, the orthodox definition of rationality presumes that intentions can be and are explicitly stated. A common analysis of implementation failure holds policy ambiguity at fault, in that goals or intentions were not made explicit, clear, and unambiguous.

However, it is also not uncommon for analysts of the policymaking process to observe that policies are often worded in such a way as to accommodate conflicting interests. To see ambiguous policy language as a problem to be solved in order to improve implementation chances is to ignore the reality of purposive ambiguity: it temporarily resolves conflicts and accommodates differences, allowing contending parties to legislate and move on to implementory actions. An interpretive approach anticipates such ambiguity as the rule, rather than the exception, since it focuses on the capacity of symbols (including the language of legislated policies) to entail multiple meanings and make possible multiple interpretations. We will continue to create obstacles for an understanding of policy implementation by assuming that implementors have been or should be the sole audiences for policymakers' communications and that in their ambiguity of expression, the latter have failed to communicate with the former. If we change our assumptions about ambiguity as failure and see it rather as inherent in human expression directed to many policy audiences, we should no longer attempt to rectify implementation difficulties by exhorting policymakers to eliminate ambiguity from their expressions.

To demand the eradication of ambiguity in favor of making meanings and intentions explicit may be a request for the ungiveable. If policies entail verboten elements (that is, meanings which at that point in time are not sanctioned for public discussion), then prescribing that they be made explicit is demanding something that societal pressures, for example, require to remain tacit—tacitly expressed (or implied) *and tacitly understood.* For to the extent that human behavior is expressive, then members of interpretive communities *are* communicating *and* understanding these tacit meanings among themselves, mostly by way of language, objects, and acts that represent and convey meaning in an unspoken way. It is, by and large, only the demands of an instrumentally rational science of evaluation which require that this tacit communication be made explicit.

That knowledge is tacit does not mean necessarily that it is private. Tacit knowledge may be known in common, whether by members of the same symbol-sharing group or by members of conflicting groups, and communication in this nonexplicit fashion may, under certain circumstances, be more effective, accurate, and powerful than explicit communication. The professional practices of teaching or of community organizing, for example, are not always easy to describe. Parts of each are done and known tacitly. However, awards are made annually to the "best" teachers, and community organizers recognize when a colleague is doing "good" work. The effort to articulate recognized practitioner traits has proved difficult: their tacit communication has been, at least in these and similar instances, more effective and accurate than attempts at explicit communication (although this fact continues to raise thorny problems for professional education and for rational evaluation, as debates about teacher effectiveness indicate). Tacit knowledge can be shared, tacitly; it is not wholly private knowledge.[4]

We "speak" many vocabularies (Rorty 1989), and some we "speak" in silence. Underlying the explicit vocabulary of material policy elements may be other vocabularies of meaning, and these tacitly known vocabularies "echo" in public discourse about explicit policy mandates and influence the implementation of these mandates. To assay implementation failures in terms of only one of these vocabularies is to turn a blind eye (to mix a metaphor) on part of human nature. We use ambiguous language in policies for very real human reasons, including political ones. Should we pretend this is not the case? Calls for eliminating ambiguity are calls to change human action, human "nature," to make us all more instrumentally rational and to eliminate the metaphoric nature of our speech. This is truly asking us to make ourselves blind as we confront policy elephants.

Put another way, the old story about the centipede whose movement was immobilized when he was asked to answer the question, "What is your 86th leg doing when your 23rd is up?" illustrates part of the cost of ignoring the reality of tacit knowledge. Implementation (indeed, the policy process as a whole) can be similarly thwarted by demands that knowledge tacitly understood be made explicit.

Moreover, when the substance of such immobilizing questions is publicly unmentionable because societal consensus on that value is tenuous and subject to conflict, or when that value is incommensurable with another that is maintained equally strongly and when both are held in suspension by means of a myth, making the tacit explicit may endanger the myth, bare the conflict, and force attention to elements that may sunder daily social life and make "walking" impossible. We want, for example, to believe that schools educate, but there are equally plausible interpretations of schools as parent-surrogates or as employment substitutes which protect the organization and efficiency of labor markets. The latter explanations, however, do not enjoy widespread public support as acceptable purposes for schooling.

To promote them explicitly as schools' major goals and, therefore, as rationales for curricular, scheduling, and budgetary decisions and evaluative measures would be to thwart the operating procedures and community relations which school committees and administrations have carefully built up over many years and which support them in their work.

In daily discourse people generally do not argue, for example, that a "pro-life" stance represents a threat to individual identity or social standing. The attempt to make such a discussion explicit becomes an effort to mention publicly that which is typically not sanctioned for public discussion. Verboten goals are more acceptably handled by tacit means, through the use of cultural artifacts whose meanings are shared and similarly understood by relevant publics, albeit not explicitly. The artifacts that express these goals or values constitute data for analysis.

Seeing agency meaning constructions in the context of communal, polity, and societal meanings adds a wider range of policy and organizational "texts" being "read." These texts include organization-scapes, languages to talk about policy goals and agency actions, and implementing acts. Policy and organizational actors and policy-relevant publics are both interpreters of meanings and creators of meaning, both interpreters of "texts" and creators of "texts" that others interpret. Policy implementation in this view is both interpretation and text: the initial interpretations of legislative texts in the form of agency actions themselves become "texts" that are then interpreted and reinterpreted, in an ongoing cycle (as diagrammed in Figure 1-7). Administrators' acts, language, and objects created during implementation may play as central a role in communicating policy meanings to clients, implementors, and others as does the language of the enabling policy document. Conflicting values, beliefs, and so forth that characterized legislative debates often are carried into implementation through these artifacts. Indeed, policy language itself often retains nuances of preexisting difference as well as of present (and perhaps temporary) consent.

This is a view of implementation as adaptive as well as iterative. Once an implementor (broadly defined) interprets a policy and acts on that interpretation, a "reader" of that interpretation is no longer dealing with the original policy. Each interpretation may yield a new view of the policy; it is modified in some way. Subsequent "readers" engage a policy different, sometimes subtly, from the one initially legislated. Such a view is more cyclical than the traditional assembly-line, machine-linear model of the policy process.

This is also an interactive view of implementation. In this view a policy designed to produce changes in the behavior of a "target" population can succeed only if the "target" agrees to the terms of the transition. Implementation of a housing policy will fail if tenants use vouchers improperly or if landlords refuse to accept them; of an educational equity policy, if parents decline to spend vouchers; of a health policy, if doctors refuse to give service; of a citizen participation policy, if citizens choose not to participate.[5]

Such a view yields some control over the success of implementation activities to actors other than those conceived of traditionally as implementors. Moving away from the central rational decision-maker model of implementation, this enlarged scope includes actors external to the implementing agency, including legislators, policy target groups, agency clients and potential clients, and other policy-relevant publics. It challenges the focus on elites or leaders that marks much work in policy, implementation, and organizational studies and that entails the assumption that sensemaking is conducted properly only by legislators or perhaps agency executives as they shape policies; all others are passive receivers or audiences or targets. The point here is not the limitations of leadership in determining implementation outcomes or controlling organizational cultures. The ICCC had a "fixer" (Bardach 1977) in the person of Hayim Zipori, a charismatic figure, a supreme negotiator with good political ties, who had inherited Minister Zalman Aranne's mantle and the political goodwill toward the ICCC that Aranne, beloved of all, had generated. The image of Zipori "flying over the rooftops" to see what development town residents were doing added to his image of the mythical hero performing an impossible task. His internal role was to generate commitment of agency members to the mission; his external role, to convince others of the organization's worthiness and draw their support. He did both well, by all accounts, a very accomplished leader. And yet the social gap was still not narrowed.

But active "readership" of policy and implementation texts— that is, the active constructions of meaning through interpretation of symbolic artifacts—characterizes all policy-relevant publics and plays a role in the determination of policy success and failure. Once we construe the policy process as an arena for the creation, expression, and communication of meaning, we come face to face with the inherent limitations on human ability to control the outcomes of implementing acts. Implementation success—or failure—also hinges on the variety of such readership and the relative compatibilities of multiple meanings, intended and read.

At all levels of the organization, and among all groups of "readers," there exists the possibility of misconveyance of meaning or misinterpretation of intended meanings, any of which may lead to implementation complications and complexities or may facilitate implementation as ambiguities and differences of opinion are temporarily smoothed over. These are problems from the perspective of ruling or administrative elites and the point of view of implementation as control. Yet none of them is solved by making policy language less ambiguous (if it even could be done). What an interpretive analysis points to is the limits of control—control over interpretations of policy meanings, control over policy "targets."

This view of implementation presents a challenge to democracy theory, because allowing for interpretation within the administrative phase of the policy process and seeing clients and others as taking active roles in determining the success or failure of policy implementation takes it out of accepted views of democratic processes and does not allow for accountability and control. But if we move to a more cyclical and long-range view of the process, we would see that policy ideas rarely begin de novo and that debates arising during implementation may be precursors to the next round of policy design. In this view, tenants, landlords, parents, doctors, and other citizens and residents are all active creators of meaning and cannot be controlled. In its own way, it is a *more* democratic theory than the control theory it challenges, in that it counters the view of people as "targets" of policies. Targets do not move, think, act, feel. They are a major silent group, as distinct from policy "actors." It is the actors who "play" with language, while the client-targets are passive receivers of meaning.[6] This is a view of objects who take no initiative, engage in no independent thought or action, and are happy to have government save them. Reader-response theory applied to a policy context leads us away from such a paternalistic view of passive readers. Interpretive approaches rest on a belief in human autonomy.

This discussion might seem to be limited in its application to the realm of social policies where the policy "object" is a group of people—illegal immigrants, welfare or Medicaid recipients, the illiterate—who are being asked to change their behavior and who may refuse to do so. There is, however, a wide range of public policies—concerning technology, the environment, health, and other issues—that entail multiple interpretive communities actively constructing meanings that are at odds with legislative meanings and each other (see, e.g., Hofmann 1995, Linder 1995, Pal 1995).

Social policies are also not the only kinds of policies that entail expressive elements in addition to instrumental ones. Environmental policies, foreign policies, and military policies are also forums for the expression of national identity. Their implementation may also be, and in fact often is, fraught with similar cycles of interpretation and reinterpretation. The implementation of defense policy to build the Polaris missile (Sapolsky 1972) is a case in point, where part of its implementation included mustering the funds to do so, for which congressional support was necessary. Coalition-building for this support included creating the impression that the missile was successful, and individual congressmen had the option to decline to be persuaded. Such a view also posits a central role for persuasion, where actors try (consciously or otherwise) to convince others to share their interpretations of events. From this point of view, implementation succeeds when voting publics or legislative appropriations committees are convinced of that success.[7]

In the face of multiple possible interpretations, one might be moved to invoke the cliché that it's a miracle anything gets done at all. As a general rule, however, we do not become paralyzed in the face of multiple interpretations; indeed, such multiple possibilities characterize much of normal daily interactions. Rather, we behave as if our counterparts understood our meanings as we intended them to be understood, and the circumstances of ensuing behavior usually corroborate that this is so. But we find in implementation the multiple meanings and interpretations that accommodated political conflicts in the legislative phase, although—herein lies the rub—we may not observe the absence of corroboration until time and money and effort have been expended. From an interpretive point of view, multiple meanings and multiple interpretations become the reason for and the explanation of such difficulties, and the task of analysis is to uncover and understand the reality of these multiple interpretations and expressive acts.

ANALYZING INTERPRETIVELY

The implication of interpretive approaches for the analysis of implementation is that a close match between policy intentions and agency outcomes is the exception rather than the rule. Interpretive analyses focus on such discrepancies, directing our consideration toward policy objectives other than those stated explicitly, and widening the scope of evaluations to include the contextual meanings by which implementation often succeeds or fails. When the validation of such qualities as identity and status are the underlying subjects of public policy debates, their implementation will likely be fraught with contested meanings and associated ambiguities. In this view implementation actions are not seen exclusively as instrumentally rational, in the sense of being goal-oriented, involving the conscious and deliberate adjustment of agency means to the realization of explicitly stated policy ends. At times, they are expressive acts.

Then, too, artifacts that symbolically represent policy and agency meanings may come to replace goals themselves as objects of struggle and attainment, and status value is transferred to them. When building the Polaris missile, the Department of the Navy's Special Projects Office found that the Management Information Systems (MIS) they had introduced (such as PERT) came to represent the success of the venture, regardless of the actual track record of Polaris developments (Sapolsky 1972). Although PERT and other such tools were "as effective technically as rain dancing," they provided a symbolic "protective veneer" that allowed technical staffs to proceed with their work unhindered by outside officials: "it was enough that those outside the program were willing to believe that management innovation had a vital role in the technical achievements of the Polaris" (Sapolsky 1972, p. 246). When the Tennessee Valley Authority's continuity was threatened by an external source of power, it co-opted that source by sharing "the symbols of power"—by extending the formal trappings of power rather than by sharing power itself (Selznick 1949).[8] The absence of such artifacts can make agency life difficult. In the takeover of the

Washington State Ferry System by the state's Department of Transportation, the absence of the formal MIS, budgeting, and accounting tools of modern, rational management was seen to indicate the agency's inefficiency (Ingersoll and Adams 1992).

If acts are expressive as well as rational, a rational analysis will not help us understand their expressive, nonrational aspects. For this, we need an appropriate interpretive science that shifts the focus from the exclusively rational, goal-oriented, machine metaphor of social science behavior to an appreciation of expression, the nonlinear, non-goal-oriented communication of identity, as an artifact of human action, both individual and organizational. In other words, organizations may seem often to be purposive and goal-oriented, but not all human action is. This expressive side of human action takes place within organizations and around and about them. For example, attendance figures and other numbers may be simple, rational devices for reporting weekly activities. In that case, an evaluator would expect the numbers to be truthful. But when otherwise-objective numbers lie, an evaluator needs to be sensitive to their use in creating impressions and expressing desired images rather than reporting objective reality.[9]

The implications of an interpretive approach for organizational and policy analysis are based on the central importance the interpretive approach places on context-specific knowledge: that is, on situated knowers and situated knowns. If the idea of the situated known—the subject of research existing within a context that is not necessarily identical with the contexts of other subjects—is taken seriously, then it can no longer be possible at the end of the twentieth century to seek to develop universal models of policy processes and practices based in one experience and export them to other situations with the expectation that they will model well the experience and context of others. We cannot, in other words, continue to search for the universally applicable theory and use it to guide action, because such universally applicable knowledge is understood in this view not to exist. Rather, the interpretive approach calls for situation-specific understandings and for attention to the meanings made by governmental, local, and other actors in the situations under study of their own actions and events.

As long as policy analysis continues to labor in the shadow of microeconomics (Harpham and Scotch 1988, Stone 1988), its explanatory capacity will be hamstrung by the conceptual limitations of the rational actor and other positivist, modernist notions of universal, nonsituated knowledge about and from the perspective of an implied norm.[10] Interpretive analysis suggests that such a model of universal laws and experience is inappropriate and that local actors must be involved in the development of models and proposals. Moreover, when researchers themselves are seen as situated knowers—that is, conditioned by their own family, community and national backgrounds, education and training, experiences, and so forth—then the knowledge they produce will be understood to be a product of those situations.

Policy analysts, in an interpretive approach, take on the role of interpreter between and among interpretive communities. The first step in analysis is to identify these communities—whether groups of experts in some field and members of the public (e.g., Linder 1995), or conflicting groups of professionals within the same field (e.g., Chock 1995, Pal 1995), or centrally located policymakers and/or agency executives and field-based experts with local knowledge (e.g., Schmidt 1993)—and their different understandings of the issue at hand. A next step is to identify the elements of each group's interpretive framework and the particular symbolic artifacts through which each expresses values, feelings, and beliefs, as well as ways in which these artifacts express different and possibly incompatible meanings for different groups. As interpreters, policy analysts learn to speak—to make sense—within each group's framework and within that framework to explain—to translate—other groups' interpretive frameworks. In this, analysts take on an educative role, attempting to help each community "see" how other groups are making different, and perhaps incommensurable, meanings out of the same symbols. It is not uncommon for central administrators and policymakers to discount the local knowledges of those traditionally conceived of as policy "targets," often with disastrous results for lives or livelihoods, as Schmidt (1995) shows in the case of bridge construction and Wynne (1992) in the case of English sheep farmers and the Chernobyl fallout. Legitimating the interpretive framework of local knowers and attempting to interpret each community to the others might forestall some of these disasters.

Let us be clear, though: translating is not simple. Aside from the technical difficulties of becoming fluent in another conceptual language, speaking does not make things so. We are human, not deities like the God of Genesis who spoke a whole world into existence. Let us not fall again into the fallacy of faith in ideal language and rational systems of signs, believing that reasoned discourse will be sufficient to overcome differences of worldview and their related practices.[11] At the same time, attempts to communicate and to interpret communications, whether through languages more traditionally conceived or through the languages of objects and acts, are all that we have.

Interpretive analysis also directs attention to the conceptual assumptions embedded in theories—that is, in the textual and rhetorical products of the academy. That much implementation analysis has assumed an "intent to implement as written" makes persuasive sense from an interpretive viewpoint. We have adopted language with which to explain or predict the functions and purposes of government, and this assumption of intent is part and parcel of that conceptual framework. Implementation analysis examines the workings of a policy process that is a human creation, and that process is assumed to operate according to theories and laws that we have posited: it is our artifice and the artifice of our theories. It is not an objectively seen reality. We have created theories to understand a world, and those theories and observations also constitute that world.

What this argument means for writing policy analytic, organizational, and implementation studies is also clear. We can no longer have texts that purport, through their use of social science rhetoric, to present a definitive analysis of a policy, organization, or agency—that speak as if from a detached, objective point of view outside of the event being analyzed, in which the researcher makes her or his presence invisible through the use of impersonal linguistic constructions (such as the voice being used here at the moment). Clients', cognate agencies', voters', and others' interpretations of and actions with respect to policy and agency meanings must also be included in any analysis. The analytic text must become multivocal, making those voices heard, and not just the univocal record of the researcher's interpretation. At the very least, analytic views must be identified as situated knowledge and the parameters of the situation identified and located in some conceptual, demographic, political, or other "space," rather than presented as universal, timeless, and hence objective and "norm-al" views.

Indeterminacy of meaning is part of the human condition. Why should we expect policies and policy discourses to be different? We cannot control every aspect of human action; we cannot always know with certainty how our meanings will be interpreted. This is the limitation that an interpretive understanding of human life poses to the positivist view: that, though we might wish it otherwise, human action is not scientific in a positivist way, subject to prediction and control. Nor can we make it so by wishing—or by writing implementation and administrative theories which prescribe conditions that run counter to human practices. We need a better understanding of interpretive science as applied to the policy arena, including the actions of organizations in implementing policies. We need to bring interpretive processes and philosophies into the realm of policy and administrative studies.

Multiple interpretations do not obviate the need to act.[12] We live in a world that we take to be real, and we act in it accordingly. How we choose to act and what acts we choose to make have to be determined by the context. If a fire alarm sounds, I will not stop to ask whether the exit door is "real." Without much active analysis in the moment, I will draw on past use of the door and move as quickly as possible toward it. In other circumstances, however, it may be better to act without such certainty. When faced with conflicting views about an organizational action, for example, we would do better to engage the possibility that conflicts stem from different views of a socially constructed "reality" than assume the ignorance or stupidity of other views. We must, at times, stop to ask whether individuals, singly or as organizations or nations, are "not waving but drowning."[13]

This is not an argument that all behavior is nonrational. We live, in fact, in a world in which the rational paradigm is quite persuasively operative. Therefore, individuals and organizations continue to conduct themselves in a rational, goal-oriented fashion. When dealing with the verboten goals of policies, the tacit aspects of professional practice, and other occurrences of nonexplicit expression as actors or as analysts, we may interpret these instances as "uncertainty" or "ambiguity," and to appear more rational we often seek to control them. Interpretive approaches, however, afford us a different view of such rational behavior, in which individuals and organizations are seen as emphasizing symbols of rationality—formal goal statements, annual meetings, etc.—to foster the image of rational behavior in a world that expects or needs to see it. Such approaches free us from the ontological quest for the ultimate essence of implementation and allow us to rethink our analysis of its success and failure, whereby we may inquire into the meanings that policy and agency events hold for relevant publics and the actors involved.

This book stands as a bridge between a positivist world and an interpretive one. The research was begun within the framework of positivist theories. It reflects their orientation toward the intended meanings of policy and agency elites, even as it seeks to step away from that orientation and explore differences between intended or authored meanings and constructed ones. The book stands—I stand— looking hopefully in the direction of other modes of thought that suggest directions for new forms of researching and writing, including those that explore how policies mean.

NOTES

1. Several efforts to quantify organizational culture(s) have been published in recent years in such journals as the *Academy of Management Journal*. Many of them, especially those seeking to explore culture in a transnational context, have based their work on Hofstede (1984). His work is more complex than most, in that he makes explicit the grounding of such rule-oriented, etic analysis on emic (contextual) data. Whether this is philosophically possible is another question.

2. Industry studies (e.g., Weiss and Delbecq 1987) are a step in this direction, in that they consider regional influences that might shape parts of that industry differently. But the ones conducted so far have begun the story with a predetermination that there is a sense of "industry," of collective identity, among the members, rather than making that a subject of inquiry. The latter would constitute an interpretive approach.

3. See Kunda (1992) on the promise and its limitations.

4. See Cook and Yanow (1993) for an example of the effective use of tacit knowledge in the practice of a firm of flutemakers.

5. Gusfield (1963) identified two types of "disinterested reform"— "divorced from any direct economic interests" (p. 2)—in the Temperance movement: (1) assimilative reform, where the reformer is confident that his values and culture will prevail and where he invites the Other to join in and "lift himself to middle-class respect and income"; and (2) coercive reform, where "the object of reform is seen as an intractable defender of another culture, someone who rejects the reformer's values and denies the legitimacy

of his life style and really doesn't want to change" (pp. 6–7). Symbols can also range from expressively persuasive to coercive. Social policies are inherently designs for reform, for change. The ICCC is an example of a noncoercive policy that assumed that its "targets" desired the proposed change. That was left unsaid, but communicated tacitly through symbols. The English-only movement in the United States is a coercive policy, in this sense, but based on assumptions about language use and employment that do not hold (*New York Times*, 6/29/93).

6. A parallel analysis could be made here from a feminist theoretical point of view that would see passive, silent, policy targets as the females of the policy setting, as distinct from policy "actors." See Ferguson (1984) for an analysis of both clients and bureaucrats as the "second sex." Another sort of feminist analysis could be crossed with interpretive analysis to explore the clash between community organizers and Center directors (COs were largely female; directors, male) or even crossed further with class analysis (COs were middle class, university educated, foreign-born or with extensive overseas experience; directors were initially army officers without overseas experience).

7. This discussion suggests a meaning of implementation similar to its usage in Operations Research, where "to implement" is to convince a client to use the system which has been designed for him (e.g., Siebert 1973).

8. It is interesting to note that some definitions of power invoke a terminology which suggests that *real* power may lie in creating and successfully managing an *impression* of having power. Specifically, a definition of power which relies on implied but invisible threat depends on signaling the existence of that threat and communicating its nature symbolically. For the threat to remain invisible, such communication must depend on a symbolic representation of imminent danger—that is, on creating, communicating, and managing a "danger-ful" and, hence, powerful image. Bachrach and Baratz (1970, ch. 2) present an interesting discussion of power and perceived and real threats. See also Pfeffer (1981, ch. 6).

9. Gusfield (1981) and Stone (1988) provide examples of such uses of numbers.

10. The assumed norm of the rational economic actor often carries with it other assumptions about race, class, and gender. Donald McCloskey (1985) has mounted a concerted effort to show that economic theories, too, are matters of written rhetoric and not objective "science."

11. Susan Handelman (1982) argues that differences between faith in words, characteristic of rationalist discourses, and faith in deeds, characteristic of practice- and action-oriented interpretive philosophies, replay distinctions between Athens and Jerusalem, between reason and faith, and between their later expressions as Christian and Jewish critical practices.

12. These matters, which often turn up as questions about the relativism thought to inhere in interpretive approaches, have been addressed by philosophers and political theorists. The question, as typically asked, has two aspects. The first is definitional: relativism exists as a problem only from the vantage point of positivist knowledge. By definition, a philosophy that posits that the world is knowable in one best way cannot accommodate multiple interpreta-

tions: all but one of them must be wrong. From an interpretive position, different interpretations *are* the reality of human life. There is no one authoritative position—not the state, not the church—to which other positions are relative. The problem, by definition, does not exist.

The other aspect of the question is moral: If you give up the possibility of objective, universal knowledge, aren't you also giving up your ability to make judgments? Aren't the Holocaust deniers right, in this view, along with those who would like equal time in school curricula for the Nazi Party's and the Ku Klux Klan's views?

These issues have been addressed by R. J. Bernstein (1983), among others. Philosophers taking their approach answer "no" to both questions. The obligation to make judgments remains, but they are human judgments made as members of communities in light of practices accepted in those communities (which may, at times, be a religious or civic entity). What is required—indeed, what is only possible—are local judgments made on the basis of contextual, local knowledge, rather than according to a set of principles abstracted from a number of local contexts. More needs to be said on this subject in the context of the actual practice of policy interpretations, at the very least because it continues to trouble many who contemplate turning to interpretive practices.

13. The reference is to a poem by Stevie Smith (1972) by the same title, in which a man—some say the poet herself—waves for help, but is mistaken as waving hello.

References

Abbagnano, Nicola (1967). Positivism. *Encyclopedia of philosophy*, Vol. 6. New York: Macmillan.

Administrative Science Quarterly (1983) 28:3 (September).

Agar, Milton H. (1980). *The professional stranger: An informal introduction to ethnography*. Orlando, FL: Academic Press.

Allison, Graham T. (1971). *Essence of decision*. Boston: Little, Brown.

Altman, Elisabeth A. and Rosenbaum, Betsey R. (1973). Principles of planning and Zionist ideology: The Israeli development town. *Journal of the American Institute of Planners* 39, 316–25.

Anderson, James E. (1990). *Public policymaking*. Boston: Houghton Mifflin.

Argyris, Chris and Schon, Donald A. (1974). *Theory in practice*. San Francisco: Jossey-Bass.

Arnold, Thurman (1935). *The symbols of government*. New Haven: Yale University Press.

Arnold, Thurman (1937). *The folklore of capitalism*. New Haven: Yale University Press.

Avruch, Kevin (1987). The emergence of ethnicity in Israel. Review article. *American Ethnologist* 14 (May), 327–39.

Bachrach, Peter and Baratz, Morton S. (1970). *Power and poverty*. New York: Oxford University Press.

Bahloul, Joelle (1993). Respondent's comments delivered at the conference "Democracy and Difference," Indiana University, Bloomington (April).

Bahloul, Joelle (1994). The Sephardic Jew as Mediterranean: A view from kinship and gender. *Journal of Mediterranean Studies* 4:2, 197–207.

Baier, Vicki Eaton, March, James G., and Saetren, Harald (1986). Implementation and ambiguity. *Scandinavian Journal of Management Studies* 2:3–4 (May), 197–212.

Bar-Haim, Gabriel (1987). The meaning of Western commercial artifacts for Eastern European youth. *Journal of Contemporary Ethnography* 16:2 (July), 205–26.

Bar-On, Dan (1989). *Legacy of silence: Encounters with children of the Third Reich*. Cambridge: Harvard University Press.

Bardach, Eugene (1977). *The implementation game*. Cambridge: MIT Press.

Batten, T. R. (1960). *The non-directive approach in group and community work.* London: Oxford University Press.

Bauman, Zygmunt (1987). *Legislators and interpreters.* Ithaca: Cornell University Press.

Beam, George and Simpson, Dick (1984). *Political action.* Chicago: Swallow Press.

Behar, Ruth (1993). *Translated woman.* Boston: Beacon Press.

Bellah, Robert (1980). *Varieties of civil religion.* San Francisco: Harper and Row.

Ben-Ari, Eyal and Bilu, Yoram (1987). Saints' sanctuaries in Israeli development towns. *Urban Anthropology* 16, 243–72.

Bennis, Warren G. (1972). A funny thing happened on the way to the future. In J. M. Thomas and W. G. Bennis, eds., *Management of change and conflict.* Baltimore: Penguin.

Berg, Per Olof and Kreiner, Kristian (1990). Corporate architecture. In Pasquale Gagliardi, ed., *Symbols and artifacts.* New York: Aldine de Gruyter. Pages 41–67.

Berger, John (1972). *Ways of seeing.* London: BBC and Penguin. Esp. Chapter 5.

Berger, Peter L. and Luckmann, Thomas (1966). *The social construction of reality.* New York: Anchor.

Berler, Alexander (1970). *New towns in Israel.* Jerusalem: Israel Universities Press. Chapter III.

Bernstein, Basil (1977). Ritual in education. *Class, codes, and control*, Vol. 3, second edition. Boston: Routledge and Kegan Paul. Chapter 2.

Bernstein, Richard J. (1976). *The restructuring of social and political theory.* Philadelphia: University of Pennsylvania Press. Quoted in George Beam and Dick Simpson (1984), *Political action.* Chicago: Swallow Press. Page 23.

Bernstein, Richard J. (1983). *Beyond objectivism and relativism.* Philadelphia: University of Pennsylvania Press.

Bialik, Hayim Nachman and Rabinitsky, H., eds. (1939). *Sefer ha'agadah*, Vol. I. Tel Aviv: Dvir. Quoted in Percy S. Cohen (1969), Theories of myth, *Man* 4:3, 350.

Black, Max (1962). *Models and metaphors.* Ithaca: Cornell University Press.

Black, Max (1979). More about metaphor. In A. Ortony, ed., *Metaphor and thought.* Cambridge: Cambridge University Press.

Booth, Wayne C. (1978). Metaphor as rhetoric. In S. Sacks, ed., *On metaphor.* Chicago: University of Chicago Press.

Bosman, J. (1987). Persuasive effects of political metaphors. *Metaphor and Symbolic Activity*, 2:2, 97–113.

Boston Sunday Globe (1981). Unsigned editorial (November 1).

Bourgeois, V. W. and Pinder, C. C. (1983). Contrasting philosophical perspectives in administrative science. *Administrative Science Quarterly* 28, 608–13.

Brown, Richard H. (1976). Social theory as metaphor. *Theory and Society* 3, 169–97.

Burke, Kenneth (1969) [1945]. *A grammar of motives.* Berkeley: University of California.

Burrell, Gibson and Morgan, Gareth (1979). *Sociological paradigms and organisational analysis.* Portsmouth, NH: Heinemann.

Campbell, Joseph (1949). *Hero with a thousand faces.* New York: Pantheon.

Campbell, Joseph (1972). *Myths to live by.* New York: Bantam.

Campbell, Joseph (1979). *The flight of the wild gander.* South Bend: Gateway.

Carroll, Lewis (1968). *Alice's adventures in wonderland and through the looking glass.* Baltimore: Penguin. Pages 267–83 passim.

Cassirer, Ernst (1946). *Language and myth.* New York: Harper.

Charon, Joel M. (1985). *Symbolic interactionism,* second edition. Englewood Cliffs, NJ: Prentice Hall.

Chock, Phyllis Pease (1995). Ambiguity in policy discourse: Congressional talk about immigration. *Policy Sciences* 18:2.

Ciardi, John (1959). *How does a poem mean?* Boston: Houghton Mifflin.

Ciborra, Claudio U. and Lanzara, Giovan Francesco (1990). Designing dynamic artifacts. In Pasquale Gagliardi, ed., *Symbols and artifacts.* New York: Aldine de Gruyter. Pages 147–65.

Clifford, James (1988). *The predicament of culture.* Cambridge: Harvard University Press.

Cohen, Erik (1970). Development towns—the social dynamics of "planted" urban communities in Israel. In S. N. Eisenstadt, Rivkah Bar Yosef, and Chaim Adler, eds., *Integration and development in Israel.* New York: Praeger. Chapter 25.

Cohen, Erik (1977). The city in Zionist ideology. *Jerusalem Quarterly* 4, 126–44.

Cohen, Michael D. and March, James G. (1986). *Leadership and ambiguity,* second edition. Boston: Harvard Business School.

Cohen, Percy S. (1969). Theories of myth. *Man* 4:3, 337–53.

Colebatch, H. K. (1995). Organizational meanings of program evaluation. *Policy Sciences* 18:2.

Colebatch, H. K. and Degeling, P. (1986). Talking and doing in the work of administration. *Public Administration and Development,* Vol. 6, 339–56.

Combs, James E. (1980). Political ceremonials. *Dimensions of political drama.* Santa Monica, CA: Goodyear. Chapter 2.

Community Centers in Israel (1971). Jerusalem: ICCC. [Hebrew and English.]

Cook, Scott and Yanow, Dvora (1993). Culture and organizational learning. *Journal of Management Inquiry* 2:4 (December), 373–90.

Cooper, Clare (1976). The house as symbol of the self. In J. Lang et al., eds., *Designing for human behavior.* Stroudsberg, PA: Dowden, Hutchinson and Ross.

Craig, Lois (1984). *The federal presence.* Cambridge: MIT Press.

Cuthbertson, Gilbert Morris (1975). *Political myth and epic.* East Lansing: Michigan State University Press.

Dallmayr, Fred R. and McCarthy, Thomas A., eds. (1977). *Understanding and social inquiry.* Notre Dame: University of Notre Dame Press.

Dar, Yoel (1969). Development towns demand priority. Interview with the chairman of the Development Town Committee of the Local Authority. *Davar* (February 21). [Hebrew.]

Davis, Stanley M. (1982). *Culture and strategy.* Cambridge: Management Analysis Center.

De Neufville, Judith I. and Barton, Stephen E. (1987). Myths and the definition of policy problems. *Policy Sciences* 20, 181–206.

Deal, Terrence E. and Kennedy, Allen A. (1982). *Corporate cultures.* New York: Addison-Wesley.

DeHaven-Smith, Lance (1988). *Philosophical critiques of policy analysis.* Gainesville: University of Florida Press.

Denzin, Norman K. and Lincoln, Yvonna S. (1994). *Handbook of qualitative research.* Thousand Oaks, CA: Sage.

Doniger, Wendy (1992). A very strange enchanted boy. Review of S. Larsen and R. Larsen, *A fire in the mind, The life of Joseph Campbell. New York Times Book Review* (February 2).

Donnellon, Anne, Gray, Barbara, and Bougon, Michel (1986). Communication, meaning, and organized action. *Administrative Science Quarterly* 31, 43–55.

Douglas, Mary (1982). A rule of method. *Natural symbols.* New York: Pantheon. Chapter 4.

Doxtater, Dennis (1990). Meaning of the workplace. In Pasquale Gagliardi, ed., *Symbols and artifacts.* New York: Aldine de Gruyter. Pages 107–27.

Dryzek, John (1990). *Discursive democracy.* Cambridge: Cambridge University Press.

Dunn, William M. (1981). *An introduction to public policy analysis.* Englewood Cliffs, NJ: Prentice Hall.

Edelman, Murray (1964). *The symbolic uses of politics.* Urbana: University of Illinois.

Edelman, Murray (1977). *Political language.* New York: Academic Press.

Edelman, Murray (1980). Systematic confusions in the evaluation of implementing decisions. Sapir Conference on Social Policy Evaluation, Tel Aviv University (Israel).

Edelman, Murray (1988). *Constructing the political spectacle.* Chicago: University of Chicago Press.

Edelman, Murray (1995). *Art and politics.* Chicago: University of Chicago Press.

Edwards, George C., III (1980). *Implementing public policy.* Washington, DC: Congressional Quarterly Press.

Elder, Charles D. and Cobb, Roger W. (1983). *The political uses of symbols.* New York: Longman.

Ellis, Richard and Coyle, Dennis (1994). *Politics, policy and culture: Applications of group/grid theory.* Boulder, CO: Westview.

Erikson, Erik (1963). *Childhood and society.* New York: Norton.

Facts about Israel (1977). Jerusalem: Israel Information Center.

Fay, Brian (1975). *Social theory and political practice*. Boston: George Allen & Unwin.

Feldman, Martha S. (1989). *Order without design*. Stanford: Stanford University Press.

Feldman, Martha S. (1994). *Some interpretive techniques for analyzing qualitative data*. Beverly Hills, CA: Sage.

Ferguson, Kathy E. (1984). *The feminist case against bureaucracy*. Philadelphia: Temple University Press.

Fernandez, James (1972). Persuasions and performances. *Daedalus* 101:1, 39–60.

Fernandez, James (1974). The mission of metaphor in expressive culture. *Current Anthropology* 15:2, 119–45.

Fischer, Frank (1980). *Political values and public policy*. Boulder, CO: Westview.

Fischer, Frank and Forester, John, eds. (1993). *The argumentative turn in policy analysis and planning*. London: Duke University Press.

Floden, Robert E. and Weiner, Stephen S. (1978). Rationality to ritual: The multiple roles of evaluation in governmental processes. *Policy Sciences* 9, 9–18.

Fox, Charles J. (1990). Implementation research. In Dennis J. Palumbo and Donald J. Calista, eds., *Implementation and the policy process*. New York: Greenwood. Chapter 13.

Fried, M. (1963). Grieving for a lost home. In Leonard J. Duhl, ed., *The urban condition*. New York: Basic.

Frost, Peter J. et al., eds. (1985). *Organizational culture*. Beverly Hills, CA: Sage.

Frost, Peter J. et al., eds. (1991). *Reframing organizational culture*. Newbury Park, CA: Sage.

Gagliardi, Pasquale (1990). Artifacts as pathways and remains of organizational life. *Symbols and artifacts*. New York: Aldine de Gruyter. Pages 3–38.

Garfinkel, Harold (1977). What is ethnomethodology? In Fred R. Dallmayr and Thomas A. McCarthy, eds., *Understanding and social inquiry*. Notre Dame: University of Notre Dame Press. Pages 240–61.

Garrison, C. E. (1981). The energy crisis. *Qualitative Sociology* 4, 312–23.

Geertz, Clifford (1972). Deep play: Notes on the Balinese cockfight. *Daedalus* 101 (Winter), 1–38.

Geertz, Clifford (1973). *The interpretation of cultures*. New York: Basic.

Geertz, Clifford (1983a). From the native's point of view. *Local knowledge*. New York: Basic. Chapter 3.

Geertz, Clifford (1983b). Common sense as a cultural system. *Local knowledge*. New York: Basic. Chapter 4.

Geertz, Clifford (1988). *Works and lives*. Stanford: Stanford University Press.

Goffman, Erving (1959). *The presentation of self in everyday life*. New York: Doubleday Anchor.

Goggin, Malcolm et al. (1990). Studying the dynamics of public policy implementation. In Dennis J. Palumbo and Donald J. Calista, eds., *Implementation and the policy process*. New York: Greenwood. Chapter 12.

Goldberg, Harvey (1987). The changing meaning of ethnic affiliation. *Jerusalem Quarterly* 44 (Fall).

Golden-Biddle, Karen and Locke, Karen (1993). Appealing work: An investigation in how ethnographic texts convince. *Organization Science* 4:4 (November).

Goodman, Nelson (1978). *Ways of worldmaking*. Indianapolis: Hackett.

Goodman, Nelson. (1985). How buildings mean. *Critical Inquiry* 11 (June), 642–53.

Goodsell, Charles T. (1988). *The social meaning of civic space*. Lawrence: University Press of Kansas.

Gottdiener, M. and Lagopoulos, Alexandros Ph., eds. (1986). *The city and the sign*. New York: Columbia University Press.

Gottschalk, Shimon B. (1975). *Communities and alternatives*. Cambridge: Schenkman.

Gray, Barbara, Bougon, Michel G., and Donnellon, Anne (1985). Organizations as constructions and destructions of meaning. *Journal of Management* 11:2, 83–98.

Greenberg, Harold (1979). *Israel social problems*. Tel Aviv: Dekel Press.

Greenwood, Davydd J., Gonzalez, Jose Luis et al. (1991). *Industrial democracy as process*. Assen-Maastricht: Van Gorcum.

Grossman, David (1988). *The yellow wind*. Haim Watzman, transl. New York: Farrar, Straus, Giroux.

Guba, Egon G. and Lincoln, Yvonna S. (1987). The countenances of fourth-generation evaluation. In Dennis J. Palumbo, ed., *The politics of program evaluation*. Newbury Park, CA: Sage. Chapter 7.

Gusfield, Joseph R. (1963). *Symbolic crusade*. Chicago: University of Illinois Press.

Gusfield, Joseph R. (1981). *The culture of public problems*. Chicago: University of Illinois Press.

Hall, Edward T. (1959). *The silent language*. New York: Doubleday.

Hall, Edward T. (1962). Sensitivity and empathy at home and abroad. Three Leatherbee Lectures. Boston: Harvard University, Graduate School of Business Administration (Spring).

Hallett, Michael A. and Rogers, Robert (1994). The push for 'truth in sentencing': Evaluating competing stakeholder constructions. *Evaluation and Program Planning* 17:2, 187–96.

Handelman, Don (1976). Re-thinking 'Banana Time.' *Urban Life* 4:4, 433–48.

Handelman, Susan A. (1982). *The slayers of Moses: The emergence of rabbinic interpretation in modern literary theory*. Albany: SUNY Press.

Harpham, Edward J. and Scotch, Richard K. (1988). Economic discourse, policy analysis, and the problem of the political. In Edward Bryan Portis and Michael B. Levy, eds., *Handbook of political theory and policy science*. New York: Greenwood.

Harrington, Michael (1963). *The other America*. Baltimore: Penguin.

Harris, Stanley G. and Sutton, Robert I. (1986). Functions of parting ceremonies in dying organizations. *Academy of Management Journal* 29:1, 5–30.

Hatch, Mary Jo (1990). The symbolics of office design. In Pasquale Gagliardi, ed., *Symbols and artifacts*. New York: Aldine de Gruyter. Pages 129–46.

Hatch, Mary Jo (1993a). The dynamics of organizational culture. *Academy of Management Review* 18:4, 657–93.

Hatch, Mary Jo (1993b). Rhetorical and narrative style in the discourses of organization theory. Presented to the Annual Conference of the European Group on Organizational Studies, Paris (July).

Hawkesworth, M. E. (1988). *Theoretical issues in policy analysis*. Albany: SUNY Press.

Hearn, Jeff et al. (1990). *The sexuality of organization*. Newbury Park, CA: Sage.

Herzberg, Arthur, ed. (1960). *The Zionist idea*. New York: Atheneum.

Hofmann, Jeanette (1995). Implicit theories in policy discourse: Interpretations of reality in German technology policy. *Policy Sciences* 18:2.

Hofstede, Geert (1984). *Culture's consequences*, abridged edition. London: Sage, 1984.

Honko, Lauri (1972). The problem of defining myth. In Haralds Biezais, ed., *The myth of the state*. Stockholm: Almqvist & Wiksell.

Howe, N. (1988). Metaphor in contemporary American political discourse. *Metaphor and Symbolic Activity*, 3:2, 87–104.

Hunter, Albert (1974). *Symbolic communities*. Chicago: University of Chicago.

Hutman, Bill (1990). Black Panthers: forgotten but not gone. *Jerusalem Post* (September 15).

Ingersoll, Virginia Hill and Adams, Guy (1986). Beyond organizational boundaries. *Administration and Society* 18:3 (November), 360–81.

Ingersoll, Virginia Hill and Adams, Guy (1992). *The tacit organization*. Greenwich, CT: JAI Press.

Iris, Mark and Shama, Avraham (1972). Black Panthers: The movement. *Society* 9 (May), 37–44.

Iser, Wolfgang (1989). *Prospecting: From reader response to literary anthropology*. Baltimore: Johns Hopkins University Press.

Jennings, Bruce (1983). Interpretive social science and policy analysis. In Daniel Callahan and Bruce Jennings, eds., *Ethics, the social sciences, and policy analysis*. New York: Plenum. Chapter 1.

Jennings, Bruce (1987). Interpretation and the practice of policy analysis. In Frank Fischer and John Forester, eds., *Confronting values in policy analysis*. Newbury Park, CA: Sage. Pages 128–52.

Katz, Elihu and Gurevitch, Michael (1972). *Israeli culture: 1970. Second report: Patterns of entertainment and cultural consumption—a national survey*. Jerusalem: Institute for Applied Social Research and the Communications Institute, Hebrew University. (March.) [Hebrew.]

Keeley, M. (1980). Organizational analogy. *Administrative Science Quarterly* 25, 337–62.

Kelly, Marisa and Maynard-Moody, Steven (1993). Policy analysis in the post-positivist era. *Public Administration Review* 53:2 (March–April), 135–42.

Kirschenbaum, Alan (1974). Selection, migration and population distribution: A study of new towns in Israel. Haifa: Center for Urban and Regional Studies, Technion.

Krefting, Linda A. and Frost, Peter J. (1985). Untangling webs, surfing waves, and wildcatting. In Peter J. Frost et al., eds., *Organizational culture*. Beverly Hills, CA: Sage.

Kuhn, Thomas S. (1970). *The structure of scientific revolutions*, second edition, enlarged. Chicago: University of Chicago Press.

Kuhn, Thomas S. (1977). *The essential tension*. Chicago: University of Chicago Press.

Kunda, Gideon (1992). *Engineering culture*. Philadelphia: Temple University Press.

Kvale, Steinar (1995). The social construction of validity. *Qualitative Inquiry* 1:1, 19–40.

Lakoff, George (1986). A figure of thought. *Metaphor and Symbolic Activity* 1:3, 215–25.

Lakoff, George (1987a). The death of dead metaphor. *Metaphor and Symbolic Activity* 2:2, 143–47.

Lakoff, George (1987b). *Women, fire, and dangerous things*. Chicago: University of Chicago Press.

Lakoff, George and Johnson, Mark (1980). *Metaphors we live by*. Chicago: University of Chicago Press.

Lakoff, George and Johnson, Mark (1987). The metaphorical logic of rape. *Metaphor and Symbolic Activity* 2:1, 73–79.

Larsen, Janne and Schultz, Majken (1990). Artifacts in a bureaucratic monastery. In Pasquale Gagliardi, ed., *Symbols and artifacts*. New York: Aldine de Gruyter. Pages 281–302.

Lasswell, Harold (1979). *The signature of power*. New Brunswick, NJ: Transaction.

Lasswell, Harold D., Lerner, Daniel, and De Sola Pool, Ithiel (1952). *The comparative study of symbols*. Stanford: Hoover Institution.

Landau, Martin (1964). On the use of metaphor in political analysis. *Political theory and political science*. New York: Collier-Macmillan. Chapter 3.

Lavi, Zvi (1979). A venture born under Gemini. In *Summaries and objectives: 1969–1979*. Jerusalem: ICCC. Pages 8–14. [Hebrew with English summary.]

Leibman, Charles S. and Don-Yehiya, Eliezer (1983). *Civil religion in Israel*. Berkeley: University of California Press.

Lichfield, Nathaniel (1970). *Israel's new towns: A development strategy*, Vol. 1. Tel Aviv: Institute for Planning and Development.

Linder, Stephen H. (1995). Contending discourses in the electromagnetic fields controversy. *Policy Sciences* 18:2.

Lipsky, Michael (1970). *Protest in city politics*. Chicago: Rand McNally.

Lipsky, Michael (1978). Standing the study of public policy implementation on its head. In Walter Dean Burnham and Martha Wagner Weinberg, eds., *American politics and public policy*. Cambridge: MIT Press. Chapter 16.

Lipsky, Michael (1979). *Street-level bureaucracy*. New York: Russell Sage Foundation.

Liron, Yocheved (1973). *Deprivation and the socio-economic gap in Israel*. Prepared for the second Assembly of the Jewish Agency, Jerusalem (February).

Luker, Kristin (1984). *Abortion and the politics of motherhood*. Berkeley: University of California Press.

Macarov, David (1974). The new role of the Community Centre. *Ariel* 36, 84, 89–91.

Manning, Peter (1977). Resources, information and strategy. Presented to the American Society of Criminology, Atlanta (November).

Manning, Peter K. (1979). Metaphors of the field. *Administrative Science Quarterly* 24, 660–71.

March, James G. and Olsen, Johan P. (1976). *Ambiguity and choice in organizations*. Bergen: Universitetsforlaget.

Marcus, George E. and Fischer, Michael J. (1986). *Anthropology as cultural critique*. Chicago: Chicago University Press.

Martin, Joanne (1990). Re-reading Weber: Searching for feminist alternatives to bureaucracy. Presented to the Academy of Management Annual Meeting, San Francisco (August).

Martin, Joanne, Feldman, Martha, Hatch, Mary Jo, and Sitkin, Sim (1983). The uniqueness paradox in organizational stories. *Administrative Science Quarterly* 28 (September).

Maynard-Moody, Steven and Stull, Donald (1987). The symbolic side of policy analysis. In Frank Fischer and John Forester, eds., *Confronting values in policy analysis*. Newbury Park, CA: Sage. Chapter 11.

Mazumdar, Sanjoy (1984). Situated societal values or architects' values? Manuscript.

Mazumdar, Sanjoy (1988). *Organizational culture and physical environments*. Ph.D. dissertation, MIT.

Mazmanian, Daniel A. and Sabatier, Paul A. (1983). *Implementation and public policy*. Glenview, IL: Scott, Foresman.

McCloskey, Donald (1985). *The rhetoric of economics*. Madison: University of Wisconsin Press.

McLuhan, Marshall (1964). *Understanding media*. New York: McGraw-Hill.

Mead, George Herbert (1934). *Mind, self, and society*. Chicago: University of Chicago Press.

Meinig, D. W., ed. (1979). *The interpretation of ordinary landscapes*. New York: Oxford University Press.

Merriam, Charles E. (1934). *Political power*. New York: McGraw-Hill.

Merten, Don and Schwartz, Gary (1982). Metaphor and self. *American Anthropology* 40, 796–810.

Meyer, John W. and Rowan, Brian (1983). Institutionalized organizations: Formal structure as myth and ceremony. In John W. Meyer and W. Richard Scott, *Organizational environments*. Beverly Hills, CA: Sage. Pages 21–44.

Meyer, John W., Scott, Richard, and Deal, Terrence (1977). Research on school and district organization. Presented at the Sociology of Education Conference, San Diego.

Miller, Donald F. (1982). Metaphor, thinking, and thought. *Et cetera* 39:2 (Summer), 134–50.

Miller, Donald F. (1985). Social policy: An exercise in metaphor. *Knowledge* 7:2, 191–215.

Miller, Eugene F. (1979). Metaphor and political knowledge. *American Political Science Review* 73, 155–70.

Morgan, Gareth (1980). Paradigms, metaphors and puzzle solving in organization theory. *Administrative Science Quarterly* 25, 605–22.

Morgan, Gareth (1983). More on metaphor. *Administrative Science Quarterly* 28, 601–7.

Morgan, Gareth (1986). *Images of organizations*. Beverly Hills, CA: Sage.

Moseley, Dan (1990). On the development of a mythological approach to the analysis of public policy formulation. M.P.A. thesis, Department of Public Administration, California State University, Hayward.

Mosse, George (1975). *The nationalization of the masses*. New York: Howard Fertig.

Myrdal, Gunnar (1968). *Asian drama*. New York: Pantheon. Vol. 3, Appendix 6 (2041–61).

Nakamura, Robert (1990). The Japan External Trade Organization and import promotion. In Dennis J. Palumbo and Donald J. Calista, eds., *Implementation and the policy process*. New York: Greenwood. Chapter 5.

Nakamura, Robert T. and Smallwood, Frank (1980). *The politics of policy implementation*. New York: St. Martin's Press.

Neuman, W. Russell, Just, Marion R., and Crigler, Ann N. (1992). *Common knowledge*. Chicago: University of Chicago Press.

Nicholson, Linda J., ed. (1990). *Feminism/Postmodernism*. New York: Routledge.

Nimmo, Dan, and Combs, James E. (1980). *Subliminal politics*. Englewood Cliffs, NJ: Prentice Hall.

Noschis, Kaj (1987). Public settings of a neighborhood. *Architecture and Behavior* 3:4.

O'Connor, Ellen (1995). Paradoxes of participation: Textual analysis and organizational change. *Organization Studies* 16:5, 769–803.

Ortony, Andrew (1975). Why metaphors are necessary and not just nice. *Educational Theory* 25, 45–53.

Ortony, Andrew (1979). *Metaphor and thought*. Cambridge: Cambridge University Press.

Oz, Amos (1983). *In the land of Israel*. New York: Harcourt, Brace, Jovanovich.

Pal, Leslie A. (1995). Competing paradigms in policy discourse: The case of international human rights. *Policy Sciences* 18:2.

Palumbo, Dennis J. (1987a). Introduction to Symposium: Implementation: What have we learned and still need to know. *Policy Studies Review* 7:1 (Autumn), 91–102.

Palumbo, Dennis J. (1987b). Politics and evaluation. In Dennis J. Palumbo, ed., *The politics of program evaluation*. Newbury Park, CA: Sage. Chapter 1.

Palumbo, Dennis J. (1988). *Public policy in America*. New York: Harcourt, Brace, Jovanovich.

Palumbo, Dennis J. (1991). Constructing policy issues. Manuscript.

Palumbo, Dennis J. and Calista, Donald J. (1990). Introduction: The relation of implementation research to policy outcomes. In Dennis J. Palumbo and Donald J. Calista, eds., *Implementation and the policy process*. New York: Greenwood.

Passmore, John (1967). Logical positivism. *Encyclopedia of philosophy*, Vol. 5. New York: Macmillan.

Patai, Raphael (1972). *Myths and modern man*. Englewood Cliffs, NJ: Prentice Hall.

Patai, Raphael (1980). *The vanished worlds of Jewry*. New York: Macmillan.

Peled, Elad (1982). The educational reform in Israel. In E. Ben-Baruch and Y. Neumann, eds., *Educational administration and policy making*. Beer Sheva, Israel: Ben Gurion University and Unipress-Academic Publications. Pages 85–108.

Perkins, H. C. (1988). Bulldozers in the southern part of heaven. Part 1: Local residents' interpretations of rapid urban growth in a free-standing service-class town. *Environment and Planning A* 20, 285–308.

Pfeffer, Jeffrey (1981). *Power in organizations*. Boston: Pitman.

Phillips, Margaret E. (1994). Industry mindsets: Exploring the cultures of two macro-organizational settings. *Organization Science* 5:3 (August), 384–402.

Pinder, C. C. and Bourgeois, V. W. (1982). Controlling tropes in administrative science. *Administrative Science Quarterly* 27, 641–52.

Polanyi, Michael (1966). *The tacit dimension*. New York: Doubleday.

Polkinghorne, Donald (1983). *Methodology for the human sciences*. Albany: SUNY Press.

Pondy, Louis R. (1983). The role of metaphors and myths in organization and in the facilitation of change. In Pondy et al., eds., *Organizational Symbolism*. Greenwich, CT: JAI Press. Pages 157–66.

Pondy, Louis R. et al., eds. (1983). *Organizational symbolism*. Greenwich, CT: JAI Press.

Portis, Edward Bryan and Levy, Michael B., eds. (1988). *Handbook of political theory and policy science*. New York: Greenwood.

Pozner, Ya'el (1967). Committee Report to Zalman Aranne. Ministry of Education and Culture. [Hebrew.]

Pressman, Jeffrey L. and Wildavsky, Aaron (1973). *Implementation*. Berkeley: University of California Press.

Preziosi, Donald (1979). *Architecture, language, and meaning*. The Hague: Mouton.

Prime Minister's Commission for Children and Youth in Distress (1973). *Summary and recommendations*. Jerusalem: State of Israel, Prime Minister's Office. English version published by the Szold National Institute for Research in the Behavioral Sciences, Jerusalem, Publication No. 545 (July).

Prottas, Jeffrey Manditch (1979). *People-processing*. Lexington, KY: Heath.

Rabinow, Paul and Sullivan, William M., eds. (1979). *Interpretive social science*. Berkeley: University of California Press.

Raelin, Joseph A. (1986). *The clash of cultures*. Boston: Harvard Business School.

Rapoport, Amos, ed. (1976). *The mutual interaction of people and their built environment*. Paris: Mouton.

Rapoport, Amos (1982). *The meaning of the built environment*. Beverly Hills, CA: Sage.

Raskin, Dr. Hillel (1979). Leisure and physical recreation at the Community Center. Jerusalem: ICCC and JDC-Israel, Monograph No. 2 (January). [Hebrew, with English abstract.]

Rayner, J. (1984). Between meaning and event. *Political Studies* 32, 537–50.

Redman, Eric (1973). *The dance of legislation*. New York: Simon and Schuster.

Rein, Martin (1983). Action frames and problem setting. *From policy to practice*. London: Macmillan. Pages 221–34.

Rein, Martin and Schon, Donald A. (1977). Problem setting in policy research. In Carol Weiss, ed., *Using social research in policy making*. Lexington, MA: Lexington.

Richardson, Laurel (1994). Writing: A method of inquiry. In Norman K. Denzin and Yvonna S. Lincoln, eds., *Handbook of qualitative research*. Thousand Oaks, CA: Sage. Pages 516–29.

Ricoeur, Paul (1971). The model of the text: Meaningful action considered as text. *Social Research* 38, 529–62.

Robertson, Oliver (1980). *American myth, American reality*. New York: Hill & Wang.

Ronnen, Meir (1980). Architectural sculpture. *Jerusalem Post* (October 17).

Rorty, Richard (1979). *Philosophy and the mirror of nature*. Princeton: Princeton University Press.

Rorty, Richard (1989). *Contingency, irony, and solidarity*. Cambridge: Cambridge University Press.

Rosen, Michael, Orlikowski, Wanda J., and Schmahmann, Kim S. (1990). Building buildings and living lives. In Pasquale Gagliardi, ed., *Symbols and artifacts*. New York: Aldine de Gruyter. Pages 69–84.

Rullo, Guiseppina (1987). People and home interiors. *Environment and Behavior* 19:2 (March), 250–59.

Sadalla, Edward K. et al. (1987). Identity symbolism in housing. *Environment and Behavior* 19:5 (September).

Sapolsky, Harvey (1972). *The Polaris system development*. Cambridge: Harvard University Press.

Schein, Edgar (1985). *Organizational culture and leadership*. San Francisco: Jossey-Bass.

Schein, Edgar (1993). *Organizational culture and leadership*, second edition. San Francisco: Jossey-Bass.

Schmidt, Mary R. (1993). Grout: Alternative kinds of knowledge and why they are ignored. *Public Administration Review* 53:6 (November/December), 525–30.

Schneider, Benjamin, ed. (1990). *Organizational climate and culture*. San Francisco: Jossey-Bass.

Schneider, Anne and Ingram, Helen (1993). Social constructions of target populations. *American Political Science Review* 87:2 (June).

Schon, Donald A. (1971). *Beyond the stable state*. New York: Norton.

Schon, Donald A. (1979). Generative metaphor. In A. Ortony, *Metaphor and thought*. Cambridge: Cambridge University Press.

Schutz, Alfred (1967). *The phenomenology of the social world*. Evanston, IL: Northwestern University Press.

Schutz, Alfred (1973). Concept and theory formation in the social sciences. *Collected papers*, Vol. 1 (Maurice Natanson, ed.). The Hague: Martinus Nijhoff. Pages 48–66.

Segev, Shlomo (1973). Community organization in the ICCC: First report. Jerusalem: ICCC. (January.) [Hebrew.]

Selznick, Philip (1966/1949). *TVA and the grass roots*. New York: Harper and Row.

Shachar, Arie S. (1971). Israel's development towns. *Journal of the American Institute of Planners* 37, 362–72.

Shamas, Anton (1988). *Arabesques*. Vivian Eden, transl. New York: Harper and Row.

Sharkansky, Ira (1970). *Public administration*. Chicago: Markham, p. 8. Quoted in Pressman and Wildavsky (1973), p. 172.

Shibles, W. (1971). *Metaphor: An annotated bibliography and history*. Whitewater, WI: Language Press.

Shokeid, Moshe (1980). Middle Eastern immigrants and the moshav. In Asher Arian, ed., *Israel: A developing society*. Assen-Maastricht: Van Gorcum. Pages 211–33.

Siebert, Glenn (1973). Implementation of evaluation and the systems approach in government. Berkeley: Institute of Urban and Regional Development, Working Paper No. 20.

Sills, David (1961). The succession of goals. In Amitai Etzioni, ed., *Complex organizations*. New York: Holt, Rinehart and Winston. Pages 146–59.

Smircich, Linda (1995). Writing organizational tales. *Organization Science* 6:2, 232–37.

Smith, K. K. and Simmons, V. M. (1983). A rumpelstiltskin organization. *Administrative Science Quarterly* 28, 377–92.

Smith, Merrit Roe (1979). MIT lectures on Technology in America. Cited in R. E. Sclove, The nuts and bolts of democracy. Delivered at the 5th Biennial International Conference of the Society for Philosophy and Technology, Bordeaux, June 29–July 1, 1989.

Smith, Stevie (1972). Not waving but drowning. *The new Oxford book of English verse 1250–1950*, chosen and edited by Helen Gardner. Oxford: Clarendon Press.

Smooha, Sammy (1972). Black Panthers: The ethnic dilemma. *Society* 9:7 (May), 31–36.

Smooha, Sammy (1978). *Israel: Pluralism and conflict*. Berkeley: University of California Press. Chapter 7.

Sopher, David E. (1979). The landscape of home. In D. W. Meinig, ed., *The interpretation of ordinary landscapes*. New York: Oxford University Press. Pages 129–52.

Spradley, James P. (1972). *The cultural experience*. Palo Alto: Science Research Associates.

Spiegel, Erika (1967). *New Towns in Israel*. New York: Praeger.

Srivastva, S. and Barrett, F. J. (1988). The transforming nature of metaphors in group development. *Human Relations* 41:1, 31–64.

Steele, Fred I. (1981). *The sense of place*. Boston: CBI Publishing.

Stein, Harold, ed. (1952). *Public administration and policy development*. New York: Harcourt, Brace.

Stoller, Paul (1986). The reconstruction of ethnography. In Phyllis Pease Chock and June R. Wyman, eds., *Discourse and the social life of meaning*. Washington, DC: Smithsonian Institution Press. Pages 51–74.

Stone, Deborah A. (1988). *Policy paradox and political reason*. Boston: Little, Brown.

Taylor, Charles (1971). Interpretation and the sciences of man. *Review of Metaphysics* 25, 3–51.

Taylor, Charles (1988). Lecture, NEH Summer Seminar on Interpretation, University of California, Santa Cruz (July 5).

Teuber, Andreas (1987). Original intent. Manuscript.

Tevet, Shabtai (1970). Too many development towns. *Ha'aretz* (2/26).

Theodoulou, Stella Z. (1995). Making public policy. In Theodoulou, Stella Z. and Cahn, Matthew A. *Public policy: The essential readings*. Englewood Cliffs, NJ: Prentice Hall. Chapter 11.

Thompson, Michael, Ellis, Richard, and Wildavsky, Aaron (1990). *Cultural theory*. Boulder, CO: Westview.

Thompson, Stith (1955). Myths and folktales. In Thomas A. Sebeok, ed., *Myth: A symposium*. Philadelphia: American Folklore Society.

Titus, C. H. (1945). Political maxims. *California Folklore Quarterly* 4.

Trice, Harrison M. and Beyer, Janice M. (1993). *The cultures of work organizations*. Englewood Cliffs, NJ: Prentice Hall.

Tudor, Henry (1972). *Political myth*. New York: Praeger.

Turner, Barry A., ed. (1990). *Organizational symbolism*. New York: Aldine de Gruyter.

Turner, Victor (1974). *Dramas, fields, and metaphors*. Ithaca: Cornell University Press.

Urban Institute (1994). A sourcebook for the immigration debate. *Policy and Research Report* (Summer), 20–21.

Van Maanen, John (1988). *Tales of the field*. Chicago: University of Chicago.

Van Maanen, John (1995). Style as theory. *Organization Science* 6:1.

van Noppen, J-P, DeKnop, S., and Jongen, R. (compilers) (1985). *Metaphor: A bibliography of post-1970 publications*. Amsterdam: John Benjamins.

Vickers, Sir Geoffrey (1968). Ecology, planning, and the American dream. *Value systems and social process*. New York: Basic. Chapter 2.

Vickers, Sir Geoffrey (1973). *Making Institutions Work*. London: Associated Business Programmes.

Warner, W. Lloyd (1959). *The living and the dead*. New Haven: Yale University Press.

Weatherley, Richard (1979). *Reforming special education*. Cambridge: MIT Press.

Weick, K. E. (1979). *The social psychology of organizing*, second edition. Menlo Park, CA: Addison-Wesley.

Weiss, Joseph and Delbecq, Andre (1987). High-technology cultures and management. *Group and Organization Studies* 12, 39–54.

Weiss, Robert S. and Rein, Martin (1969). The evaluation of broad-aim programs. *Annals of the American Academy of Political and Social Science*, 133–42.

Westerlund, Gunnar and Sjostrand, Sven-Erik (1979). *Organizational myths*. New York: Harper and Row.

White, S. K. (1986). Foucault's challenge to critical theory. *American Political Science Review* 88, 419–31.

Whyte, William Foote (1955 [1943]). Appendix. *Street corner society*, second edition. Chicago: University of Chicago Press.

Whyte, William Foote (1981 [1943]). *Street corner society*, third edition. Chicago: University of Chicago Press.

Whyte, William Foote (1984). *Learning from the field*. Beverly Hills, CA: Sage.

Whyte, William Foote, Greenwood, Davydd J., and Lazes, Peter (1989). Participatory action research. *American Behavioral Scientist* 32:5 (June), 513–51.

Witkin, Robert W. (1990). The aesthetic imperative of a rational-technical machinery. In Pasquale Gagliardi, ed., *Symbols and artifacts*. New York: Aldine de Gruyter. Pages 325–38.

Wynne, Brian (1992). Sheep farming after Chernobyl. In B. Lewenstein, ed., *When science meets the public*. Washington, DC: American Association for the Advancement of Science.

Yanay, Uri (1989). Reactions to domain overlap. *Administration and Society* 21:3, 340–56.

Yanoov, Binyamin (1974). Urbanism as a factor in Jewish group survival. Manuscript.

Yanow, Dvora (1976). Intellectual roots of the idea of "community center." Unpublished manuscript.

Yanow, Dvora (1987a). Toward a policy culture approach to implementation. *Policy Studies Review* 7:1, 103–15.

Yanow, Dvora (1987b). Ontological and interpretive logics in organizational studies. *Methods* 1:2, 73–90.

Yanow, Dvora (1990). Tackling the implementation problem: Epistemological issues in implementation research. In Dennis J. Palumbo and Donald J. Calista, eds., *Implementation and the policy process.* New York: Greenwood. Chapter 14.

Yanow, Dvora (1995a). Built space as story: The policy story that buildings tell. *Policy Studies Journal* 23:3.

Yanow, Dvora (1995b). Writing organizational tales. Introduction. *Organization Science* 6:2, 225–26.

Yanow, Dvora (1996). American ethnogenesis and public administration. *Administration and Society* 27:4, 483–509.

Young Members of the Kibbutz Movement (1970a). *The seventh day.* New York: Scribner's. [English translation of *Si'ah lohamim.* Tel Aviv: Young Members of the Kibbutz Movement, October 1967.]

Young Members of the Kibbutz Movement (1970b). *Among young people: Talks in the kibbutz.* [English translation of *Bein ze'irim.*] Tel Aviv: Kibbutz Movement and Am Oved, 1969.

Zeisel, John (1981). *Inquiry by design.* Monterey: Brooks/Cole.

Zipori, Hayim (1967a). Survey of Culture, Youth and Sports Centers in development towns and in immigrant cities. Report to the Minister of Education and Culture. Jerusalem: Department of Culture, Ministry of Education and Culture (March). [Hebrew; carries 1966 date, but see Chapter 1, Note 1.]

Zipori, Hayim (1967b). Survey of culture, art, recreation, and sports activities on Sabbath eves [Friday nights]. Jerusalem: Department of Culture, Ministry of Education and Culture (September). [Hebrew.]

Zipori, Hayim (1971). Report and background material: Definition of purposes. Report to the Director-General of the Ministry of Education and Culture. Jerusalem: ICCC files (April). [Hebrew.]

Zipori, Hayim (1972). The emergence of the ICCC Community Centers in Israel and their development. Lecture to the Schwartz Program to Train Community Center Directors and Senior Staff. Baerwald School of Social Work, Hebrew University of Jerusalem (November). [Hebrew.]

Index